He Restoreth My Soul

The Personal Testimony of

Maurice Sklar

Unless otherwise noted, all Scripture quotations are from the King James Version of the Bible.

Scripture quotations marked NKJV are from the Holy Bible, The New King James Version. Copyright © 1979, 1980, 1982, Thomas Nelson, Inc. Used by permission.

Copyright © 1998 by Maurice Sklar
Maurice Sklar Ministries
6702 E. 95th Street
Tulsa, Oklahoma 74133

Printed in the United States of America

ISBN 0-9666944-0-6

Dedication

This book is dedicated to my wife, Debbie, and to our children, Rebekah and Josiah.

Contents

Contents

Foreword

He Restoreth My Soul is a story about the love of two fathers for a very special and gifted son, Maurice Sklar.

One father, Charles Sklar, gave all he could, but made mistakes and fell short along the way. This father's love was generous, his commitment total, but it was also imperfect and human, causing hurt and brokenness.

Through a second Father, the Heavenly Father, Maury found and experienced perfect love that restored his bruised and broken life.

It is a beautiful love story. A story of the power of love—God's love, and the love of people God providentially placed in Maury's life—to restore and heal a wounded and confused young man.

It is a story of faith—the power of Maury's faith in God. The enormous pressures from peers, mentors, and family to perform with perfection led to insecurity and eventually to thoughts of suicide. But Maury's tenacious, bold faith and dogged determination in believing God helped him overcome his feelings of rejection and enormous and overwhelming emotional problems.

It is a story of healing and restoration. In choosing Christ, Maury experienced the rejection of family and friends, and gave up an opportunity for a brilliant career in the classical music field. Ironically, however, he gained the very things he desperately needed—perfect love, acceptance, and forgiveness...and an anointed ministry that takes him around the globe, performing on the violin and ministering to the lost and needy of the world.

I have known Maury as a friend and dear brother for many years, and our relationship has been a real joy and pleasure. His bold faith and prophetic anointing have profoundly impacted my life. His loving and giving spirit have been an inspiration to me and my family.

You will see Jesus in Maury's story—His tender mercies, His loving kindness, and His wonderful ability to create "beauty for ashes." And as you read this testimony of God's amazing grace, you too can experience His perfect love. No matter what you are facing, or how your life may have been broken, you can say with Maury, "He Restoreth My Soul."

—*Ben Ferrell*
Tulsa, Oklahoma

I waited patiently for the Lord; and he inclined unto me,and heard my cry. He brought me up also out of an horrible pit, out of the miry clay, and set my feet upon a rock, and established my goings. And he hath put a new song in my mouth, even praise unto our God: many shall see it, and fear, and shall trust in the Lord.
—Psalm 40:1-3

The Lord is my shepherd; I shall not want. He maketh me to lie down in green pastures: he leadeth me beside the still waters. HE RESTORETH MY SOUL...
—Psalm 23:1-3

And they overcame him by the blood of the Lamb, and by the word of their testimony...
—Revelation 12:11

Chapter 1

My Family Before Me

So much of who I am and who I have become is the result of my early life and my parents, particularly my father, Charles Burrowes Sklar. A remarkable man in many ways, he has left his mark on my life in both positive and negative ways. Our relationship has always been particularly intense because of his great desire to see me succeed as a concert violinist. This desire—and near obsession—came from his own past. I've been told little about my dad's past, but I know enough to understand much of what happened to him...and later to me.

My father was born in the mid-1930s—the first son of Harry and Georgia Sklar. Harry was a first-generation American. His father, Frank, was a Jewish immigrant who had come from the Ukraine to the United States around 1896 to escape the horrible pogroms and anti-Semitism there prior to the 1917 Revolution. He escaped Russia as a stowaway in a freight boat. Although he was caught several times, Frank always managed somehow to escape. Finally, he made his way to Ellis Island in New York City where he found freedom from his old life of poverty and the ever-present shame and fear of anti-Semitism that pervaded his former existence.

9

Frank worked as a butcher in Brooklyn, New York. He spoke almost no English and was a hard-working, immigrant Jew. His son Harry, my grandfather, was a musician of sorts. He played the saxophone and jazz violin in those early days of the Big-Band Era, although he earned his living as a salesman.

Harry had little place or regard for religion other than respect for his father's cultural Judaism. After all, this was America where you can make it big. Who needs to be tied up with an old-fashioned religion that gets you nowhere? So when he fell in love with a Gentile girl named Georgia Hyer, who really knocked him off his feet, he married her shortly thereafter. She was a stunning blond with beautiful, blue eyes and a gentle disposition. He and Georgia had their first child, my dad, in Perth Amboy, New Jersey, on December 19, 1934.

Georgia was a loving mother and a good wife. She was athletically inclined and loved horseback riding and swimming. She taught physical education for eighth graders in a public school in New Jersey.

Georgia had a Dutch Reformed Church background. If she was anything like her sister, my great-aunt Frances, she was a godly woman indeed! Frances loved the Lord with all her heart and played the organ for her church for over forty years (and very well, I might add).

When my dad was seven, tragedy struck. After some severe health problems, both mental and physical, Georgia was institutionalized several times and unexpectedly died! So my father lost his mom at a young age. Just days before she died, Georgia gave birth to a baby boy, my Uncle Peter. It is a mystery what actually happened to Georgia. All I know is the little snippets I have been able to piece together from my memory of what little my father and relatives told me.

Rather abruptly after Georgia's death, Harry married a sophisticated Jewish girl named Miriam who worked for him. After the marriage, Harry took my dad up to his room and told him, "Miriam is your new mother now. I do not want you to mention your previous mother ever again in this house. We have burned every picture of her, and she shall never be remembered by you or by us again."

Not long after that, Harry and Miriam had another son, my Uncle David. My Uncle Peter was just a baby when his father remarried, so Miriam was the only mother he ever knew. Miriam was determined that Chuck, as they called my father, would be raised along with her sons in a real Jewish home. Unfortunately, she showed a great deal of favoritism toward the younger two sons at Chuck's expense. After all, she was raising them right, and they would be much truer to the tradition that was her ideal. My dad must have experienced some real rejection. I'm sure he felt left out of this new family with a new mother who was so drastically different from his real mother.

A love for music

My dad had a great love and talent for music. He started studying the piano with his Aunt Frances and practiced very hard. He spent much time with her as she taught him to play the piano. Aunt Frances took him to audition at the Juilliard School of Music in New York City when he was twelve. She had received a Master's Degree in Organ from Juilliard, and she wanted Chuck to play for her former teachers. They listened to him and said, "There are so many fine young talents on the piano. Why don't you play another instrument such as the cello, which isn't so competitive?" So Aunt Frances began trying to find a cello for my dad.

She located an old cello that had been abandoned by the public schools and was in awful condition. She decided to strip off the varnish and to restore it as best she could. It was a success. When she put new strings on it and my dad began to play, he fell in love with the cello!

My dad plunged himself into music and began to dream of a career in classical music. He often practiced for hours. As a result, he began to encounter some strong opposition from his parents. They told him, "Why can't you be like other boys and go out and play baseball? What's wrong with you? You'll never amount to anything in music! You should be a lawyer or a professional person instead!"

Harry and Miriam were disappointed in their oldest son whom they felt was wasting his life. Nevertheless, my dad was determined to prove them wrong and make it in the music world. He would show them! So he practiced and practiced.

Unfortunately, my dad had a late start on the cello. It is best to start learning a stringed instrument such as violin

11

or cello by the age of five or six. Even so, my dad left home a few years after he started playing cello to study in a more serious way. He was determined that hard work would make up the difference. He went to the Brevard Summer Music Camp as a young teenager for three summers in a row. It was there that music became his great love and consuming passion and desire. He studied with several world renowned teachers including Heinrich Joiachim and Lorne Munroe during these summers.

Joiachim asked him to come to New York and study with him after his second summer at Brevard. My dad's Aunt Nellie had a boarding house in New York where he could stay, so at the age of fifteen, he decided to go to the Big Apple and study the cello. I don't know to this day whether his parents threw him out of the house or he just left because of his ambition and love of music. Either way, it was clear that they were *not* interested in Chuck's cello career and would not support him much, if at all. After he left home, my dad was never close with his parents again, as far as I can tell.

Harry died of a heart attack in his fifties, so I never knew him. I think he was a hard, driven man who made a good life for himself and his family but had very little capacity to love and nurture them.

The music world seemed a magical place for my dad. It drew him like a magnet into its glamorous concert life in New York City. He got into a fairly important orchestra, playing in Carnegie Hall, and he continued to attend music camps during the summers. He studied with several well-known teachers, including Lorne Munroe who was at that time principal cellist in the Philadelphia Orchestra and Gordon Epperson who had just been appointed as cello professor at Louisiana State University in Baton Rouge, Louisiana. Epperson offered my dad a big scholarship for the fall at LSU. So my dad left the East Coast and went to Baton Rouge, Louisiana. He had no money, and this was a great opportunity for him to go to college on scholarship.

During this time, Dad auditioned for the Curtis Institute of Music in Philadelphia, Pennsylvania. It was very hard to get in this conservatory because it was so selective. He played for the great cellist Leonard Rose and all of the cello faculty present at the Curtis auditions that year. They told him, "We would like you to come back and audition for us next year. We think you play very expressively, but your technique isn't developed enough at this time."

So Dad left and practiced and practiced. The next year he returned to play for the great Leonard Rose in his hotel room. Dad was hoping that Mr. Rose would be favorable toward him and invite him to study with him at Curtis. Then he would have a chance in the auditions that spring! But it was not to be. Dad had to carry his cello for two hours just to get there, and then he had to play without warming up and with sore hands.

Disappointment...change...tragedy

Mr. Rose wasn't impressed with Dad's audition and told him, "I think you ought to look into another vocation. You are not good enough to make it professionally on the cello, and I do not think you will be able to make your living playing the cello. Keep it as a side vocation instead, and forget about Curtis!"

These words hit my dad very hard. They shattered his dreams. This was probably one of the worst experiences of rejection he has ever had in his tragic life. But there was some truth in Leonard Rose's evaluation of my dad's music. He openly said what all of Dad's teachers had expressed concern about. His teachers agreed that he had a fine talent but thought he had started the cello too late to be able to have a professional career in the music business.

After five years with not many doors opening in music, Dad decided to take his father's advice and go into accounting and law, but he still continued his cello lessons. He is very smart and did extremely well in school. He worked his way through college and law school at Louisiana State University, and he played in the Baton Rouge Symphony. At his graduation, he was ranked as the top student in the law school and had the sixth highest grade point average in the entire university! The other students complained about him because he set the grade curve for his classes so high that other students who should have passed failed. Such was the drive and the ability of my father.

Socially, Dad didn't fare as well. He was quite a loner. His whole life was studying law books, practicing the cello, taking lessons with his music teacher, and working to support himself. He never felt like he fit in, so he immersed himself in his books and his work. Even so, one day he met a bright and attractive girl named Gloria Rosen who was also in school at LSU. He started dating her and before long fell in love with her. The daughter of a Jewish Rabbi from Wichita, Kansas, she had frail, blonde features and a beautiful smile. Before long, Dad and Gloria were engaged and then married in a simple Jewish wedding. Dad found a lot of comfort in Gloria, and they began their life together with God's blessing as Gloria sought to make a fine Jewish home. I don't think my dad has ever been happier than he was at that time.

After only a very short time, however, tragedy struck again! My dad was honored one evening during graduation ceremonies at the LSU Law School. After the ceremony, he and Gloria got into their car to return home. At an intersection, a car swerved in front of them. Dad was driving, and he hit the brakes as hard as he could and pulled sharply to the right. There was quite an impact as their car lunged to a violent stop in a ditch. Dad was okay, but when he looked over, he saw Gloria lying motionless beside him. She wasn't breathing.

She was rushed to the hospital where the doctors discovered she had broken her neck upon impacting the dashboard. Gloria Sklar was dead! I read a newspaper clipping years later that I found hidden away in an old box in our attic. It read, "LSU LAW STUDENT GRADUATES WITH TOP HONORS AND LOSES WIFE IN SAME DAY." What a profound loss that must have been for my father! His life went from one rejection and loss to another.

The devil was doing all he could to kill, steal, and destroy all that my dad held dear. I am sure the Lord reached out to him, but somehow he didn't come to a saving knowledge of Jesus as the Messiah and his Lord. Instead, the devil lied to him and told him God had done these things to him.

Perhaps Dad reasoned, "My mother died, and she believed in the Christian God. She died because my father married her, a non-Jewish woman, and was cursed by God. Then Gloria and I served God in our Jewish faith, and my sweet wife was killed. There must not be a God...or if there is and He has done this, I refuse to serve Him. If He would allow this to happen, then I will never bow my knees to this God."

When I was in graduate school, I had a vision of my father shaking his fist at God at the grave of Gloria Rosen

Sklar. I believe that is exactly what happened. My dad shook his fist at God, buried Gloria, and walked away alone.

My dad left Judaism and only recently has returned to some form of the Jewish faith. He has never accepted the God of the Bible or the Bible's authority that I know of during my lifetime. It is so sad to see the devastation that the devil inflicted upon him, not to mention his family, since he turned away from God. But I believe that in the end, he will repent and turn to God and escape the damnation, fire, and darkness of hell. I believe that one day he will recognize that it was not God who destroyed his life but the enemy.

Picking up the pieces

My father got up from Gloria's grave and picked up the pieces of his life as best he could. He passed the Bar Exam, became a Certified Public Accountant, and began his professional career. Of course, his cello playing also continued, and he performed with the Baton Rouge Symphony and in chamber music as much as he could with a full-time job. He soon went to work for the federal government as a CPA and punched a clock to make a decent living.

Not long after, he decided to take a better job in New Orleans, Louisiana. There he met a shy, delicate Jewish girl named Audrey Siegel. She was very beautiful, but she also seemed as fragile as a porcelain figurine. Dad was drawn to her and soon they were dating. Before long Dad fell in love and asked for Audrey's hand in marriage. She said yes, and Dad and Audrey were married.

Audrey struggled with insecurity and inferiority. Dad didn't make things easy for her with his authoritarian and perfectionistic personality. She felt that she could never do anything well enough for him and that he was constantly finding fault with her. Dad felt that she was too sensitive, that she had an enormous guilt complex, and that she brought all her problems on herself. Needless to say, they weren't very happy, but they managed to hold things together for about eight years.

Then Audrey became pregnant. She was very happy about it but also felt completely overwhelmed at the thought of being a mother. Still, she prepared her home for the new arrival. Dad had purchased a piece of land and had an architect design a beautiful, modern house, which he had built over the river outside of New Orleans. Shortly after, I was born into this world in New Orleans, Louisiana, on June 11, 1963.

My parents couldn't decide what to name me. Grandmother Mimi insisted that I be named Harry after her deceased husband. Audrey's father was named Maurice Siegel, and "Maurice" was more to my parents' liking. So they compromised and named me Maurice Harrison Sklar after my grandfathers. Everybody was happy and called me "Maury."

Chapter 2

My Early Years

I was two and a half when my parents separated. Dad took a new accounting job, and he and I moved to Greensboro, North Carolina. He wanted to make a clean start with his life in a new place. We found an apartment in an old building, and it became our home. I remember the wonderful camaraderie we had together. We were a team—Dad and me. We were going to face the world together. I knew three things down deep in my spirit, even from my earliest childhood: my dad loved me, he was very needy and lonely, and he hurt a lot deep inside. He needed me, and I needed him. I loved my dad very much.

My mom and dad tried to get back together several times while we lived in Greensboro, and sometimes she even stayed over at our apartment. But these tries were never too positive, and they failed to get back together. Their marriage, like Humpty Dumpty, was broken and could never be put back together again.

In late 1966 or early 1967, Dad took another accounting job, and we moved to Atlanta, Georgia. We moved into a two-story townhouse apartment. I had a big room upstairs with nice, wooden floors. I really liked my new room, especially that it was upstairs. It was fun to play on the stairs.

Dad worked during the day and then did freelance cello playing in the evenings and on weekends. Atlanta was a much larger city and had more opportunities for his music. He played in civic orchestras and for visiting musicals, shows, and even entertainers such as Chet Atkins and his orchestra. But his greatest love was classical music. I remember listening to him practice his cello, playing from *Bach's Unaccompanied Suites*, *Boccherini's Concerto*, the *Brahms E Minor Sonata*, and other wonderful pieces. I loved listening to him! I would sit and listen sometimes for hours and play with my toys as he practiced in the living room downstairs.

He bought me an LP record of Haydn's *Surprise Symphony* and played classical music for me quite a bit. We also enjoyed listening to the record of "The Sound of Music." My favorite sing-a-long record was "Tubby the Tuba" narrated by the wonderful comedian/singer Danny Kaye. It was a favorite of ours for years!

By this time, I had gotten used to living without a mother and thought it was normal. Dad hardly ever spoke of Audrey, and when he did it wasn't too positive, to say the least. He said I was better off without her, so I believed it. I remember having very ambivalent and confusing feelings toward life and particularly toward Dad and Audrey. She visited me several times in Atlanta at our apartment, but I only remember one of the times. She took me swimming at the pool, and things evidently got out of control. I must have said something inappropriate to her because she got very upset. She was crying hysterically on the phone to Dad and saying that I hated her and wanted nothing to do with her. She said it was because he had brainwashed me against her.

Part of the problem was that Audrey was always very insecure around me, and that made me extremely uncomfortable with her. But I also felt compassion for her in my little boy way and wanted to be nice to her. I knew down in my little spirit that she loved me and felt very guilty for not raising me, but I also knew that she couldn't handle having me as her son. Somehow I felt I was to blame, and I felt guilty and bad about this. How else could I interpret these events as a three year old?

The "big hole"

So I grew up with "a big hole" in my life. There was this strange woman who I saw very little and somehow was not capable of accepting as my mother. Dad did almost nothing to encourage any positive association with her. Yet she was my "mother," whatever that meant. I felt like the little bird in the children's book *Are You My Mother?* The baby bird asks all the animals in the barnyard, "Are you my mother?" but none of them are. Ironically, I didn't think I wanted a mother. In my young mind, I concluded that people were better off without mothers. And yet I felt very lonely for something that I didn't know I needed.

I didn't know I needed a mother. My father didn't even acknowledge this as a legitimate need in my three-year-old world. Dad made it clear that he was more than enough to raise me, and he was going to prove it to me, to himself, and to the whole world, if necessary. Since I believed him so much, I accepted these things as absolute truth and drank them deeply into my inner life. I could not deny that some horrible, deeply embedded pain seemed to never leave me, but Dad also had the same inner pain, and we simply didn't talk about it.

Dad was very impatient with me, and sometimes if I didn't obey him instantly, he would get very angry. I never knew exactly when this would occur. I'm not saying I didn't provoke him at times, as any three- or four-year-old boy might do, but his discipline of me was erratic, sudden, and sometimes severe. Physically, he never did more than spank me, but the words he spoke into my spirit were so full of anger and fear that I would simply lie down and shake in shame and fear.

After Dad got over being angry, he would come into my bedroom before I went to sleep and tell me that he loved me very much and everything was going to be all right. This almost Dr.-Jekyl-and-Mr.-Hyde behavior hurt me deeply and confused me terribly. One minute he would go into a tirade and scream at me, and the next he would hug me, kiss me, and try to comfort me the best he could. I once heard a man say that hurting people hurt people. We will hurt others if we ourselves are hurting unless Jesus comes in and heals our broken hearts. Such was the case with my father and me growing up.

As a child, I believed with all my little heart that there was something horribly wrong with me deep down in the core of my being. That was why I felt the way I did. I didn't deserve to live or even to breathe the air of this world. I was bad in the most depraved sense of the word. I didn't belong. I wasn't wanted, just tolerated, and Dad's response to me proved that this was true.

When I was good and could meet his standards, Dad liked me, and life would be better, calmer, and happier for a little while. Then I would once again be confronted with another failure in my behavior, and the proverbial ax would fall. Once again I would have to admit my guilt. The "truth" of my shame and unworthiness always returned in the form of Dad never entirely approving of me or of what I did. The one person I wanted to please the most was the one I was failing the most. I never measured up for very long.

The Lord revealed to me when I was older that a spirit of rejection—among other generational curses—was transmitted into me before I was even born, and I grew up with those same demonic spirits that afflicted my parents and who knows how many of their ancestors before them. Because of my gifting toward worship and the calling on my life, I knew them even more intimately and drank their poison into my spirit many times more deeply than my parents did.

The devil fought to destroy me from my earliest childhood, and he nearly succeeded. He fights dirty. He doesn't wait until you are old enough to fight back. He sows seeds of destruction from the womb if at all possible. The Bible says that the sins and the iniquities of the fathers shall be visited on the children (see Numbers 14:18). I can testify to the truth of that scripture. I was in close personal communion with those demons and their curses from my earliest memory. I drank their cups of bitterness and inner agony into my spirit and drained them to the dregs.

Was I a morbid and despairing child? By no means! I actually had much joy and happiness because the Lord was always with me in spite of everything. Dad and I had many great evenings and weekends together during this time. When he was in a good mood, we would build big towers to the ceiling with my blocks or construct large Tinkertoy ferris wheels and rocket ships. We flew kites and made paper airplanes or listened to music and sang together with the records. He could be enormous fun!

I am with you

Something wonderful happened to me one evening in early summer. There were fireflies blinking outside every-where. I went out and chased them and ran around until I was exhausted. Then I went into the house and got ready for bed. After Dad kissed me good night and turned out the light, I remember looking out my window and seeing all those fireflies blinking as far as I could see into the dark-ness.

Suddenly this Presence came into my room. A gentle, soft voice spoke to my spirit and said, "Everything is going to be all right. I am with you." I replied, in my little-boy way, that I was glad He was there and that I needed His pres-ence with me. I asked Him not to leave me ever. And the voice said, "I will never leave you or forsake you."

Such peace filled my heart! I didn't know who had spo-ken to me at the time, but I knew He was good. I accepted this wonderful Presence as my friend, and He stayed with me even until now, just like He said He would. I know who He is now, and I love Him even more each day of my life. He is a friend who sticks closer than a brother and loves me more than anyone else. His name is Jesus.

I am so thankful to God that He came to me when I was a small boy. If He hadn't, I am sure I would not be alive today.

Chapter 3

The Afternoon
That Changed My Life

One day at a musical gathering, my dad met a young lady named Deanna Lewis. She played the violin in the Atlanta Symphony Orchestra. She was very attractive, with beautiful, long, brown hair, brown eyes, a slender figure, and a sweet smile. With her outgoing, vivacious personality and her love and devotion to music, it was not hard to see why Dad would be attracted to her. She could talk your ear off about many things, but it all seemed so interesting.

Dad and Deanna shared so much together. Deanna liked Dad because he was a successful attorney who also shared her love of the music world without threatening her with his ability on the cello. He understood and respected her as a professional musician. But most of all, he was amazed at how she and I hit it off so well together. I believe she had been given a special love for me from the Lord, and she treated me as if I were her own son. I enjoyed all this new attention, of course, and she actually began to minister to

23

my heart in the area of abandonment and rejection that had come as a result of losing Audrey. Just like a flower begins to flourish and blossom with the warmth of the sunlight, the proper soil, and watering, I began to respond to Deanna's love and warmth toward me. In fact, the next four years of my life were to be the best of my whole young life. Out of those years came much of the formation of who I am as a musician and a person today.

After a brief courtship, Dad asked Deanna to marry him, and she said yes. They became engaged, and a new "mommy" came into my life.

Deanna attended a Unitarian church in Atlanta. Dad and I started to go to church with her, and I became a "project" of sorts to Deanna. This was the late sixties (around 1967) and an optimistic time for what was called "progressive education." The world was trying desperately to divorce itself from anything traditional as far as God and morality were concerned—especially concerning the Bible.

After his experiences with tragedy and the seeming failure of God and religion to help him at all, my dad eagerly embraced this watered-down, secular, humanistic religion. After all, it was respectable, even "Artistic," with a capital "A." It was tolerant of any religion. In fact, you could believe anything and still be accepted. "There are many paths to God. And man is basically good. We just need the right environment, the right education, and the absence of anything considered oppressive and inhibiting, and man can solve his problems on his own." Such was the message of the Unitarian Universalists.

My introduction to music and the arts

Music and the arts became our gods. We worshipped and bowed down to the music world—its artists, its concerts, and its creations. There was a clear hierarchy of people within this world. The local Atlanta musicians and artists, such as those in the Atlanta Symphony, were not really admired much by Deanna and Dad. They weren't as holy and exalted as the visiting artists and soloists from New York and Europe who came to Atlanta to perform. These people were the giants among all the gods of the music world.

Granted, this was a small and elite world where only a few could enter...and only if they had enough talent. My parents believed they knew and could judge accurately who had or didn't have this exalted status. So our lives revolved around the culture of the performing arts world. It was the hub of our family fellowship and conversation for a number of years.

As a four-year-old boy, I had very little understanding of all this, but I could pick up very quickly what was important and what meant the most to Dad and Deanna. I was very good at adapting to what they wanted me to be, so it wasn't hard for me to adopt their tastes and standards as my own. They took me out to the finest restaurants. They dressed me up and took me to the symphony, the ballet, and the opera. We went to museums and saw fine paintings and sculptures. We read books and listened to fine musical recordings. I was introduced to the visiting soloists who performed with the symphony. I was invited to receptions after concerts to be with all those people who were the underpinnings of the fine arts community in Atlanta.

The Wedding

Dad and Deanna's wedding was a very confusing experience for me. I remember sitting in the circular sanctuary of the Unitarian Church in Atlanta, watching my dad get married. I remember wondering why I was watching his wedding when I wasn't supposed to be born yet. I didn't fit into the scheme of things. I belonged and yet I didn't belong. Deanna was my "mom," and yet she wasn't. I felt like I was losing Dad to this new woman in our lives. No longer would Dad need me as his best friend. Now I was just a part of his life, along with this lady who had worked her way into our lives.

According to the Unitarian minister, the "Inner Light" was witnessing this holy marriage ceremony as Dad and Deanna were joined into conjugal bliss amid the candles and all the religious trappings that could be allowed in this progressive, late-sixties, secular but elegant mess of a wedding. Unfortunately, the "Inner Light" of which the minister spoke wasn't enough to keep Dad and Deanna's marriage or home from falling apart later on—but the service was certainly beautiful and unique.

Deanna had some of her symphony friends perform a particular slow movement from a late Beethoven string quartet. For her, this represented the holiest thing she could think of. Dad was so taken with her that it didn't matter to him what kind of wedding it was. After the failure of two Jewish marriages, he wasn't even sure there was a God. He loved her, and that was enough of a "religion" for him. He was happy to enter into her world since his was so dark and lonely.

I knew somehow that this new family would be a good thing for Dad and me. At least we weren't alone in this wretched world any longer. I also knew we would be happier with Deanna—and we were a pretty happy family for the next several years. I am thankful for those years and all that the Lord put into my life through my dad and Deanna, for they would be the only real dad and mom I would ever know.

A special present
One afternoon an event happened that would change my life. Deanna came home with a little violin case under her arm. She said to me, "I have a special present for you, Maury." I watched as she placed a little 1/8-size violin case on the sofa.

"What is it?" I asked.

"It's a violin," she told me. "Come over here, and let's see if you can play it. You have such marvelous fingers for the violin and such a fine ear for music that I went and bought this violin for you."

I ran over to the sofa and looked at it. I felt very excited, and I didn't know why. Maybe I could play this beautiful, strange instrument.

"Do you want to try it, Maury?" Deanna asked me. I picked it up very carefully, and she put it under my chin. Deanna had taught strings and music in the public schools in Raleigh, North Carolina, before moving to Atlanta to join the symphony, so she knew how to introduce the violin to me.

She showed me how to hold it. I thought it was horribly awkward, and it hurt to twist my left hand all the way around the finger board. It hurt my fingers even more when I placed them on the strings. It was really painful to play the violin! But as I held the bow for the first time and finally managed to bring it across the strings, something clicked on the inside of me and I was able to draw a nice sound out of the open strings. I seemed to have a knack for being able to do whatever Deanna said to do with the violin, but it hurt so much to be in this awkward position that I soon stopped.

Then that special Presence filled the room. Deanna felt it, too. She said to me, as she did so many times after that, "Maury, you are a very special and gifted child, and I think you have a great gift in music."

I didn't know what to make of the violin except it sure hurt a lot to play it!

When Dad got home later that day, Deanna took the new violin out and showed it to him. He inspected it and asked about its price and quality. He seemed satisfied when Deanna told him where she had bought it, how much it had cost, and who had made it. It was a nice instrument, even by his standards.

Then the torturous thing was again placed under my chin. Dad insisted that I be taught how to play the violin properly from the very first, so Deanna put me into all kinds of contortions until I was finally in the right position. After getting the fingers of my right hand in the proper position, I once again began to draw the bow across the strings while Deanna moved the fingers of my left hand around to play a few notes. It hurt so much that I started crying, but I passed that first inspection and lesson!

After a few minutes, I threw a temper tantrum because it hurt so much and I wanted to stop. I was feeling both excitement and pain at the same time.

Why was Dad so demanding? I wondered. I just wanted to try the violin again, and he was already seeing how far I could go. I did manage to do some things that really impressed him, though. For the next few days, all he could talk about was how talented I was on the violin. And not many lessons and weeks after, Dad and Deanna decided that I was going to be a world-class violinist when I grew up. They were amazed because I caught on to the instrument so easily, and they thought I played so "musically and expressively." And always, whenever I played, that unusual Presence would come and fall on us like a blanket.

After that, I became a "holy cause" for the Sklar family, who determined to help me become a fine violinist. My "giftedness" even advanced me a little bit onto the sacred ground of my parents' worship of artists. I relished the attention but resented much of the expectations placed upon me. Dad was determined that I must have the proper training and all the things that he never had. For Deanna, I was a shining example of what the proper environment and education could do for children. I was especially a demonstration of how successful she was at teaching a "gifted" child, for I could do whatever she and Dad wanted me to do.

So began my career as a violinist. By far, this period of my life as a young boy was the most profound in shaping my future years. It was a positive and, for the most part, happy time for me.

Chapter 4

Lessons With Dad
and Deanna

*T*he next few years were fairly happy ones. We bought a house on Channing Drive, and my time there was the best of any that I had in my young life. There was a new stability in my life, and I was able to put behind me the tragic loss of my mother and other traumatic events that had so marred my young life.

Perhaps things will really be better now for me, I thought. *If I can play the violin well enough, I will really belong in this new family and they will love and accept me. We will have a good life together.*

I loved to go play in the park that was adjacent to our house. One day I was walking in the park down near the creek when suddenly I felt a familiar Someone with me. I couldn't see Him and didn't know who He was, but ever so often I would sense His presence. He would talk to me and tell me wonderful things about His love for me. He even answered any questions I had running through my five-year-old brain. This time He came and walked along beside me. He told me that I had something very special to do in my life and that He would always be with me. He said He would always be my Friend and I could count on Him no matter what. I thought it was kind of strange to hear this from Someone I couldn't see, but I was glad to have this Friend anyway and I told Him so. He said He was glad I wanted Him in my life because many people didn't want Him and turned Him away.

I asked, "Why? You're so nice that anyone who met You would want You as their friend. Wouldn't they?"

He told me that many people liked other friends more than Him. He was sad when He said that, but I told Him I knew what He meant because sometimes people didn't like me either. He said He knew that, which is why He wanted me as His friend always.

My interactions with my invisible Friend touched me deep within my being as a five year old. I didn't understand them, but I needed to talk about them. Somehow I figured this must be God who was talking with me, so I began to ask my parents questions about God. I didn't tell them about my conversations with Him because I knew they would not approve of them.

Learning about the gods

When I wouldn't stop talking about God, Dad and Deanna decided that they needed to do something about my inquisitiveness. So Deanna decided that she would read me a book she found from the Unitarian Church. I still remember what the cover of this book looked like. It was light beige with red letters that said, "Finding God in all the Religions of the World." It was written for inquisitive kids like me who wanted to find out what God was like. Deanna read me a chapter one night, and Dad read me one the next. I learned about all the different names and kinds of gods there are in the world. I learned about Buddha and who he was, and I learned about the millions of Hindu gods.

After mentioning every religion that the authors could think of, they finally put in a chapter about Jesus. According to them, He was a spineless, weak, pansy-type man who walked around, talking about flowers and birds and saying, "Love, love, love" all the time. But He was a very good moral teacher and a good man, the book said. He taught people to be nice and sweet to each other in this milk-toast way. Then people came along after He died and made another god out of Him.

The book also had an opinion about the Jewish religion and the "mean" God of the Bible. It said He kills, murders, and sentences people to hell even when they don't know they are bad. The rest of the religions seemed nice and sweet, but the Bible was a bad book that told about a mean God who couldn't be trusted. He was obviously the worst god because He said we were all sinners and were going to hell, while the truth is we are all good people and there is no such thing as hell—so the book said.

The authors said hell was a superstitious belief of people hundreds of years ago before we learned the truth about the universe through science. They stated that all people everywhere are good no matter what they believe. Everyone is right and nobody is wrong. All we need in life is to help each other and to make the right choices, and then we will live in heaven right here on this earth. We don't need to wait for anything when we die. It is right now—this life—that matters because that's all there is to existence anyway. When you die, that's it. It's all over! This is what the authors of that book said.

My parents told me I could choose whichever god I wanted or I could invent my own if I thought that was better. According to them, there were no bad choices—except maybe the God in the Bible—but it was my choice. However, they told me that religion is for people who need help coping with life...people who need a crutch to help them get through. They told me it was only for weak and dumb people, not for the culturally elite people like me and my family. They assured me that I had a lot of talent and would be a great violinist and a very smart person when I grew up, so I really didn't need religion.

After several months of hearing this, my hunger for God was quenched almost entirely. I soon forgot about this Friend who came to me at times in a special way. My parents told me I just had "an overactive imagination." Since I was able to learn new things quickly and was doing well on the violin, I determined that the gods of music and the violin would be my gods, too, just as they were for my parents. After all, my parents loved me best when I was playing the violin well. Sad to say, I did not hear much from my Friend for quite a long time after that.

My parents placed great value on education, particularly on my musical training. I am thankful in many ways for the constant nudging and guidance they gave me growing up. Without their faith and relentless resolve to make me into a concert violinist, I probably would have become something else. They were extremely determined about my musical training, and the seeds of their ambition eventually grew into the musician I am today. My parents were set on me being a fine musician and violinist.

For Dad, it was a deeply personal agenda—my success would prove that he wasn't a failure as a musician. I would be what he never was. I had the "goods." I was the proverbial goose that laid the golden eggs of musical talent. That was the negative side. The positive side was that he really was proud of me when I played well, and I delighted in that approval. He would light up like a Christmas tree when I would meet with his goals in our practice sessions and in family performances for his friends.

Unfortunately, to please him in that way wasn't easy. Even after I had jumped through whatever hoops he had put in front of me during practice, Dad never remained satisfied for very long. Once I could do what had been impossible for me to do two days earlier, my accomplishment was forgotten and new hoops were presented for me to jump through. That is not a fun way for any kid to grow up. However, I am thankful for the challenges that were placed before me. Without them, I would not have been able to master the violin as I did.

I believe the Lord placed me in the family He did precisely because He knew that my talent would be developed in that way. The Lord causes all things to work together for our good when we turn toward His grace through our prayers and intercession (see Romans 8:28). God's grace was on me in spite of the emotional trauma I was subjected to during my childhood. I thank God for whoever prayed for me in my young life!

More training in music and the arts

At first, it was a real blessing for Deanna to teach me academics and the violin. She recognized that God had given me special gifts, and she had a genuine desire to see me rise up and conquer things at a young age that others couldn't do. She really did love and care for me, but she also wanted me to succeed for two other reasons. Deanna knew that Dad was so bent on my doing well in life—and particularly on the violin—that he would not be happy unless I did, and she wanted to make him happy. Second, she wanted to prove what she could do with someone like me to teach. I gave her a purpose, a great quest in which she could prove what could be done with the right environment, the right education, and a great talent. Deanna believed it would all mix together into a fantastic stew, and she could be the cook!

Of course, I only recognize this now; it was not something I understood growing up. All I knew was that I got a lot of attention and praise by doing what others wanted me to do. My life went much more smoothly when I was able to score another point on my parent's list of projected accomplishments. Of course, I knew they really wanted the best for me and that was the way they showed me their love.

When I started my lessons with Dad, he just taught me on open strings instead of having me play music. This was so I would learn to use my bow arm perfectly. He had me do exercises to work on my bow changes to make them so smooth that they would be imperceptible. He wanted me to be able to control my bow at any position and at any speed. He worked on my hand position to make it just right. To this day, one of the strongest aspects of my playing is my right hand and my bow control.

Dad's favorite phrases were, "Do it again," "Bend your thumb," "Parallel to the bridge," "Don't go around the corner at the tip of the bow," "Straight bow," and "Smooth bow changes." When I lapsed at all in my concentration, he would say, "Turn your brain on!" and "I'll stay here until midnight if I have to until you do it right!"

Deanna quickly realized that she would not be the one to teach me the violin. Dad completely took over and only once in a while asked advice from her. I was a daily project with him. It was rare that I did not end my violin practice/lesson in tears and with tremendous frustration. I often went into a rage and argued with him.

Eventually, a problem began to emerge between Deanna and Dad. I took so much of his focus and attention that she began to feel neglected. It was always "Maury this" and "Maury that."

Finally, after nearly a year of these intense lessons, I could play very well with my bow. I could even do some virtuoso bowings such as a four-stringed ricochet, spiccato, and others. It almost made me angry that I could do it! But somehow, in spite of my stubborn resistance toward my dad, I learned it anyway.

Then I was ready to start playing with my left hand. Once again, I had to put my fingers down onto the finger board. I hadn't liked doing it the first time I had picked up the instrument, and I didn't like it any better this time. It still hurt! I complained pretty loudly about it, but that just caused another argument. I was tired of it all, so after about a year of lessons, I refused to play my violin anymore. I quit. I could not endure it any longer. After I made the decision to quit playing violin, the strife level in our house decreased considerably. Deanna wasn't as threatened with my talent or my pull on Dad's time, energy, and devotion. He could spend more time with things other than perfecting me on the violin.

Meanwhile, Deanna and Dad taught me other things like reading with flash cards, mathematics, chess, geography, history, and, of course, humanism. I grew up on educational TV. I learned that we evolved from primates over millions and billions of years from Bronowski's book *The Ascent of Man*. We read beautiful, illustrated books on great artists such as Michelangelo, Leonardo Da Vinci, Van Gogh, and Monet.

My parents read me books on many different subjects, including science, poetry, and literary masterpieces. I was to have the best of everything in every realm and in every way. Nothing could be drab or mediocre. Then if I failed in life, my parents would know it wasn't their fault. After all, what other child had been given as much as Maury? They were determined to be five-star parents, first class all the way.

A new addition to our family...and a move

One day Deanna came home from her orchestra rehearsal, beaming from ear to ear! She looked like she was floating. She said, "Maury, I am going to have a baby! I just went to the doctor, and he said that a little baby is in my tummy. You are going to have a little sister or a little brother! Isn't that exciting?"

I was very excited and a little confused over this news. When Dad got home from work, we all threw a party and got very happy about a new child coming to our home. Very soon, however, the dynamics of our family began to change. As Deanna began to grow larger and larger around the middle and the spring season was drawing to a close, she knew she would have to take a leave of absence from the orchestra to have the baby. She was also having strong maternal and hormonal reactions that were redirecting her motivation away from the concert life. She longed to stay at home, be a mommy, and raise her baby.

Even though the new baby wasn't fully on the scene yet, her presence was keenly felt. Things normally change when a new baby comes. In all the preparation for Deanna's own child, slowly but surely I became secondary to the main attraction. Of course, that naturally happens to any firstborn child when a new brother or sister comes, but my situation was magnified considerably by several unique features. First of all, Deanna was obsessed with being a perfect mother. If she would give me so much, then her own flesh and blood would have even more! She had all kinds of new security needs, and Dad's preoccupation with me was threatening to her.

Dad had an authoritarian hold over me, but I also had a kind of control over him. He would always be at my beck and call if I behaved in certain ways. I was a master at "pushing his buttons," which I am ashamed of today. I could get his attention whenever I wanted, even if it was of a negative nature.

I was also threatened by this new baby. *Would my life be altered yet again? Would Deanna stop wanting me now that she had her own baby?* Many such thoughts rolled around in my subconscious mind. Actually, Deanna was determined to not favor the new baby over me. It did not fit into her motherly agenda to be so base as to fall into such a blatant trap. No indeed, she would prove all the child psychologists and family therapists wrong—she was enlightened and could raise us both in utopia and endless familial bliss.

As I mentioned earlier, I had quit the violin out of sheer frustration, but it had left a pretty major gap in my life. I had been demoted several levels in my parents' estimation. The violin had been my trump card. It had gotten me loads of attention, especially from Dad, and had made me much more lovable and important to them. At times I had even ascended into the throne room of the "evolutionary elite." I had that magic touch, and when I had played, the music flowed from my violin in a beautiful way, even on exercises with the open strings. My parents had "oohed and ahhed," looked at each other with that expert, knowing look, and raised their eyebrows as I jumped through more of their hoops.

But all that was over for me. Playing the violin simply wasn't worthwhile to me anymore. The reaction I got from my parents didn't satisfy me. After all, I had my parents' attention anyway. I had a happy home life now that Deanna had made our house into a home, and I enjoyed school. For now, it was as good as it would ever be. They surely didn't love me just for my violin talent, did they? That turned out to be the biggest question in my life.

However, stormy waters were approaching. Even then, things were not as secure as they had once been. There were mild disagreements between my parents almost every day, and ever so often Dad and Deanna had screaming arguments with each other. That was unsettling enough, but it was even more unsettling that I was no longer the center of Deanna's affections. No matter how hard she tried to conceal it, I knew that the new baby was far more important to her. When my sister, Gloria, was born, I adored her, but I knew that if I didn't do all I could to show Deanna that I was totally comfortable with her, she would feel bad. Then things ultimately would turn out for the worse.

One day Dad found out about an opportunity to be the personnel manager of an orchestra in Cedar Rapids, Iowa. He thought about it and finally decided that he wasn't happy with law and accounting work anymore. Maybe this was just the thing he needed. He could have a career in music, even if it was on a much smaller scale. He could play in the orchestra and be a big fish in a little pond, and he could work in the administration for the symphony. Besides, it cost a lot less to live in Iowa than in Atlanta. He could leave the nine-to-five grind with the daily traffic jams and be involved in music. He could also be at home more with his family.

Perhaps the change would be good for Deanna, too. Tensions were mounting, and Deanna wasn't as happy as she used to be. Maybe the professional world was too much for her. She could be more of an "at-home mom" in Iowa. She could also play in the symphony, since the concert schedule wasn't nearly as intense as that of a major orchestra like Atlanta's. Dad and Deanna were now the parents of two kids. They should be raised in a nice community, etc., etc. So went the thoughts of Charles Sklar.

He went to Cedar Rapids, interviewed for the job, and was accepted. They liked the added bonus of Deanna playing in the orchestra, I am sure. So less than eight weeks after Gloria was born, we sold our house, packed all our belongings into a big U-Haul truck, and set out for Iowa! Little Gloria was nursing at Deanna's breast, and Dad drove as we made our way into the great Midwest. Talk about a sudden and drastic change!

I have moved and changed my life so many times that it is a good thing the Lord gave me a disposition for it. Otherwise, I would have been miserable growing up. Every year or so from this time on, I lived somewhere different or went to another school or lived with a different family. Life was pretty unpredictable, but I seemed to enjoy it. I didn't have much stability in my young life as a result of all the change, but at least it brought some added fun and adventure. At least my life was not dull and boring!

Chapter 5

Dad's Growing Obsession

I turned seven in June of 1970, as we arrived in Iowa and entered a new phase of life. I didn't feel so helpless against the negative forces that seemed to swallow up my earlier life. In spite of the arguments and difficulties that were beginning to emerge in my parents' relationship, I was happier now. The nightmare of the abandonment and the collapse of Dad's first marriage were beginning to fade into the past.

I was also relieved to be away from the strain of "the music world" and its pull on my parents. There was nowhere near the same level of pressure on Deanna, and she could be home more with us. The Cedar Rapids Symphony was just a small, regional orchestra with a limited schedule, so she wasn't having to play in a concert every week of the year as she had in Atlanta. I felt like we could be "normal people," whatever that is. We were doing our best to adapt and fit into the mindset of Midwestern, small-town, rural America.

Several months into my second grade year, I asked Deanna if I could play the violin again. I said that if I could study with someone other than Dad, I would like to try to play again. I told them that I was very sorry that I'd had a bad attitude before, but that I would like to try again if there was someone who could teach me. They jumped on that, of course, and immediately found a man named Jack Ranney who taught strings in the public schools in Cedar Rapids and played in the symphony. He seemed nice and patient to my parents, and so I began taking private lessons with him.

Playing the violin...again!

It had been a little over a year since I had quit playing the violin, but all of it came back to me very quickly. I had grown quite a bit and was much stronger now, so the left-hand fingers didn't hurt when I placed them on the strings. Mr. Ranney was very nice and patient indeed. He started me on a high-school level, beginning violin method book. I had learned to read music from flash cards in Atlanta, so I didn't have any problem reading the music in the book. I learned things so quickly that Mr. Ranney was quite amazed. He had never had a student who could do what he wanted with as much ease as I could. He always complimented my lessons and said, "Maury, you sure are a natural on the violin. You're going to go far in music if you keep it up." He was very nice.

I practiced in the afternoons down in the basement, with only an occasional intrusion from Dad when he couldn't stand it anymore and had to give me a few pointers. Whenever I practiced in the house, I could literally feel the ears of both Dad and Deanna monitoring my every note. It wasn't easy, but they really tried to stay out of my practice time. I had demanded that if I played the violin again, they were not to interfere with me. I was going to do it myself. For a time, they did admirably in giving me enough leeway so that I could do it more on my own.

Soon, however, Dad felt he just had to get involved again. He felt morally obligated to train me hard on the violin because I had what he considered to be the kind of talent that only a few people in the world have ever been given. He told me that if I had had only a little ability on the violin, he wouldn't have interfered. He would have just let me enjoy piddling with the violin. But after only a few weeks of leaving me alone, he started working with me again because, as he said, he didn't want me to learn bad habits.

So we were at it again. This time, however, it was better because he backed down if I got too upset during his lessons. Deanna also argued with him and told him not to go overboard. At those times he would back down a little bit, and I would have a few days respite before the next onslaught began. I am thankful now for what God put into my father to help me and train me, though at the time I didn't like it much. I continued to play my little songs perfectly for Mr. Ranney, and he was very pleased.

Dad did another thing that really set the course of my life. He always "spoke a word of faith" over me. He told me that when I grew up, I would become a great violinist. I would do what he had always dreamed of doing and "make it" as a soloist in the music world. I just had to practice very hard, and it would surely happen.

Deanna was beginning to really get upset at Dad because of his obsession with me and the violin. He would have these long conversations with me and describe the glories of "the music world" that I was "heir apparent" to. When I was a little older, Deanna often said to my dad in derision and heavy sarcasm, "What do you think Maury is, anyway— God's gift to the violin? Leave him alone and let him be a normal boy. You don't want him to become a totally warped person, do you?" She had my best interest at heart, but I think she also became jealous of me because I had such a hold on Dad.

The first thing he asked her when he walked in the door each night after work was, "Did Maury do his practicing today? How much did he do?" So Deanna had a genuine concern for me because of Dad's obsession concerning my music, and more and more she felt like she had second place in his affections. Dad's world always revolved around me and the violin. This created problems for her and aggravated the already strained relationship between all of us. Deanna's reaction was to build a strong relationship with Gloria and to favor her over me at times. This added to the sibling rivalry that had already developed between us, even though Gloria had just begun to walk.

As time went on, Deanna felt she had been robbed of her career with a major orchestra. There was so little for her musically in Iowa, and she began to develop a festering resentment toward Dad because of this. It did not surface until later, but the seeds were being planted at that time. I was really oblivious to all of this except the strife in our home, which at times was quite high between my parents.

Making memories

Nevertheless, there was still much that was warm and pleasant about our home life in Cedar Rapids. Dad took me out to a lake that had frozen over and taught me how to ice skate. After a few falls and some awkward and wobbly attempts, I got to where I could skate fairly well. I loved the winter activities there in Iowa that I was able to participate in, such as tobogganing, sledding, ice skating, and even snow-shoeing, which I was introduced to. During that winter, there were several big snowstorms, and it was great to be able to stay home from school and play in the snow with the other kids in the neighborhood.

I remember we had a very big and steep hill at the end of our street. Red Fox Road dropped severely at the other end, creating quite a dare-devil hill to sled and toboggan down after it iced over and snowed. I remember nearly getting killed going down that hill! We probably approached speeds of seventy miles an hour and more as we plummeted to the bottom. I got scared once when I nearly lost control, and I only tried it once or twice after that. But it was sure a whole lot of fun!

I received several letters from Audrey, my real mother, during my time in Iowa. Since I could read them, she addressed them directly to me. She had moved to Germany after marrying a man named Art Hille who was stationed there in the military. She seemed like a very far-away person. Her letters made me uncomfortable, and I wasn't encouraged by either of my parents to pursue much of a relationship with her. Dad never talked about her except in negative terms of how she had abandoned me, so I did not think very highly of her. But her letters had a sincere ring to them.

She said she felt guilty and was very sorry for not being there for me. She had a new baby boy named Louis who was supposed to be my brother, and she wondered if we could keep in touch. She asked that I please write back to her because she really missed me. I couldn't help thinking that if she missed me so much, why wouldn't she come and see me? It really didn't make a whole lot of sense. I tried to write back to her out of duty, but I never really enjoyed it, so I wrote her very little. Deanna had become my mother now. Even with all her faults and her favoritism of Gloria, I had accepted her as my mother. She really did treat me well most of the time.

Gloria was so cute when she was learning to walk and then toddling around with her curly blond hair and her sweet giggles. I loved playing with her inside the house during the long winter hours.

I thank God for the memories of our family at that time. I had a reasonably "normal" life for the next couple of years, playing with my precious baby sister and enjoying some of the benefits of a normal childhood. Unfortunately, those times would quickly pass into memory as my life started to take on the great quest of fulfilling my dad's dreams and the Lord's plans during the coming years. But just prior to that time, life had been as secure as it would ever be for me, even though many successes and triumphs were up ahead. That was the foundation that held me up through the first twenty-two years of my life. I thank God for what He did for me and for all the good that was a part of my parents' attempts at raising me without the Lord. By His grace, God made up much of what I needed. Praise His holy name!

Things weren't going so well for Dad at the Cedar Rapids Symphony. For whatever reason, they were not happy with him and the job he was doing. He didn't seem to fit in with the hometown, laid-back, Midwestern pace of life and was probably too demanding on the musicians. Dad had a short temper and wanted everything done perfectly. He demanded it from himself and expected everyone else to do likewise. They wanted an easy-going, farmer type who would just go with the flow. He was so frustrated with them that he would come home and be ready to tear out his hair because of their lack of competence. The problem was that they were convinced they were quite competent, thank you, and they didn't need his input or his suggestions. He just turned them off. So they fired him. Unfortunately, that wasn't too convenient for us.

The entire summer of 1971 was pretty hard on all of us as a family. Since Dad was unemployed, he was at home all the time, except when he traveled for interviews. We couldn't wait until he was working at something—any-thing—again! He was so irritable and felt really down on himself because he wasn't providing for his family. He kept saying he made a big mistake when he left Atlanta.

Since I was home all the time, Dad decided that would be a fine opportunity to teach me daily on the violin. That was the most intensive summer we ever had together. He took out his frustrations on me. He would practice with me sometimes for over three hours at a time. We would repeat passages of my music over and over again until it was good enough for him. I was really excelling in my studies, but I was beginning to hate and dread each day when I had to get my violin out of the case.

Dad's temper was at an all-time high. His fuse was as short as I had ever seen it. He was getting more and more exasperated at failing to find a job. When he was gone, it eased up considerably, but when he returned after not find-ing anything, it was bad. Deanna would nag him and com-plain about Iowa, asking him why he had taken her away from Atlanta and her career. She was being affected by the financial pressure also and reacted by coming down on Dad and me. So no one was more relieved than I was when the position in the law firm opened up in Baton Rouge and we said good-bye to Iowa forever.

A new start in Louisiana

Now Dad could reclaim his place in the upper-middle class as a respected attorney in the community. He proba-bly was getting the best salary he had ever received. Dad had many friends from his college days at LSU, and this was a tremendous help to him in getting established. Most of the attorneys and all of the professional community oper-ated on the "good-old-boy" buddy system. Being "some-body" was determined by whom you knew and what family you came from more than by how brilliant you were or how good a job you did in your profession. You had to go hunt-ing and fishing with the right people, own a lake-side camp-ing home on False River where you invited the "who's who" for crawfish boils and long weekends of water skiing, and generally hobnob in the right way with the establishment. That's how the moneyed people "lived and let live" in the bayou land of Louisiana.

Nothing turned Dad off more than this type of political stuff. Nevertheless, he was and still is so brilliant in Louisiana tax law that to this day he is one of the most respected attorneys in all of Louisiana. He still is practicing law in Baton Rouge at the time of this writing.

Thank God, the financial pressure was gone—and so were the relentless and tormenting violin lessons I had endured that summer in Cedar Rapids while Dad was unemployed. Now, with him back at work, I could escape and do some other things after school and on weekends. I enjoyed riding my bike through the immense and labyrinthian subdivision we had moved into! I would meet all kinds of people—both adults and children—during my outings. I had quite the adventures!

Baton Rouge wasn't Atlanta, but it was a whole lot better for my parents. They began to return to their preferences and their convictions. They could be "artists" again, and because Dad had landed such a good job, the finances were there to make us comfortable. They were now respected in the community, and that meant a great deal to them. Dad was a part of an elite law firm and had a lot of perks that the position allowed him, including membership in the exclusive "City Club" with it's old-South hospitality.

Deanna and Dad both had positions in the Baton Rouge Symphony Orchestra. Deanna could still play the violin well and was in the symphony and the local music community. Dad still plays in the symphony at the time of this writing—and has every season since 1971. The Lord has blessed him with a good life in Baton Rouge.

Failure formula

Since it was September and school had already begun, I was put into the public elementary school in our area. Let me tell you a formula that will guarantee failure for an eight-year-old in the public school system in Baton Rouge, Louisiana. I know—I tried it. First, be an outsider coming in after school has begun. Second, don't be good in sports. Be on the weaker side and physically skinny. Third, add to that a smart alecky attitude in class as you demonstrate how much you know. Fourth, become the teacher's pet. Always add to the discussions and answer every question right, and thus make the other students look dumb and foolish. Fifth—like cherries on top of a nauseating sundae—play the violin, wear thick glasses, and be Jewish. That's it—the sure-fire formula for hell on earth in school.

Now, I knew nothing about being Jewish at that time, and I don't want to magnify something that I was totally unaware of. But I know that it is like wearing a badge in the spirit realm, saying, "Please do your best to persecute me."

Well, I managed to get all of the appropriate negative responses that were humanly possible from one group of kids during the next three years. It got very familiar for me, for it had happened over and over. Why did this happen? It happened for several reasons. I was living in a family with a very warped sense of values. They considered that the more I demonstrated my "precociousness," the more value I had. I was admired for my violin playing and my intellectual abilities with all Dad's and Deanna's adult friends. I was once again providing more fuel for their social ascension through my clear demonstration of his superior rearing and genetics.

On several occasions, when I arrived home beaten up with my clothes torn, Dad would say to me, "Maury, you can't just let them do this to you. Take a brick and throw it at them and hit them in the head or something. I can't stand this 'turning the other cheek' business. What's wrong with you? Fight back! I don't blame them for doing that to you when you act the way you do. You deserve it. If you don't fight back, you'll be the laughingstock of the school. I guess you are that, anyway."

When he had calmed down and was not so angry, he would say, "Maury, you are different than other kids your own age. It's not your fault. You have a special talent on the violin, and you are very smart. I never fit in with my schoolmates, either. When you grow up some more and can be with other musicians and artists like yourself, they will accept you and like you. Don't worry about it. You'll have the last laugh one day when you are playing violin all over the world and they are stuck in some grocery store, punching a clock, and reading about you in the paper. But if you don't practice and develop, you'll just be like them. We'll see how well you'll do in music.

"If I had had your talent, I could have made it in music, even though I started late. But you will have everything that I can give you—then if you fail, you'll have nobody to blame but yourself. Stop being so talkative with those classmates of yours. Stand up like a man and fight them. If you can't do that, maybe they are right—maybe you really are just a sissy violinist. Take a crowbar and whack one of them in the head and send them to the hospital, and they will stop giving you trouble."

It's hard to find a crowbar when you don't know what one is, much less taking it with you to school without being noticed. Besides, even if I'd had one, I would have gotten so paralyzed with fear that they could have taken it away from me and finished me off with it. So I never tried anything like that. I wasn't capable of proving my manhood by sending someone to the hospital. I was really a case!

However, things were not all bad during that year. I had some good times at home with Gloria when we played together. I really liked her very much. My violin playing was continuing, of course. I was learning and growing quite a bit on the violin. It was an escape for me from the awful days in school. I really believed what Dad said—that I would be a great violinist and when I "made it," I would be happy. It was the only thing I had to hope for. The music world held my salvation from the horrors of the real world.

One evening as I was riding in the car with Dad, he began telling me about a very special school. He said, "Maury, there is a school where the most talented children from all over the world go to study their instruments. I think you may be good enough on the violin to go there one day. A few of the kids are only ten or twelve years old, and they get to leave regular school and go to this school because they are so good. It is the Curtis Institute of Music in Philadelphia, Pennsylvania. I auditioned to go there once, but I wasn't good enough.

"If you really work hard, perhaps you can audition there and get in. If you make it and they accept you, it is free tuition. Some kids get to study music all the time. You would like that because then you would be with others who are as talented as you, and you would fit in much better.

"Maury, if you reach sixteen or seventeen years of age and you don't have a solid technique on the violin by then, you can just forget it—you'll never make it! Then you would have to play in an orchestra like Mommy and I do, and you would be miserable. But I know you can make it as a soloist. So it is very important for you to develop to where you can play the big violin concertos by the time you audition. If you are really great on your instrument, you will get into Curtis before you are out of high school."

I thought, *What a wonderful school!*

It sounded like fairy-tale land. If only I was so good that I could be there, people would like me and wouldn't make fun of me. That had a powerful influence on me as an eight year old. I determined right then that I wanted to go to that special school where I wouldn't be so unhappy. If only I was good enough on the violin, then I would be happy. That was the clear and ever-present message that Dad gave to me. So the stock in my becoming a fine violinist was rising. I simply *had* to succeed musically in order to survive in life.

Chapter 6

Laying the Foundation For My Life

Shortly after we moved to Baton Rouge, my parents began looking for a violin teacher for me. They wanted someone who could challenge me and teach me correctly while being gentle and compassionate at the same time. They found an older graduate student studying for his doctorate at LSU. His name was Harvey Olin. He was very nice to me and saw right away that I had great potential on the violin. He took a very loving interest in me right from the first. I liked him very much. I was so happy to get away from having to work every day with Dad the way I had all the previous summer in Cedar Rapids. It was such a relief to finally have a teacher outside the home again! I was truly nourished by his love for music in general, his love for me and my talent in particular, and his tremendous devotion to violin pedagogy.

He treated me like a priceless Fabergé egg most of the time. He felt that I was so fragile I could break if he didn't teach me correctly. Please understand, I never thought I was good enough on the violin. No matter how good I played, I wasn't good enough for Dad. There was always the next plateau to reach. I never seemed to "arrive" very long before embarking on the next violinistic challenge. I felt like a failure on the instrument and as a person. But for Harvey, I was a dream come true. He really enjoyed teaching me. I looked forward to my lessons because he was very encouraging to me. He was a methodical teacher who taught me to practice patiently until I mastered something.

I have never known a more dedicated teacher of the violin. During my lessons, I was always aware of his great friendship and respect. I knew that he loved me very much. In fact, he, and especially his wife, Esther, touched my life spiritually in a profound way then and also in the years ahead. They were strong evangelical Christians. They probably are responsible for praying me into my salvation and awesome conversion that occurred several years later. I thank God for allowing them to impact my life from such a young age. The Lord sent Harvey Olin to be my teacher at a time when I needed someone just like him. I needed someone who could share Jesus' love with me in a practical way through my music—planting the seeds of the gospel that would come up later in my life and bear much fruit.

My first music camp experience

One day my parents found out that a friend from Atlanta was going to be teaching at a summer music camp in Greensboro, North Carolina, called "Eastern Music Festival" (EMF). Dad thought it would be a good experience for me to attend this music camp the following summer. I was very excited at the thought of being big enough to leave home and be away from my parents for a whole summer. It was a six-week program, starting at the end of June and going into August. I was very vocal about my desire to attend, and with Dad's high ambition for me, it wasn't too difficult to convince my parents that this was indeed a fine opportunity. However, looking back, it is shocking to realize that they allowed me to be away from home for an entire summer when I had just turned nine. They let me live almost entirely unsupervised in a college dormitory with a bunch of high school and college kids at the end of the drug and hippie era!

I applied for and was accepted at EMF for the summer of 1972. I turned nine years old in June, and we drove up to North Carolina about a week and a half later. Dad and

Deanna got me situated in the dorm where I was to room with a clarinet student. They introduced me to their friend, Derry Drinkall, who was going to be my violin teacher. They showed me where the bathroom, the cafeteria, and the concert hall were, and then they said, "Good-bye! See you at the end of the summer!"

Dad wrote to me once a week on his law-firm letterhead. He dictated his letters and had his secretary type them. That was the primary way Dad communicated with me from then on. Sometimes his letters contained a check! If there was one, it was usually small enough to keep me in financial anxiety, but I did read his letters faithfully when they came. He tried his best to communicate his love from a distance after banishing me from his life and into the world he thought was best for me.

Somehow, I survived that summer. The kids I lived with at EMF thought of me as the little kid who got into trouble without even trying. I was simply too young to be in that type of situation alone, but I could adapt easily to new things, so I managed to make it through the summer. At least the kids didn't make fun of me like the kids did in school. I thought they liked me and believed I was a really good violinist for my age. I even thought they respected me! Actually, most of the kids put up with me because they realized I was far too young to be there.

Ironically, I left EMF thinking "the music world" was a much nicer place than "the real world" I had to return to that fall when I went back home to Baton Rouge. I concluded that if this was the music world of which my father spoke, I was indeed much happier in it and could fit in far better among musicians than anywhere else. He was right!

I played so much in the lowest student orchestra there at EMF that I began to develop some bad habits. I developed some stiffness in my right arm and was raising my shoulder too high for my bow arm to be positioned properly. When I returned to Baton Rouge, Dad immediately noticed this and was alarmed. He and Harvey Olin began working with me to help me get over it. My parents were sure that I hadn't practiced as I should have.

They were also concerned about the profanity that sometimes came out of my mouth without my realizing it. For humanists who didn't believe in God, they quickly became moral when I didn't "speak right." They thought swearing was vulgar and beneath both them and me. They decided that I would not go back to the festival unless circumstances were a whole lot different. They blamed the EMF administration for their lack of care for me.

When school started in the fall, I was assigned to Mrs. Nolan's fourth grade class. I really liked her! I sat right in the front across from her desk. She was the nicest teacher I had ever had in school. I liked Mrs. Nolan because she had something very special about her. I know now that it was her spirit. She knew Jesus. I couldn't put my finger on it at the time, but there was a special love in her heart that was apparent in the way she looked or smiled at me. I knew that she really liked me, and I did my best to really do well in my studies for her.

One day, a couple of men came to our class and talked about the Bible. They said they were Gideons and would give each of us a free copy of the New Testament if we would like to have one. They loved the Bible and wanted to give it to as many people as possible. I thought they were rather boring at first, but I found myself raising my hand when they offered their Bibles.

I remember taking that Bible home and reading some of it. It was a pocket-sized King James Version of the New Testament. It had a bright red plastic cover and very-hard-to-read small print. I kept it by my bed, though, and started to read some of it. I read from the book of Revelation, and it scared me. I somehow knew that this was no ordinary book. So I asked Dad about it. He said I shouldn't believe the stories in the Bible because they were made up by people and were not true. We never went to church anymore—even to the Unitarian one. We just stayed at home on Sundays.

A few weeks later, Dad decided that I should go to a service at a Jewish synagogue because I was asking about God again. It was a Jewish New Year's service. Dad told me that Judaism was my heritage, and he said if I was going to believe in religion or God, the synagogue was the place to find out about Him. It was a strange service, I thought, with the Rabbi dancing around with the Torah scrolls and everybody following him and singing in a strange language. They did give out candy, and I liked that! The rest of the service was boring. The Rabbi didn't even talk in English most of the time, and when he did, he mumbled so much I couldn't understand him anyway.

Dad told me he thought I was old enough to go to this special service, especially since I was asking about God. He wasn't about to let some "fanatics" who came into the public schools convert me. He had also arranged for the Rabbi to meet with me to discuss God. The Rabbi gave me a book of prayers and told me to remember that I am Jewish, which meant almost nothing to me. Then he said if I wanted to know God, I must learn that He is the God of Abraham, Isaac, and Jacob. That was the only Jewish service Dad ever took me to.

Now I had two religious books on my shelf—my little Gideon's Bible, which I knew Dad didn't approve of, and this Jewish prayer book that no one ever explained to me. The prayer book made absolutely no sense when I tried to read it. Every once in a while, I would take the little Bible down and try to read it—also without success. It was written in old Elizabethan English, which I couldn't understand, even if I could decipher the tiny print.

A visit with my mother

The school year ended, and we had decided that summer music camp was not the way to go for me that year. The summer of 1973 was the only summer I did not attend a music school or camp until I was nineteen years old. That year, Audrey invited me to come and visit her for my birthday. At that time, she was living in Albuquerque, New Mexico, with her husband, Art Hille, and her young son, Louis. So I flew out to visit her for a couple of weeks in June, and she was very happy to see me.

Audrey and Art Hille were anxious that my stay with them be as trouble-free as possible. But because of our tumultuous past, there was simply too much emotional baggage attached to every conversation and interaction with my mother. It was like living with nitroglycerin. If you shook it too hard, it would explode. She meant well, but I was increasingly more uncomfortable with each passing day.

No matter what I said, I felt Audrey construed it as some kind of an insult toward her. If I started to talk about anything concerning Dad or my home life in Baton Rouge, she would walk out of the room or start crying and say that I hated her. She said that Dad and Deanna had put all kinds of lies in my head concerning her and that I would never be her son in the way she wished. She felt so bad about leaving me as a baby. She said that she had to because Dad was so mean to her and forced her to leave. Then she would start to cry again and look at me with her big brown eyes filled with pathetic tears and tell me that she loved me. I truly did feel compassion for her. But at the same time, I felt smothered. I tried as much as a ten year old can to get along with Audrey, but it wasn't working out well. So because of that, we decided I would return to Baton Rouge earlier than we had planned.

After my trip, I was happy to get back home. However, Deanna and Dad weren't getting along too well. There were more and more arguments with the resulting slammed doors and screaming. Deanna wasn't very happy in Baton Rouge, and she again began to accuse Dad of taking her away from Atlanta and her career. She kept a record of wrongs done to her and would read the long list to Dad several times a week.

I never fully agreed with Deanna; I was just confused about her. I had made a commitment that Dad was right about life and especially about the music world. After the EMF summer the year before, the music world seemed to be my salvation and my only ticket out of the crazy, confusing, and painful world of my childhood.

Nevertheless, I hated the occasional lessons Dad inflicted upon me. Even worse were the comments if I missed a note, was practicing too fast, or played a passage out of tune. Occasionally, I got so angry I kicked the walls in frustration and cursed! I wanted to run away and somehow get out of my home. I didn't want to live there anymore, but there was nowhere for me to go. I also didn't want to keep playing the violin, but I knew it was my ticket out of that house, if I was good enough. It was all I believed I could do. If I quit, I thought my parents would be terribly upset with me and tell me that I had wasted my life and thrown away this great gift they had never had. I was afraid I would be banished from their affection and would never receive anything but everlasting contempt and shame from them. So I was stuck. I had to play the violin, so I endured for the next few years as best I could. The consequences for quitting were simply too devastating to even consider doing so.

The fall of 1973 came, and I had to return to school. I actually stayed in one school for three entire years! That was the last time I would do so before college.

Scheming my way out of practicing

Deanna had to pick up Gloria from school each afternoon and run errands, so she was usually gone by the time I got home from the bus stop. Most of the time, I would go to the kitchen and get some kind of snack for myself out of the refrigerator. I was then supposed to practice for at least two hours. However, I liked watching "Star Trek," which came on at six o'clock, and before it aired, there was "Gilligan's Island," "The Partridge Family," and "The Brady Bunch."

Now, our TV set was in the den next to the stairs. I was supposed to be practicing in my room, which was upstairs, opposite the stairs. I usually went into the den, turned on the TV, and watched my shows. Sometimes Deanna would be out until close to six o'clock, but most of the time she returned home between four o'clock and five o'clock. Of course, as soon as she entered the kitchen, she would be listening for my violin. That was because of Dad's BIG question, which he asked every day after work: "How much did Maury practice today?"

I devised a scheme that allowed me to watch TV, turn it off, run up the stairs and across the house to my room, pick up my violin, and start practicing before Deanna entered the back door. Most of the time I successfully made it. For those times when I didn't hear the car entering the garage, I would jump up off the sofa in the den, punch the TV knob off, dash up the stairs and into the upstairs bathroom, and flush the toilet. I could make it to the bathroom at the top of the stairs in time, even without hearing anything more than her hand on the door latch. That way, she only thought I was going to the bathroom and that gave me time to get to my room where I was "practicing" before she came in. I think I saw a whole lot of episodes of "The Brady Bunch" only halfway through!

I did practice diligently, in spite of this. Even with my dishonest scheme, I still had to practice whenever my parents were home. Sometimes when I got to playing I liked it, and that made it easier. But most of the time, it was hour after hour of drudgery as I practiced my scales and studies and whatever piece I was working on for Dr. Olin.

I spent my entire sixth-grade year working on *Introduction and Rondo Capriccioso* by Saint-Seans. It was way above my level, both technically and musically, but he insisted that I play it. So I worked and worked on this piece. Finally, after nearly nine months of practice and with Dad's coaching, I was ready to play it for what I felt was a big competition in New Orleans. It was the young artist competition for the New Orleans Philharmonic. I played for it, and I won! That gave me a chance to play it with the orchestra for one of their children's concerts.

I wanted to please Dad, and in order to do that, I felt I had to play at a certain level before "it was too late." He played recordings for me of great violinists such as David Oistrakh, Jascha Heifetz, and Isaac Stern. He told me that this was how I had to play. He said that the "greats" on the violin could all play anything by the time they were in their mid-teens. If I didn't practice now, he said, and gain the kind of technique they had, I could just forget a solo career.

That was Dad's great dream for me—a solo concert career! When he spoke of it, his eyes would light up and he would describe what a wonderful life it was to travel all over the world, playing concerts, making lots of money, and having everyone falling over you wherever you went because you played so beautifully!

Then he would look at me very sternly and say, "You have everything it takes to make it. I could never play the way you can. You have a shot at a major concert career, but if you don't practice, you can just forget it. If you have to settle for playing in an orchestra, it's worse than anything else. I know. I've been with them and seen those fiddle players in orchestras. They are miserable. They feel like slaves—like Ben Hur chained to the galleys and pulling the oars for some stupid, idiotic conductor's musical interpretation. But you have a chance to be even greater than the violin soloists playing today. If only you would turn your brain on and go for it instead of playing so halfheartedly."

Of course, I had heard the same litany from Dad for years. It was nothing new. I never really wanted to play the violin when I got away from Dad and was alone, but when I was with him and under the spell of his proclamations concerning my musical "destiny," I was swayed into thinking and dreaming with him. I got to where I really believed his words, as any eleven-year-old would.

Back to EMF

In the spring of 1974, Dad and Deanna were talking about the Eastern Music Festival once again. Deanna wanted to do some real orchestral playing again. There was a faculty orchestra that met there for the summer each year, and she was interested in playing the violin in it. We encountered some resistance from the administration as to whether or not I should be admitted again as the youngest student (I was still only eleven years old) after their experience with me in 1972, but they finally agreed to accept me on the condition that Deanna would be there to supervise and to chaperone me.

So Deanna, Gloria, and I drove up to North Carolina in late June of 1974. I was very happy to be there again, but it was kind of strange having my mom just across the lawn in the faculty dormitory. I practiced very little that summer—in fact, almost none—but I had a blast! I realized that the music world was truly where I fit in. I loved being there even though I wasn't really ready for it. God somehow preserved me through at lot of difficult and trying experiences.

I had a bubbly, unsinkable enthusiasm that seemed to carry me through anything. I was so optimistic about life and music that nothing seemed to bother me. Criticism and misunderstanding just rolled off me like water off a duck's back as long as I had a few friends who would comfort me when I felt bad. Yes, life seemed to be good, and the world was a sunny place for me at EMF. I was living in that particular fantasy that Dad had painted for me of a wonderful and glamorous music world where I could live happily ever after. That would be my "pretend world" for many years to come.

From my summers at Eastern Music Festival and from my early life with my parents came the foundation for my perceptions of life, music, and my place in both. By the time I was eleven years old, they were solidly in place in my inner consciousness. They were built so strongly by my father's words of faith spoken over me (thank God for the good in that) and reinforced through my experiences at home and at EMF that they lasted all the way into my early adult life. It is remarkable how powerful and strong the perceptions had been built into me by my father! Life was a wonderful, scary, unpredictable, and awesome experience for me.

Chapter 7

Studying With Fredell Lack

As I began school the next fall, life at home remained much the same as it had always been. I arrived home in the middle of the afternoon and had to practice as usual. Harvey Olin had moved to New Orleans, so I went down there every other week with my parents for lessons. I began to dream more and more about leaving home when I was older, going into music, and about the wonderful times I would have then. Dad and Deanna were fighting more and more, and I really wasn't happy at home. I talked about EMF all the time and how much fun it had been for me to be there. I forgot how hard it actually was. I romanticized it to the point that it became a distorted fairy tale. I lived for the time when I could leave home and be at EMF again. I hated the strife that was becoming more prevalent in our family. Dreaming was my way of escape.

I realized that the violin was my only ticket out, so I began to practice more and to take a little more interest in my playing. As I did, I began to play better and better. I had a lot of trouble really believing that I could play all those impossible-sounding pieces I listened to constantly, but I gave Dad the benefit of the doubt that he knew best.

It was like listening to some kind of Darth Vader inside of my conscience, breathing sinisterly and constantly saying, "Violin is your Destiny, Maury Sklar." In a certain way, that was true. God was in the training I received and in the details of my upbringing far more than I can even perceive at this time. The Lord is able to use everything in our lives—even what the devil sends to destroy us—and turn it to our good. However, at the time, I felt trapped. I had very ambivalent feelings toward the violin, as you might understand. At times I wanted to quit altogether, but like some kind of poker game that I had played too long to quit, I had to play to the finish, bluff and all!

Everyone else thought I played well, but a morbid, almost paranoid fear that I wasn't good enough on the violin began to dog me then and for the next fifteen years of my life. For better or worse, however, I had decided that music would be my life. I was in too deep and had, even at that time, invested too much of myself in it to give it up. I would do all I could to fulfill Dad's dream for me and his vicarious obsession to live his life through me. I had no choice. The die was cast and my fate was sealed. I was going to be a violinist, and that was that.

Meeting Miss Lack

One night that spring, I went with my parents to the Concert Hall to watch a rehearsal of the Baton Rouge Symphony. There was a special soloist playing violin with the Symphony by the name of Fredell Lack. She was in her fifties at the time and was performing *Symphonie Espagnol* by Lalo. It is quite a virtuoso piece. Dad and Deanna wanted me to hear her in rehearsal in addition to the concert so I could watch how a real artist works with an orchestra to prepare for a concert.

Miss Lack had studied in New York years ago with the great Armenian violin teacher Ivan Galamian. He was the greatest violin teacher of the early and middle twentieth century. He had produced most of the famous violinists of the previous twenty-five years, and she was one of his first artists. Fredell Lack was in her prime in the 1930s and '40s when she lived in New York. She taught and headed the violin department at the University of Houston in Texas and was one of the most respected teachers in the southwest.

I don't remember much about her performance, but I do remember meeting her for the first time. I was practicing that day and working down in the lower level of the auditorium near her dressing room. I was practicing on my Saint-Saens piece. She heard it, flung open her dressing room door, and exclaimed, "You sound wonderful! What a beautiful sound and from such a small boy!"

Miss Lack was such a great lady, but she was so melodramatic and gushy that she bowled me over. At first I didn't know who she was, but finally I recognized her as the violin soloist.

She said, "You know, Dearie, you are practicing too fast! You have to listen more carefully. But what a wonderful talent you are. What is your name?"

I told her it was Maury Sklar and that my parents played in the orchestra. I had come to listen to her part of the rehearsal, I said, and I really liked her violin playing. She smiled in her matronly way and exclaimed, "I think you are quite a talent on the fiddle yourself! I was listening to you for a while before I walked in. Such fingers! But you need a good teacher. How old are you, Sweetie?"

I told her I was eleven years old. She just looked at me and smiled with great affection. Her eyes twinkled, and as she closed the door she said, "It was wonderful to meet you and to hear you play. I hope I can hear you again sometime." And then she was gone.

My last summer at EMF

I returned to Eastern Music Festival in the summer of 1975 for the last time. I had made significant progress on the violin that year and now could play in the more advanced orchestra. I was very frustrated with my life at home in Baton Rouge, and the summer came as a welcome relief! My parents could not stop fighting, and I knew it wouldn't be long before they would split up. The strife at home and the pressure on me was enormous, and I just wanted out.

I decided that as soon as it was possible, I would leave home. I knew that if I played on my father's desire to see me succeed as an artist, I could leave home and study the violin. I had reached the point where Harvey Olin couldn't really teach me anymore, and I was ready for a more advanced teacher. I wasn't improving as fast as Dad would have liked. After all, I was nearly twelve years old! From the way he talked, you would have thought that soon I would be "over the hill" and my life would end. I was so thankful when the summer finally arrived. I could get away from it all and have fun in my now familiar North Carolina oasis of summer rebelliousness.

One day I wandered into an academic building that was next door to the library. I started thinking how wonderful it must be to be grown-up and going to college. I figured the students who attended there in the fall must have a great time. I thought, *I wish I could be one of them. I could just be "normal" and not have to play the violin.*

I began to daydream about running away from home and living in some college—maybe this one. I could hide out in the library, find meals in the cafeteria, and sleep in some basement where no one could find me. But I knew that was ridiculous and impossible. I guess I just didn't want the summer to end. I liked it there.

As I was resting in one of the chairs near the doorway, I realized how quiet it was in the building! I wondered, *Is anyone watching me? Is anyone out there?* As soon as I asked myself that question, I felt that Presence come into the foyer where I was. *What is that?* I wondered. I looked around but nobody was there. Even the janitor was off that day. Still, I knew Someone was watching me. Someone was with me. The room was filled with peace. I decided that whoever or whatever this was, I wanted it to never leave.

I didn't move for several hours. I didn't want to leave there. I knew it was something very special. I never heard a word, but I talked with this Presence and asked Him to help me because life was so hard for me. I began to cry as that Presence got stronger and stronger all around me. It was as if it was hugging me and holding me in its grasp. I felt such indescribable love and peace! Like a warm blanket, it covered me from head to foot. It was awesome! I knew that was a special place.

After that day, I returned to the room from time to time to see if that experience would happen to me again—but it never did, and I soon forgot about it.

I was having some serious emotional problems at that time, although I didn't speak much to my parents about them. I would sometimes walk the hallways of Milner Hall or go into the basement to be alone and just cry and fall into a feeling of hopelessness. What was going to happen to me? Could I ever escape? There was simply no way out. I intuitively knew that if I didn't quit playing the violin now, I could never quit. It was my last chance. Maybe it was still possible for me to be a "normal" kid...maybe I still could escape from this whirlpool of expectation and pressure that I was being sucked into. I realized that for me to continue the violin I had to get serious about it and that meant living up to the standards that were rising rapidly in Dad's estimation.

In his mind, time was getting short. I was now twelve years old and my teen years were about to begin. In order to "make it," I had to play like those records I had heard in the library and on the eight-track tapes that Dad played constantly in the car. It seemed impossible to me that I could ever sound that good on the violin. Dad said I had to play that way before I reached my last year of high school or I could just forget it! The vortex of that whirlpool and the gravity of that "black hole" was pulling me in fast. I knew that once I started school in the fall, there was no turning back. There was no way out and no escape.

Finally I decided that I would go for it. I would only be held in shame and contempt by my parents if I quit, and I couldn't handle that. So again I plunged on toward my solo career on the violin.

The summer ended, and again I returned home to Baton Rouge. During the summer, Dad had contacted Fredell Lack, the lady violinist from Houston, Texas, thinking she might be a good teacher for me. He had decided that I should go and play for her, even though it would mean a five-hour drive from Baton Rouge to Houston every other weekend, if she agreed to take me as a student.

Studying with Miss Lack

Miss Lack was an artist through and through! She had a lovely personality, even if it was a bit smothering. She was a "Yiddische Mama" in the truest sense of the word. I became like her musical son. This was to be a relationship that would continue for many years to come. I thank God for Fredell Lack and all she taught me. She was a non-religious but very Jewish lady who saw great potential in me.

Without her teaching and impartation, I would not be the violinist I am today. She will always remain one of the most important people ever to cross my path in this lifetime.

God definitely arranged for me to study with her! It was an honor to have such a teacher. If there is such a thing as royalty, I first saw it in her. I admired her greatly. She carried herself in a regal way and always treated me with tremendous devotion and respect. God bless Fredell Lack for what she has been in my life. Musically and emotionally, she was the closest thing I ever had to a mother during the next several years and into my adult life.

Once again, school began and I plunged in. Fortunately, I managed to get through the school year with far less problems than I had had in the past. There were still some of the kids who made fun of me, but gone forever was the agony of my elementary school days, thank God!

I traveled to Houston every other weekend for my lessons with Miss Lack, and they were quite a production. Now it wasn't just an hour-and-a-half drive to New Orleans; it was a weekend-long trip with a five-hour drive each way and an overnight stay. Also, my parents weren't getting along any better, and sometimes the hours in the car were nearly unbearable as the arguments and the strife reached record highs. Many times Dad would get frustrated and take it out on me and Gloria. I just tried to lie down in the back seat and sleep or at least pretend I was sleeping.

The lessons themselves were great for me musically, however. Often I would get to fly to Houston from Baton Rouge or New Orleans and stay at Miss Lack's house when Dad and Mom were busy and we couldn't drive. Dad would drive me to the airport, give me the ticket, and drop me off. I really enjoyed flying on the airplane by myself. I felt very mature and quite satisfied with myself for getting to and from the airport and negotiating all the logistics involved. It was fun.

I worked on scales and studies and the *Bach E Major Violin Concerto* for several months after starting to work with Miss Lack. I was practicing more for her than I ever had before, and she seemed pleased with my progress. I felt very nurtured by her teaching and her love for music. It entered into my spirit like water into a fertile garden. Since I was from out of town, she gave me really long lessons. They always lasted at least two hours and many times would go as long as three hours. She would leave all of Saturday afternoon open for them.

She really believed in me and told me she thought I had all it took to "make it." (There was that terrible phrase once again!) And I believed her. Still, she was one more person whom I had to please and for whom I now had to prove that I could do it. I was a little intimidated by her, but I started making significant progress.

I started playing some local concerts and in a few small competitions. Once I even played for my high school assembly. I played solo violin for the entire student body of fourteen hundred kids! I played a march etude of Kreutzer. Then I played a version of the bluegrass tune "Orange Blossom Special" that a boy had taught me by ear at EMF the previous summer. The kids listened politely to the first selection and went wild when I played the last one! It brought down the house! They loved it! Now everyone in school knew I was a violinist. They liked the bluegrass-frenzied piece very much. It was a great victory for me to be affirmed in such a situation.

I had also felt an unseen hand come over me and help me play. I always felt it, but this time it was unusually strong. I remember thinking, *What is helping me to play the violin in these situations? I don't play that well in my practice.* But I told myself, *It's just my imagination. That's just me playing. Don't be ridiculous!* So I dismissed the feeling and chalked it up to the fact that I must be as talented as Dad and everyone said I was. Even so, I knew I wasn't really able to cause that kind of response myself. I just knew Something was helping me every time I performed. But I didn't like to think about it for very long, so I dismissed such thoughts very quickly.

My home life was deteriorating at an alarming rate. By now, Deanna was quite jealous of me, in addition to being genuinely concerned about Dad's obsession with me. More and more I heard her say, "Chuck, leave that boy alone. Do you want to ruin him? It's not worth it! What do you think he is anyway—God's gift to the violin? Give me a break!" She hated that she could never occupy the place in his heart that his obsession toward my music had. So she began to favor Gloria openly and to really spurn me at times. I knew Deanna, however, and I understood that she couldn't help herself when she got into certain emotional states.

Dad began to talk to me about how unhappy he was and how he couldn't live that way any longer. In his mind, he never did anything wrong and had never done any wrong either toward me or her. It was no use trying to point out his part in it all—it fell on deaf ears. He could not see it. So I began to hear hours and hours of accusations from both of them toward each other.

Their confiding in me put me in a very awkward position! I was their twelve-year-old marriage counselor. This produced such confusion and frustration in me, that I didn't know what to believe anymore about my parents. All I knew was that each of them thought the other was worse than the scum of the earth. They wanted me to agree that they were in the right and the other one was evil to the core. It got to where I nearly hated both of them. I thought they were both evil!

A new summer challenge

As summer approached, Miss Lack told me about a very special summer music school/camp that she thought I should attend called the Meadowmount School of Music. It was in upper-state New York. A whole group of her students was going there, and she was to be teaching there. She said Ivan Galamian, a great violin teacher with whom she had studied as a child, taught there. She wanted me to study with him. She told me she would introduce me and maybe he would take me as a student that summer.

She said the very best students from all over the world went there to study and perform concerts in the beautiful mountains near Lake Champlain just south of Lake Placid. She thought it would do me well to be in such a musically rich, intensive environment. There was no orchestra playing there, just solo and chamber music concerts. There was nothing to do but practice all day long. The most shocking thing Miss Lack said about Meadowmount was that everyone was required to practice five hours a day! I had never practiced that much in a day! How in the world did anyone practice like that? It sounded like torture! I finally agreed to go, and I told Miss Lack that if she would help me, I would do my best up there.

Miss Lack had told me not to be discouraged if I wasn't the best player there for my age. She said there would be many great young talents and prodigies there who studied with Mr. Galamian. She said I was just there to learn, not to impress them or to be better than they were—because I wasn't. I would be just one among a number of others my age—a talented group of young people from all over the world. I had never seen that before. I had always been the best for my age group everywhere I had been.

So I prepared my heart the best I could for this big change in my life. I was now entering a much bigger pond. I wouldn't be the "big fish" prodigy like I had been at EMF anymore, and I knew it. The summer would prove to be not only challenging, but would have eternal significance for me. I wondered, *Will I be good enough?*

Chapter 8

Accepting Jesus
As My Savior

A group of Miss Lack's college students and I attended Meadowmount that year. We drove up from Houston right after my thirteenth birthday during the third week of June. The day after our arrival, I auditioned for Mr. Galamian, and he accepted me as one of his students. I found out later that this was an honor that didn't come easily for outsiders who were not hand-picked to study with him in New York City. His time was limited for new summer students, and he certainly wasn't getting any younger, so he was in great demand.

I called Dad, of course, and told him of the success. He was pleased and told me that I had better practice really hard that summer so I wouldn't blow such a tremendous opportunity. I promised that I would.

Private lessons were given by the assistant teachers, Mr. Galamian himself, and the cello and viola teachers, and they began at the same time and went all day long. The focus here was not orchestral playing but on solo and chamber music playing. String quartets and other types of groups were formed for those desiring to play chamber music, and they rehearsed in the afternoons. Concerts were at night in the screened-in concert hall and started at 7:30. There were two concerts open to the public on Wednesday and Sunday nights.

Looking back, it seems a lot like the way we attend church now. Actually, it was church. The concert hall was the "temple" where all of us went to worship the big talents, the great music, and the composers. We were inspired to practice and were mesmerized by such a high standard of violin playing that we began to worship those things instead of God. Music was our god.

I was quite amazed at the incredible string playing I heard at the concerts. I had never heard such mastery of the violin, viola, and cello as I heard that summer. Miss Lack kept drilling me in the proper form and assigned the *Mozart Concerto #4* and some Bach and etudes. It was a lot of work. I felt so discouraged up there because it seemed that I wasn't so good any more. I worked harder up there that summer than I had ever worked before, mainly due to the peer pressure and the great stress of violin lessons with Mr. Galamian.

The concerts were probably the hardest things for any mere mortal to endure if you were performing in them. Can you imagine having to play a half-hour-long piece (or more) by memory in front of someone like Mr. Galamian, all of your fellow students, and the faculty? The performers were very nearly worthy of worship for such feats. The performers should have gotten the Purple Heart just for making it through the concerts. It was a rare concert when you didn't hear bows stuttering and shaking across the strings in the soft spots because of fear. I am convinced that the spirit of fear and terror was so strong over the stage that few emerged from a concert unscathed, even if they had nerves of steel!

I had—and still have—an ability to bounce back very easily from things, even in an environment of this nature. The Lord gave me the grace to go through the training I received there so He could accomplish His purpose for my life. I don't regret this training. There was much that was good in it. Mr. Galamian was a great teacher of the violin, make no mistake about it. He just needed Jesus, as we all do. I was very thankful that I didn't have to play in those concerts, but I began to dream of a time when I could. Was it possible to be good enough to play like that? It seemed like an impossible dream. Nevertheless, I felt like I had no choice. If I didn't, there was nothing else I could do in life.

Maybe that seems like a lie to you, but if you have read this far, you can understand the kind of prison my father had put me in. These were no physical bars—only bars in my mind and spirit. I realized that playing the violin was my only hope and my great quest in life, no matter how difficult. I really believed my dad. He was the only person I had been able to count on in my life. I really did love him, and I was going to go all the way for him, even if it killed me. I would prove to him beyond any shadow of a doubt that I loved him. I was in this for the long haul, and it almost did kill me.

As a thirteen year old, however, I was so enamored with the great music going on that I lost myself in it. There is something wonderful about this realm of music. I had learned to identify with it and even to love its great beauty. It is no wonder to me that people are trapped in it their entire lives. The devil really has stolen a treasure out of the church and created an idol from it.

All I knew at the time, however, was that I had a whole lot to learn on the violin and that my confidence in my own ability was very low. I did my best to keep up, which wasn't too difficult because I was good for my age. At least I had that going for me, and I wasn't too old to have a shot at a solo career. My dad had seen to that. So I endured and dramatically improved during the summer of 1976 at Meadowmount.

Eric—A Christian witness

One afternoon in late July, I was looking for a friend with whom to play Ping-Pong. There was a whole lot of Ping-Pong tables around the dorms, and I enjoyed playing during the afternoons. I was pretty good at it, and I would sometimes play for hours and hours. I loved the game and still do to this day.

Since my friend was out, I was leaving to go to lunch when I saw this tall fellow with a big beard and a gentle smile leaving his room after morning practice. He said, "Hello, Maury! How are you today?" He told me that his name was Eric Samuels and that he played the cello. I had seen him around, but I hadn't met him. He seemed like a quiet kind of guy. There was something different about Eric, although I couldn't put my finger on it. He seemed happy in a deep sort of way that I had never experienced, at least not in a long time. He asked me how my lessons were going and was very impressed that I was studying with Mr. Galamian.

As we talked, we really hit it off. He was so relaxed and peaceful, and I felt totally unafraid of him. He said he would be happy to play a game of Ping-Pong with me, so we played a match. Then we had lunch with a girl he had been dating.

He and his girlfriend took a real liking to me. They invited me out to visit the town of Essex on Lake Champlain the following Sunday. It was always great to get off campus, and all of us students tried to go on outings as much as possible! Meadowmount was such a pressure cooker and so boring at the same time. It was so peaceful riding out to the lake with Eric and his girlfriend. I will never forget the wonderful time we had that day. We even went to the lake beach, which was covered with black and gray shale rocks. The water was clean, and the sun was shining brightly on the water. The weather was perfect!

Eric had a car, actually, a very unusual car. It was a bright orange Volkswagen "Beetle." It had seen better days, that was for sure! The unusual thing about it was that it was covered with bumper stickers. In fact, it almost looked like it was held together by those bumper stickers. They were all over it. They said some strange things like, "Warning: In case of Rapture, this vehicle will be unmanned," "Honk if you love Jesus," "Jesus Saves!" and "Are you born again?" Jesus' name was all over this car.

I asked him about this, and he told me he was a Christian. I said, "What is a Christian?" He told me that he and his girlfriend had had an experience where this man Jesus came into their lives and met them. I told them that that was impossible because Jesus had been dead for a long time and they must be very confused. They assured me that this wasn't the case, that they really had met Him, and that He had changed their lives.

I didn't agree very much with their strange mystical version of meeting Jesus, but I liked them, so Eric and I became friends. He was very nice to me. He would talk about things other than music, and he seemed to have a vast love and knowledge of the Bible, a book that I had long ago given up on ever understanding. Now, I knew a whole lot about religion because of what I learned as a little kid. In fact, I was shocked by how much information about this Jesus I had been fed growing up! I suddenly remembered all kinds of conversations with Dad in which he discredited the Bible and blasted anyone who dared to be "one of those Bible-thumping preachers!" I had forgotten all about those conversations, but they came back to me very quickly. I was able to fend off many of Eric's beliefs, or so I thought. I argued that Jesus was a good man and a good teacher, but that was all—that the rest was only a legend that had been made out of His life.

For several weeks after our trip to the lake, I hung around Eric. He liked me, and I was comfortable around him. I didn't like his crazy Jesus beliefs, but I kept hanging around with him. He said things to me that helped me to cope with Meadowmount. He encouraged me and told me things from the Bible that helped him when he felt bad and scared like I often felt.

Most of all, I liked that Presence who came when we were together. I never mentioned it to anybody, but I knew when the Presence came. Many times it had come when I was playing the violin and had made people cry. I knew that. Sometimes it came when I was really sad, overwhelmed, or in a situation that was too much for me. I couldn't figure out, however, why when I was with Eric the Presence was stronger than I had ever felt it. I would get extremely uncomfortable whenever Eric talked about being "born again." I loved that Presence so much, though, that I would put up with a little of that just to be around that peace. It made me feel better.

Sometimes, however, I felt a hatred when Eric talked about the Bible and Jesus. A voice would scream inside my head, "Get away from him! He is a Jesus freak and a nut! What will everyone say about you?" Again and again those thoughts came into my mind. A couple of times, I did get afraid and ran away from Eric.

Well, naturally, people were beginning to notice that I was spending a lot of time with Eric. His car was hard to hide. I guess I was too naive to even understand that he was not liked at all up there. For me, Eric was such a good person that I thought everybody surely liked him. It didn't even enter my head that he was actually ostracized by nearly everyone. Meadowmount was a predominantly Jewish and "artistic" place. The people I knew were mostly humanistic, music-worshipping heathen. Most of the time, religion wasn't even something that had any place in anyone's conversation. It just didn't have anything to do with anything important.

As it turned out, word got out that I was being proselytized by Eric, which probably was true. Even Mr. and Mrs. Galamian had gotten wind of this, and they weren't very happy about it. However, I wasn't aware of any of this, and the things Eric told me didn't bother me that much. I just thought of him as a friend.

When I first met him, Eric had given me a little booklet about that strange born-again, mystical, Jesus stuff. I didn't read it at the time, but I was polite, took it from him, and put it in my pocket. It stayed in the pocket of my jacket for several weeks, and I forgot about it. One Saturday afternoon, I went on a long walk by myself all the way down to the concert hall. A master class was going on, and several cars were parked out on the grass opposite it. I decided to lean up against one of the cars and to listen to the cellist who was playing. Then I suddenly remembered the little booklet tract that I was carrying in my windbreaker pocket. I pulled it out and began to read it.

It said that everyone had sinned and fallen short of a holy God. It said I was a sinner, and I didn't like that too much. Then it showed this little drawing about how my sin had separated me from this God. On the next page I saw that God had sent His Son Jesus to pay the price for my sins and to bridge the chasm that had separated us. God did what we could not do for ourselves. He sent Jesus who died on a cross and shed His blood for our sins. The booklet said this was the only way God could get us back to himself. Then there was this verse from the Bible, *For God so loved the world, that he gave his only begotten Son, that whosoever believeth in him should not perish, but have everlasting life* (John 3:16). The booklet said we have to ask God to forgive us of our sins and ask Jesus to come into our hearts.

There was a little prayer on the last page that went something like this: "God in heaven, I come to You now and ask You to forgive me of all my sins. I am a sinner. Thank

You for sending Jesus to die on the cross for my sins. Come into my heart, Lord Jesus, and change me and make me into the person I ought to be. I receive You now as my Lord and my Savior. Amen." The booklet said to pray this from your heart out loud.

A life-changing prayer

I was so moved by the booklet that I totally forgot where I was. I didn't hear the music anymore. All I could comprehend was this little booklet. The whole world seemed to stop for me. After some initial reluctance, I decided that, even though I didn't fully understand what this was all about and didn't accept everything Eric had talked to me about, I needed to pray this prayer. So I said, "God, if You are there, I am going to pray the words on this page to You. Show me if You are really real." Then I prayed that prayer to God.

After I prayed the prayer, it seemed like something inside me exploded. It felt like a dam had burst and floods of water were washing over me! I felt as though a two-ton weight had been taken off of my shoulders. I looked up and the grass was greener than I had ever remembered seeing it before. In fact, all the colors were brighter. The sky was bluer, and the music coming from the concert hall was more beautiful than I had ever heard before. I was overjoyed! I had never felt like this before!

I ran all the way back to my dorm. I wanted to find Eric and tell him how awesome this was! I knew that what he had told me was right! Jesus really was in my heart. I had never experienced such joy and peace before. Oh, what a wonderful experience it was. I couldn't stop laughing and running! I knew now that I would be with the Lord forever! He was with me! Praise the Lord! Hallelujah! I would never be the same again! It was an amazing experience!

Eric wasn't in his room, so I had to wait until he returned to tell him. I wanted to thank him for giving me that little book about Jesus, and I wanted to know more about Jesus. I wasn't just in a good mood—I felt entirely different than I had before. Maybe this was what Eric meant by being "born again." Finally Eric arrived back at his room, and I ran in and told him what had happened. He was very happy, and he gave me a big hug. He said, "Praise the Lord! Maury, we are going to be friends forever in heaven!"

I had so many questions to ask him that I didn't know where to start. Finally I blurted out, "Will Jesus help me to play my violin better?"

Eric said, "Of course, He will. He gave you the gift of music. Certainly He will help you to play it for Him."

How prophetic and true those words were and have been for me. Jesus has indeed helped me to play better than I ever could in my own strength and ability. Eric and I rejoiced together. It was then that he told me about a Bible study he was leading that met on Tuesday evenings in one of the practice cabins. He invited me to attend the next one. He told me there were a few others who were also "born again," and that they met to pray and read the Bible together. That sounded great to me.

For the next few days, I marveled at how changed I felt down deep inside. I was also very uneasy because the teachers were looking at me funny, and some of the other students who once were friendly toward me wouldn't talk to me anymore. *What's wrong with them?* I wondered. They sure were treating me different.

Trouble in the camp

Then Eric started acting strange toward me. When I tried to meet him or sit with him in the cafeteria, he would try to sit somewhere else. He seemed almost embarrassed to be with me. Finally, only three days after my conversion experience, Eric and his girlfriend came and sat down with me. He explained that he was sorry he couldn't be with me anymore. He had been asked to leave Meadowmount. The "powers that be" had decided he was not very healthy to have around. He said he was very sorry if he had done anything wrong and he hadn't meant any harm to me. He said he was glad I had found the Lord but that I shouldn't go overboard about it. He said some of the teachers had told him to leave me alone. He was very sorry if he had caused any trouble.

Trouble? What trouble? I was so thrilled at what had happened to me. I didn't feel in trouble at all. I felt like I was out of trouble for the first time in my life! What was he talking about? And why in the world did he have to leave so suddenly? I just could not understand.

I remember our last meeting there at one of the tables in the cafeteria during lunch. He told me that the summer would be over in a couple of weeks anyway and that it was probably best for him to leave now. He apologized over and over and was nearly in tears. It made absolutely no sense to me, but I felt very uneasy. Now I was beginning to feel like I was in trouble with my teachers from the way he spoke. We said good-bye to each other, and I never saw him again at Meadowmount. He never returned there. He said he had gotten into trouble and was not welcome there anymore. He said he was going to send me something special very soon in the mail. Then he said, "God bless you," and left.

I found out several days later that rumors had been circulating about him being in his girlfriend's room after hours and that he had been caught in bed with her. I knew Eric, and there was no way that had happened. Someone was trying hard to discredit him. It was crazy! Eric never broke any rules. I broke rules left and right and never got caught, it seemed, but he was so innocent, clean, and morally upright that he nearly squeaked. In fact, I thought he was boring because he never did anything "out on the edge." I knew that someone had made up lies about him, but he was gone and that was that. It was a big mystery to me at the time.

I had my last lesson with Mr. Galamian the following week, and it went well. I had been practicing more than I ever had before, so I was well prepared. Miss Lack went with me to my lesson, and she was pleased. After the lesson, she looked at me with great concern and asked, "Maury, dear, are you doing all right?"

I said, "Yes, I'm doing great!"

As I said that, we went into the "rec room." The mail had just been delivered, and someone said, "Maury, there's a package for you." I was always happy to get mail, and I figured it was a care package or something from Deanna and Dad. They often sent me cookies and things like that.

Miss Lack waited for me because she wanted to review the things that Mr. Galamian had said. The package was from Eric! I wondered what it was. Then I was struck with fear. I didn't want Miss Lack to see that I had gotten something from him. She had walked in just as I was opening it. It looked like some kind of book to me. Of course, it was a Bible. I tried to hide it from her, but it was too late. She had seen it!

She sat me down in a quiet part of the room and said almost hysterically, "Maury, that boy Eric was trying to convert you. He is a bad person. We found out about him too late...that he was here at the camp. He should never have come here. Oh, dear me! Maury, don't you believe one word that he said to you! I know that you came from a broken home and don't realize who you are. It's not your fault that you weren't raised as a Jewish boy. Sometimes I feel really sorry for you. You are Jewish, don't you understand? That Eric was trying to make you into a *Christian!*"

She spewed out that last word with such force that it shocked me.

"Let me see that book he gave you!" she demanded. When I showed her the Bible, she said, "This is horrible! This is disgusting! This is an outrage!"

She became bright red in the face. She threw the book back at me in disgust and said, "Don't you believe a word he said to you, do you understand? How dare he try to do something like this! Mr. and Mrs. Galamian and I and all of the teachers were horrified when we saw that fanatic Eric with you all the time. He has a lot of problems. Don't ever hang around people like that anymore, do you understand?"

I said, "Yes, ma'am" in almost a whisper.

Then in a tone of voice mixed with disgust, anger, and fear, she asked, "You didn't actually believe what he was telling you, did you?"

"No, ma'am," I said with regret. I had never ever seen her this upset.

"How dare that boy try to convert you!" she kept saying under her breath. Then she calmed down a little and said, "Well, at least I'm glad you didn't believe all that garbage he was feeding you. Just forget about everything he ever said to you. You're such a good boy, Maury. I would hate to see you turn out like him. Just remember that you are Jewish. I hope your father teaches you something about this before it is too late. What is the world coming to these days?" And with that, she stormed out, got into her car, and drove off. I didn't see her until my lesson the following week.

That really shook me up. I just sat there stunned for about an hour. What had I done? She had never spoken to me like that before. Her words had just ripped through me. Why was it so bad to believe in Jesus? I decided right then and there that I wouldn't say anything about my experience. Whatever had happened to me, it wasn't worth risking everything for. I was surprised because I thought Miss Lack was going to take the Bible from me, but she didn't. So I finished opening the brown paper wrapping and took it out. It was a beautiful, dark green, hard-cover Living Bible. I still have it in my office, and I am looking at it now as I write this. Inside, Eric had written this message:

To Maury, with love! Summer of '76
May the author of this book be your constant guide, may
His inspiration lead you to great achievements, and may
He always bless you with friends, beautiful music, and love.
"...be filled with the Spirit..." (Ephesians 5:18-20).
My dear brother, be receptive to God's abundant life
(John 10:10).—there is much to gain, Right Now!!
In Jesus,
Eric

After I read that, I started to cry. What a wonderful and loving gift. Why was Miss Lack so upset about it? It made no sense to me. I was going to miss Eric. I even prayed and thanked God that He was so kind to give Eric to me as my friend for those few short days that summer. He was someone I would never forget.

The last week was soon over, and I got on an airplane and returned to Baton Rouge. I was so scared Dad would find the Bible that I hid it in the bottom of my trunk. He never did find it. I decided never to talk about what had happened again. Maybe it was just my imagination after all. I probably just got emotional and blew things out of proportion. I just tried to put it out of my mind, but God remembered the prayer I had prayed. My life *had* changed, and Jesus *was* with me in a new way from then on...at least to the degree I would let Him be. Thank God, He *is a friend who sticks closer than a brother* (Proverbs 18:24).

He promised me, *"I will never leave you nor forsake you,"* and *"I am with you always, even to the end of the age"* (Hebrews 13:5; Matthew 28:20).

Chapter 9

My First Recital Tour

*W*hat an intense summer it had been! I didn't really understand what had happened to me spiritually, but I knew that whatever it was, it sure wasn't something I was going to share with my parents! I knew that Dad would prefer I was anything other than a born-again Christian! He wasn't a big fan of either the Bible or of born-again Christians. The devil wasn't silent or inactive either. He was working hard on me, telling me that my experience wasn't real and to forget what had happened. He was telling me to keep it a big secret, and I was pretty convinced that keeping it quiet was my best course of action.

He said to me, "You don't really want to become a fanatic like Eric, do you—and be ostracized and kicked out of the music world? And what will your dad think? You know how he hates all those kinds of beliefs! Besides, that was just your imagination anyway, all that 'born-again conversion' stuff. You just did it to make Eric happy. It isn't real, you know."

On and on the enemy persisted with these thoughts, suggestions, and lies. Of course, I didn't know anything about where those thoughts were coming from, and I accepted most of them as truth. By the time I arrived home, I had firmly decided that I should shove this "Jesus thing" under the rug and never mention it to anyone, especially my parents! A part of me felt a twinge of regret and even shame at having to hide Jesus this way, but the oppression and pressure of those thoughts were so great that I could only get relief by agreeing with them. So that is what I did...at least on the outside. I never mentioned the Bible or my experience to my parents until long after I had left home, and since I had no way to share or feed my tiny faith, I soon forgot that Jesus had ever entered my life at all. The joy and peace I had experienced that summer faded from my life almost entirely for quite some time.

The Lord never forgot me, however. Bless His holy name! He was with me! I was different than I had been before, way down deep inside, and I knew He was there. Whenever I felt overwhelmed, angry, frustrated, or sad, I would find myself praying to Jesus and asking Him for strength and help.

The very first question I had asked Eric after I had gotten saved was, "Will Jesus help me to play the violin better?" I began to notice that I was able to play better than before. In fact, I started improving at a dramatically increased rate. The Lord was blessing my music in a marvelous way as I continued playing over the next several years. That undefinable Presence I had felt when I played the violin publicly became even stronger now. In fact, sometimes it came even when I was alone practicing, like a heavy blanket falling all over me in my room! A few times it was so strong that I had to stop playing because I was weeping uncontrollably, but I thought it was just because the music was so beautiful.

Is this my ticket out?

An interesting event occurred when I returned to Houston for my first lesson with Fredell Lack. School had not yet started, and Dad was talking to me quite a bit about my needing lessons with Miss Lack every week. I had so dramatically improved over the summer that he was almost ecstatic. This was what he had been waiting for. Finally I was beginning to sound like a real violinist. He had been in touch with a couple in Houston about the possibility of my coming to live with them so that I could take lessons once a week. They were agreeable to the idea, and when I heard about it I was so excited I could hardly stand it! This was it! I had won a ticket out of my home! Maybe I could be a part of their family. I immediately said that I wanted to do it.

I was unhappy at home because Dad and Deanna fought so much. When they got angry, they would either attack each other or me—and sometimes both at once. There was very little peace in the house. Ironically, instead of Dad being less critical of my violin playing now that I had improved so much, he was just the opposite. The better I did, the more he expected of me. I felt like a high-jumper who would clear the bar at one height, only to come back the next day and find the bar one notch higher! I was never good enough.

Now that I was a teenager, however, Dad had to back off somewhat or I got so angry with him that I wouldn't speak to him. Even he realized that he had to change his tactics from what he had done when I was younger. I wouldn't allow him to practice with me much anymore, so he had to be content to listen from downstairs and yell up to me if he felt my playing wasn't good enough. When this happened, I would go into a rage! When he left the house, I would kick the walls, curse, and scream.

If Deanna heard me, she would start in on Dad as soon as he returned, with her tiresome litany. "Why don't you leave that kid alone?" she would say. "What do you think he is, anyway—God's gift to the violin or something? You've probably already destroyed his future. He's so warped in his personality that I hate to see how he's going to turn out when he grows up. Maury will either be one of the greatest violinists in the world or he'll wind up as a drunkard on skid row if he fails. And if that happens, it will be all your fault. Wait until he wakes up to the reality of the REAL world. I hope you're happy then, Chuck!"

Dad would take all he could. Then he would fly into his own rage and say how disrespectful both Deanna and I were to him and how I never appreciated all that he had done for me. Then he would come back upstairs and scream at me until I was literally shaking with fear. Sometimes I couldn't stop shaking for nearly an hour!

Events like this happened every few days or so in some form...and had been happening for years. Of course, in a matter of a few hours, my parents would forget that anything had ever happened and would go on for several days like everything was okay. Then they would blow up again—either at me or at each other—over some stupid thing. I wanted out of this craziness, and if possible, I never wanted to live at home again. The outside world seemed warmer and much more inviting than the turmoil of our house. I was determined to escape and to find a better home! So, naturally, an opportunity to live in a different environment in Houston sounded like a dream come true.

In late August of 1976, I packed my belongings and my violin, and my parents drove me to Houston. However, things didn't work out like I had hoped. School in Houston was not a pleasant experience for me. I was attending a large school and didn't know anyone. I got behind in a couple of classes and was having trouble concentrating. There were also problems with the family I was living with. They seemed strange and chaotic, and living with them was difficult for me. Finally, after a few months, I asked to return home.

Since it was the middle of the fall, I returned to my old school and joined the eighth grade there. The rest of the year was fairly uneventful academically, and I continued commuting to Houston every two weeks for my lessons with Miss Lack. She began preparing me to do a recital that was to be a full-length program. I had never performed so many pieces on one program, so it was quite a challenge to learn.

Dad "coaches" my concerts

Dad immediately began going full-steam ahead in planning a recital "tour" for me in the late spring of 1977. I was to perform at Loyola University for Harvey Olin and the music school there. Then I was to play in downtown Baton Rouge at the Paramount Theatre a week or so later. Finally I was to play at Dudley Hall at the University of Houston for Miss Lack to finish up my little tour. Dad had spent weeks making all the arrangements for the piano, the programs, and the publicity. He was extremely excited as the dates for the recitals approached. It was almost as if he was playing it instead of me.

When I played in these concerts, I realized that the Presence seemed to have been magnified. When I started to play in Baton Rouge, a tremendous heat came over my body, even though it was not hot in the theatre. Clearly something was enabling me to play far better than I ever had before. I know now that this was the anointing of the Holy Spirit, but then I just thought it was very strange that I could play so well. I had prayed to the Lord and asked Him to help me to play my best, and He answered! Of course, I didn't tell my parents about it. I just prayed quietly. The anointing was even stronger because I was now a born-again Christian and Jesus had full authority to do as I asked. I had not mentioned anything about this to my parents, but they could tell that something was different. As always, however, they chalked up this supernatural anointing to my being especially talented and gifted.

I remember Dad being backstage with several quarts of ice-cold orange juice. In retrospect, I felt somewhat like a prizefighter. I would go offstage between pieces and have orange juice shoved in my mouth and my face wiped by Dad amid profuse encouragements and pats on the back. Then the bell would ring, and I was thrust back out for the next "round." Nevertheless, even with my father's ego feeding off my performances, I felt that there was another Father who was being glorified and who took great pleasure in my playing.

Dad really was proud of me, and I was glad I was able to please him in such a profound way, but I resented the way he was living through me. I didn't feel that he really cared about me. He was just happy because he had finally "made it" in music through my success in these concerts. He wore it like a badge of honor.

Life at home continued to deteriorate. It was worse than ever. The only thing my parents couldn't stop was time itself. I was getting older, and they were both losing control of me. I wasn't their "show pony" anymore. All I wanted was to get away from home. I had some pleasure in my recitals, but it was counteracted by the sense of exploitation I had to endure along with it.

Dad had immersed himself in the "holy cause" of preparing me for my recitals. Now that they were over and he couldn't live vicariously through them any longer, the pain and emptiness he felt returned with a vengeance. He was thinking about leaving Deanna. That was all he talked about to me. She just wasn't good enough for him anymore. He spent a whole lot of time trying to convince me that he was right in separating from her. He desperately wanted me to morally sanction it by agreeing that Deanna was incorrigible and that the marriage was beyond repair. I finally agreed with him. What other choice did I have?

Divorce strikes again!

I had heard many hours—even days—of his grievances against Deanna. Dad is a lawyer and could present his "case" against her with the utmost skill. He would "prove" to me hour after hour and day after day how right he was to leave Deanna. I tried to be impartial, but finally Dad appealed to the one thing that ran deeper than anything else in my relationship with him. He said that he and I would always be together. I didn't want to hate Deanna at first, but I was sucked in to this "covenant" that Dad and I were inseparable and that he was always right, no matter what. I had to side with him or lose the only relationship that had any semblance of permanence in my life. So I accepted as reality and truth that Deanna was despicable and that she was the reason why we were so unhappy.

Finally Dad couldn't take it anymore. One sunny morning, Dad told Deanna he was leaving her. He explained in his best impartial, professional voice that the movers would be at the house in a few hours to pack up his furniture. He had found an apartment across town, and the marriage was over. Deanna was dumbfounded with shock at first. When the reality of what he had said finally hit her, she became hysterical and began running around the house, screaming like a tormented, trapped animal.

I was so indoctrinated with Dad's months and years of indicting Deanna that I was actually happy this was happening! Looking back upon it now, I am ashamed at how wrong this was, but at the time it seemed like the right thing to do. I felt that our leaving Deanna was justified and the only solution to all our problems. I had Dad back again! He really wanted me more than anyone else. That is how my warped thinking was running that day. It seemed like a great victory.

I was packing my things upstairs when Dad told Deanna we were leaving. She started screaming and ran upstairs and into my room. When she saw me packing, she ran, tackled me, and knocked me to the floor. She grabbed my hair and started beating my head against the floor. She screamed, "You are the cause of this! This is what you wanted, isn't it? You destroyed my marriage and my home! I hope you are enjoying this! You knew your father was leaving me, and you never told me! It's all your fault!" Then she crumpled on the floor and sobbed uncontrollably.

My head was hurting pretty bad from her beating it on the floor. Little Gloria didn't understand what was going on, and she was crying and holding on to me. She was scared at how Mommy was acting. I don't remember much about the rest of the move. I was in a state of emotional and physical shock for the next several days.

Dad and I moved into an apartment across town, taking the furniture Dad had meticulously chosen for the movers to take. We took all of the furniture Dad had before he married Deanna. It was old and beat up, but it was "ours." Deanna watched helplessly as each piece of furniture was loaded into the truck and we drove off. Dad was very upset about my experience with Deanna. He told me he would never let anything like that happen to me again as long as I lived, if he had anything to do with it. We moved into a modest two-bedroom apartment, and I finished the last couple of weeks of my school year.

My family had been blown apart and would never again be together. I wish now that there had been a way to save our family, even with its many problems. After that day, I never saw much of Deanna or my little sister Gloria again. I somehow knew, even then, that my life would never be the same again.

Chapter 10

New Experiences —Good and Bad

*I*t was a strange experience to live in an apartment again. I knew Dad had been miserable for a long time with Deanna, but I really didn't think he would actually follow through with separating from her as he had threatened to do for so long. It was a shock for sure, and it took me some time to get used to going home from school to an empty apartment.

I felt an odd exhilaration. I felt happy and free. I knew that what had happened to my parents was tragic, but I didn't feel like my security or happiness had been in my family for a long time. For me, the world looked like a wonderful place, and the farther I could get away from Baton Rouge and my parents, the happier I would be. Of course, I still loved Dad, and I tried my best to comfort him. He was really hurting and was leaning on me for strength. I felt very mature—like an adult—for the first time in my life. I knew that I had finally made it out of childhood, and Dad couldn't control me anymore.

I turned fourteen in June, right before I returned to Meadowmount for the summer. Many of the same students had returned, and the summer progressed much like the previous one had. I had one really memorable experience, however. One night I couldn't sleep. I had brought my *Living Bible* with me and decided to get it out and read it. It was nearly midnight, and everyone had gone to sleep. The only sound I could hear was the distant hum of trucks driving up the Interstate about a half mile away from the campus. It seemed so peaceful.

My first experience with "tongues"

I was reading in 1 Corinthians. Suddenly I came to the passage where Paul talks about praying in "tongues" and how we are to ask the Lord for all these "gifts." None of this made any sense to me. I thought Paul was a really strange writer. He seemed confused most of the time. He would say one thing and then two verses later say the opposite. He seemed very arrogant and full of his own opinions, which he said were God's opinions. And he had opinions about everything! Most of them I didn't like very much, but this passage about tongues seemed to leap off the page and grab me. I felt that Presence come into my room. I thought to myself, *I don't know what this is, but I'm going to do what this says and pray and ask God for whatever this is that Paul is talking about.*

I got down on my knees beside my bed and said, "Lord, I don't like this Paul guy very much, but he said to ask You for this 'praying in tongues.' I think I want this, whatever it is. Would You please give it to me?"

Suddenly I felt something like warm molasses on the top of my head, flowing down my body. It was like someone was pouring hot oil over me from a pitcher. My whole body got hot and I began to shake. Tears started flooding my eyes, and I began to weep almost uncontrollably. Then my mouth and my jaw started to shake, and I had a really strong desire to say something out loud. As I began to speak, to my amazement, it sounded like gibberish. I started saying this same strange phrase over and over. It never changed. That is all I said for nearly an hour! When I got up off of my knees, I felt completely different. I knew that something spiritual had happened—I just didn't know what it was.

All during that time, I heard voices in my mind saying, "This is just you. You're making it up. What are you saying anyway? This is ridiculous! You sound like an idiot! How long are you going to kneel there, saying that nonsense?"

Normally, I would have stopped at such an onslaught, but the experience had been so overpowering that it didn't even matter what my mind was screaming at me. I was weeping so hard, and those syllables were just rolling out of me from somewhere deep inside like a mighty river. I couldn't seem to stop—it just felt too good. I went to sleep that night feeling like I was floating on a cloud. Whatever had happened to me, I hoped it would last past that night!

As it turned out, I promptly forgot all about my experience. It didn't make any sense to me, and I was too embarrassed about it to tell anyone, so I just let it go. I found myself wanting to read the Bible more, however, and I made friends with several of the Christians who were there that summer.

Summer soon drew to a close, and I returned to Baton Rouge and Dad's dreary apartment. He didn't seem a whole lot happier than when I left. The whole place seemed to be filled with oppression and hopelessness. It gave him a little satisfaction when he heard me practicing, and he thought I had improved a lot over the summer.

I went to Houston every two weeks for my lessons as I had done before. This year, however, I was flying there more. I started attending the local magnet school as a freshman in high school there in Baton Rouge. For the first time, the classes were very hard for me, and I was having trouble keeping up because I hadn't learned good study habits. Suddenly I had to do homework! The other kids had caught up with me academically. I was no longer the best in my class.

I was unhappy living with Dad. All he and I talked about was my going away to study music and leaving Baton Rouge. He said that I needed to go to Houston as soon as possible. He wanted to find a family I could live with. Of course, I wanted to do this, too. He wanted me to go out there and "make it" in the music world. I just wanted out, period. Since I had decided long ago to take the first available opportunity to leave Baton Rouge, I was all for leaving that dismal apartment any way I could.

Dad talked to Miss Lack, and she advertised in the local Jewish newspaper in Houston for a family who would take me in so I could live in Houston and study with her. Within a few weeks, we had found a family and I again moved to Houston.

The couples' names were Bob and Edith Zinn. From the first moment I met the Zinns, I liked them very much. Bob owned his own petroleum company and specialized in speculative geological surveys. He found oil and gas wells for big oil companies. Edith was a quiet, gracious lady, and I have never known a kinder or more giving person in my life. She seemed to really enjoy my company. In her quiet way, she brought a wonderful stability to my life that I had not known before.

I lived with them for the next eight months, and they took me in as a part of their family. There was more peace in their home than anywhere I had ever been. I never once heard an argument between Bob and Edith. In fact, I don't think they even knew how to argue. I breathed a sigh of relief! At last I could be somewhere that was secure. Each morning Edith knocked on my door in her sweet, quiet way and awakened me for school. She had my breakfast ready for me, and I would eat it and walk to school. In the afternoon, I practiced my violin, and once a week Edith would drive me to my lesson with Miss Lack at the University of Houston.

So my year went. For the most part, I had a wonderful year in the sheltered and peaceful home of Bob and Edith Zinn. I pray that God will bless the Zinns for their kindness and generosity to me!

That fall Miss Lack entered me in the Houston Symphony Youth Competition with the *Mendelssohn Violin Concerto*. I won in the high school division and was scheduled to play with the orchestra that fall. Later in the spring, I entered and won several competitions in Louisiana and Texas. I played the first movement of the *Lalo Symphonie Espagnole* with four different orchestras in the spring of 1978. My playing was improving quite nicely, and I was happier than I had ever been.

A few weeks before the school year ended, I was in Midland-Odessa, Texas, at a competition. I was staying with a host family who had a son a year or two older than me. He invited me to go with him to a party the Saturday night after I had played. This was the only competition I had not won that year, and I was feeling really rejected.

My introduction to drugs

There were several kids from his local high school at the party, and they were drinking pretty heavily. I felt like I really shouldn't be there, but I was feeling so low that I decided to have a couple of beers with them. When they went to the back of the house into one of the kid's bedrooms, I went with them. One of them pulled out a long, thin thing that looked like a small stick wrapped in white tissue paper.

I asked them, "What is that?"

They all looked at me and laughed. One kid said, "It's a joint."

"A joint?" I said.

They said, "Yeah, man. It's pot. You know, marijuana!"

I said, "Oh." Something inside of me was screaming to run away from them, but I didn't want them to think I wasn't cool like they were. After all, they were high school kids. Several of them were seniors, even. They lit the marijuana cigarette and started passing it around. It finally came to me, and I told them I had never smoked anything before. They told me to try it, that it would make me feel good and I would forget all about the competition. Well, I knew it was wrong, but I ignored my conscience and took a deep drag on the joint. I nearly passed out from the smoke going into my lungs. It had such an acrid, sickly-sweet smell that I nearly threw up. I fell on the bed and just lay there for about five minutes. I couldn't move or even open my eyes.

At first the other kids just laughed at me, but then they got scared that I had become ill and a few of them left the room to get help. After about five minutes, I regained my faculties somewhat, sat up, and even started to talk with them again. I knew I had done something terribly wrong. I had crossed a line that God clearly did not want me to cross. At the same time, somehow I did not care.

I was feeling kind of weak and dizzy—not the way other kids said they felt when they talked about "getting high" and "feeling stoned." I just wanted out of there. So I told the boy who had brought me to the party that I wanted to go home. He was embarrassed. His mother was a strong Baptist, a born-again woman who had even talked to me about the Lord, and he had led me to this pot-smoking party. He kept begging me not to say anything to her about what had happened...to just forget about it. I told him I wouldn't say anything...not to worry about it.

When I got back to my room at their house, I was feeling kind of strange. I was having trouble thinking straight, and everything seemed kind of foggy. I got scared and fell on my knees beside my bed. I asked the Lord to forgive me and to protect me from any bad consequences from smoking marijuana. I felt so dirty inside, but I also seemed to enjoy the party in a way that scared me even more. I liked those cool guys and wanted to be like them. I was tired of being a wimpy, violin-playing weirdo at school. I wanted to fit in. The experience with the marijuana had greatly affected me. It was like a veil had come over my mind that clouded and darkened my thoughts and perceptions. The whole experience fascinated me in a troubling way.

Marijuana seemed to hold great promise for me in the social arena. All I had to do was to inhale that sickly-sweet smoke and PRESTO, life was totally awesome. Maybe this was the way to be cool and to enjoy enhanced experiences with friends. Those I had spoken to all said that marijuana was harmless, so what was there to worry about? I did notice that I had trouble remembering things for the next few days after I had gotten high, but I didn't worry about it too much.

I finished the school year and returned to Baton Rouge a few weeks before heading to Meadowmount for my third summer. The summer of 1978 was a turning point for me. I knew that I could never really return home to Baton Rouge and be happy. Dad had enough problems without me, and he wanted me to succeed as a violinist away from Louisiana. I didn't know where I was going to go, but I put all of that out of my mind and tried my best to fit in with the other students there.

Again that summer, I took lessons with Mr. Galamian. During one of my lessons one day, Mr. Galamian mentioned that he would take me as a student in New York City that fall at the Juilliard School of Music if I wanted to study with him. I was really happy about that, so I called Dad on the phone and relayed the news to him. He was thrilled with the idea, of course, but he also had a lot of questions. He said he would drive up to Meadowmount at the end of the summer to pick me up. He also told me he had met a lady named Susan Selby, and he was pretty seriously involved with her. She wanted to come up and have a vacation with Dad and me for three weeks in August. Dad said it would be perfect to combine the vacation with getting me situated in the New York area with a family. He could also help me apply to Juilliard.

Meadowmount quickly drew to a close and everyone left. I was one of the last to leave because it took Dad longer than he had planned to drive all the way from Louisiana. I was feeling pretty lonely by the time he arrived. There were only a few other students still there, and they were leaving before me. It was like a ghost town, walking through some of the dormitories. I had started smoking cigarettes, and I remember lighting a cigarette, walking around the grounds, and thinking, *This place sure seems dead with everyone gone.*

Finally Dad arrived with his new girlfriend, Susan. She was pleasant enough, with short, blonde hair, a sweet smile, a gentle disposition, and a very positive attitude toward me. I liked her very much. I could tell that she was very much in love with Dad, and he seemed to be quite taken with her.

Dad had arranged a meeting with Mr. and Mrs. Galamian in their apartment at Meadowmount. I waited for him and Susan downstairs in the library room. I marveled that Dad and Susan were meeting with the Galamians for so long. I thought to myself, *Maybe I am in trouble or something!*

A return of the "funny language"

I was sitting on the couch in the library, and it was so quiet that I must have dozed off for a few minutes. Suddenly I awoke and instantly knew that Someone was with me in the room. That Presence was there so strong that I didn't move! I didn't dare do anything. I just sat there. I knew that God was in the library with me right then. I closed my eyes in reverence as His holy Presence engulfed me. Of course, I didn't understand it, but I knew that God wanted to talk with me somehow.

Suddenly, before I could think, I heard a voice speaking. Then I realized it was my own voice! I was talking in that funny language again. It had only happened to me that one night and a couple of other times after that when I was deeply distraught. I thought, *Oh no! Here it goes again!* It was flooding out of me so fast and strong that I didn't dare stop it! After a while, it stopped—just like that! Like someone had just shut off a faucet. I was shaking all over. This was some kind of power that I didn't understand!

Then suddenly I began to speak out loud in English! And these were the words that I said: "My son, I love you, and I am pleased with you. I am with you always. I will never leave you or forsake you, ever, no matter what. You shall become the greatest violinist in the world, by My grace. There will be none like you before you or after you, BUT IT WILL NOT BE BY MIGHT NOR BY POWER, BUT BY MY SPIRIT, SAYS THE LORD. The next five years of your life will be the hardest ones you will ever go through. They shall be a dark time. I will protect you, preserve you, and deliver you out of all that shall come against you. Then you shall serve and glorify Me. My Spirit is upon you, and I will not leave you until you have accomplished all that I have ordained for you to do. Do not fear, for I am with you!"

After those words came out of my mouth, I sat there stunned—without moving—for nearly fifteen minutes. I had never had anything like that happen to me before. I thought that maybe I had lost some marbles or something. I was embarrassed, and I finally got up and checked the next room to see if anyone had heard me. I had been talking very loudly, but nobody was around. It was as deserted as before. Then I heard voices coming down the hall. Dad, Susan, and I got into the car, left Meadowmount, and headed for New York City.

MAURICE SKLAR
Family Album

My mother, Audrey, was beautiful but fragile. Although she loved me very much, motherhood was overwhelming to her, and she and my father split up when I was just three years old.

So much of who I am and who I have become was influenced by my remarkable father, Charles Burrowes Sklar. My stepmother, Deanna, was a violinist, and she lovingly helped shape my early life. My half-sister Gloria was a joy to me.

Happy 10th Birthday, Maury! My mother kept in touch and we got together occasionally for visits.

Early Performances and Training

I started learning how to play the violin at age 5. By Christmas 1974, I played well enough to perform in a church program.

My family sacrificed to enable me to study with the finest instructors at Meadowmount and the Juilliard School of Music in New York, and at the Curtis Institute in Philadelphia.

From the time my hands were strong enough to hold the instrument, my dad had a dream and a plan for me to become a great violinist.

School Days, 1977

By the mid-70s, I was already an accomplished soloist, performing major violin concerti with various Philharmonic Symphonies in New Orleans, Baton Rouge, Houston, and other cities.

A rare photo of Dad, Mother, and me. They were so proud when I graduated.

Graduation Day

An important milestone—graduating from the Curtis Institute of Music in Philadelphia on April 25, 1983. That's me in the first row, second from the right.

Another visit with my mother during my music study days.

On My Own

Moving out on my own was not really very liberating! The endless hours of study and preparation for various auditions and competitions were draining. The unrelenting pressure eventually drove me to a complete nervous collapse.

I met Debbie Salatti at Living Word Christian Church in New York City. From the moment I saw her, I recognized something very special about her—she was beautiful inside and out. We were married on November 26, 1988.

"God has a special anointing on your hands!" Benny Hinn ministered to me at an ORU meeting—then invited me to play my violin in his crusade services. I've enjoyed a wonderful and intense relationship with this man of God, playing in many of his meetings.

Ministry Begins

The greatest music in the world belongs to God…and I love playing for His glory around the world.

I am so blessed to have such a beautiful, loving family. Here we are in Uppsala Sweden, Christmas 1995—Maurice, Rebekah, Josiah, and Debbie.

I have found my purpose for being on this earth! Thank God for the thousands upon thousands of lives touched and changed as I have ministered and performed for the Lord.

During concerts and meetings throughout many nations, I play my violin, preach, and teach the Bible, and see a constant stream of healings and other gifts of the Holy Spirit flowing to others.

With a grateful heart, I thank God for restoring my soul and satisfying me with goodness from His heart and hands.

God bless you!
Love,
The Sklars

Chapter 11

The Big Apple and the Juilliard School of Music

I had never seen the Big Apple before, although I had heard about it since I was very young. All the way there, Dad was telling me of his experiences when he was my age and had lived in New York. As he shared his stories in great detail, it almost seemed that he was there in his mind. Dad made New York City sound like such a wonderful place.

I was overwhelmed to finally see New York City and Juilliard! The school is located at 66th and Broadway on the west side of Manhattan. It is included in the Lincoln Center for the Performing Arts and is its northernmost building. The Metropolitan Opera, The State Theatre for the New York City Ballet, Avery Fisher Hall for the New York Philharmonic, and the Alice Tully Recital Hall make up the rest of the buildings, along with a huge performing arts library adjoining the buildings toward the back. It was an impressive sight to see, especially in 1978 when it was far newer than it is now.

I liked the busy streets and the lights and the hustle and bustle of the city. New York City seems to have an energy all its own. It never sleeps. Night and day it just keeps going with a ferocious tenacity. I loved the feeling of being in the center of it all. This is where music at its best took place. This is where careers were made and lost. Worldwide renown was beckoning for those who had what it took. There didn't seem to be any room for second best. Only the "great talents" could make it here. It was a wonderful and really scary experience at the same time! I couldn't wait to be left alone to explore in this amazing place.

Since Juilliard did not have dorms at that time, we set about finding a family for me to live with. We decided to go to Susan's hometown, Madison, New Jersey, which is about an hour's commute by train from New York City. Susan thought it would be a good place to find a family for me. Dad had already been in touch with the Unitarian Church there and had received a response from a family who was interested in taking me in for the year.

We drove to Madison, met the family, and made arrangements for me to live with them. Since the Juilliard Pre-College met all day on Saturdays, for the next year I took the train into New York early on Saturday morning each week, stayed all day, and then returned late in the evening to Madison so I could attend school the following Monday morning. I had never had a more demanding schedule in all of my life! But I was happy to be in New York and getting to study with Mr. Galamian.

It was a tremendous opportunity, Dad told me, and it was important that I do well. On our trip to New York City, Dad had said over and over again, "I wish I had had the opportunity you are getting to study in New York at Juilliard. It is what I wanted to do when I was your age and living in New York. I wasn't good enough to make it, but you are. You can do what I never could. You get to study with the greatest violin teacher in the world. Make the most of it. You only get one chance when you are young, and if you blow it, it's too late. You'll never get the chance again. If you don't succeed now, you will regret it for the rest of your life."

I didn't know whether to feel encouraged by Dad's pronouncements or overwhelmed. I did know that he was proud of me and wanted the best for me. I told him that I would do the best I could. He seemed almost satisfied with my comment and let it go at that.

I felt very mature and capable of handling the big city alone. I really felt like I was on cloud nine! I had made it into Juilliard at age fifteen, and I was away from home and all of the hell that was going on there. I was thrilled at being in New York City, and more than that, I got to be there on my own even if it was just for one day each week. It was such a feeling of exhilaration!

That first Saturday, I made it to the city for my audition at Juilliard, which was scheduled for 10:30 that morning. After I had played for the jury of violin faculty, Mr. Galamian asked me to be at his apartment that afternoon where he would be scheduling his students for the year. I would also be studying with Mr. Galamian's assistant, Miss Pardee, and she also told me to come to her studio to receive my lesson times. So I was "in," I concluded. I was surprised that they could get the ball rolling so fast after my audition to get me into school. But I knew that since Mr. Galamian had already accepted me, playing for the other teachers was just a formality. However, I was glad they seemed so positive in their response.

After registering for my classes, I went to the cafeteria to get something to eat. I saw the familiar face of a cellist who had spent the summer at Meadowmount. He was in college and had just arrived back in the city. His name was Scott, and he was a very disheveled looking human being, with his long, stringy blond hair hanging in his eyes and his lanky six-foot, four-inch frame covered with extremely rumpled clothing. But he was a magnificent cellist! He had proven what a great musician he was over and over again during the concerts at Meadowmount. He was definitely revered by many. When he saw me, he waved and invited me over to his table by the window, so I went over and had lunch with him.

When we finished, Scott said, "Hey, I'm having a few friends over to my apartment tonight for a party. Maury, would you like to come?"

I said, "Sure!"

Developing a new lifestyle

He wrote down the directions to his place and said the party would start at about 7:30 that evening and probably would go until the early morning. "Just ring the buzzer and come on up!" he said.

This was a great day for me, I thought to myself. *Wow! What a life in NYC!*

I was happy, to say the least. A college student wanted me to come to a party! That was totally cool by me. The last train back to New Jersey at night left at 11:35, so I couldn't stay too late. Since I was expected home earlier, I had to call and ask if it was okay for me to stay late. I figured I could sleep late on Sunday.

The evening finally came, and I made my way to Scott's apartment. He lived in a dingy apartment with gray walls and almost no furniture, but he had brought in some folding chairs. Some of his friends were already there, clutching bottles of beer and sitting wherever they could. Everyone seemed quite comfortable in these sparse surroundings, and they were "talking shop"— talking about their instruments, the upcoming year, the pieces they were working on, their teachers, etc.

Smoke from their cigarettes was rising in giant clouds, filling the room. Someone finally opened the door and the windows and let some air in. It seemed like everyone was smoking cigarettes in there! I was no exception.

We started listening to some new recordings of several great classical pieces that Scott had put on. The beer and hard liquor were flowing pretty freely, and after about two hours, the room was beginning to spin whenever I stood up. I stepped outside onto the roof with a few of Scott's friends, and we all passed around a joint. By about 9:45, I was really drunk and high, and suddenly I realized that I had to catch a train! I had forgotten all about it! I was tired, stressed-out, intoxicated on alcohol and marijuana, and had to find my way home to Madison, New Jersey! Somehow, I had to get home.

I don't know how, but I managed to make it home by 1:30 in the morning and fall into my bed. I slept in an unconscious stupor until nearly two o'clock the next afternoon. I thought the party was great the night before, but when I awoke, everything was aching from my head to my toes.

Somehow, I got through the fall. I don't really know how. I repeated the same scenario every Saturday. Very often, I would stay over at someone's apartment after a party and take the train back on Sunday. I lived for those Saturday nights when I could go out and find some party with other Juilliard students. I did my practicing, but my music and my school work began to slip some because of my intense schedule. I rarely did my high school homework...unless I was trying to cram it in at the last minute. I wasn't getting enough sleep, and I have always needed about eight hours of sleep each night. Most of the time I was only getting six hours or less.

A couple of Saturdays I called in sick to Juilliard because I was so tired. But out of respect for Mr. Galamian, I don't think I did that on his lesson days. I would just sleep on the train on my way into the city and drag myself through my classes. But for some reason, when the evenings rolled around, I seemed to perk up and come alive. All tiredness disappeared. Then I would party with the other kids until late and blow off all of the pressure from the week before.

Sometime in November, Dad called me and told me about the Christmas String Seminar that was held every year in New York. Alexander Schneider, the great violinist from the former Budapest String Quartet, conducted a concert on Christmas Eve every year at Carnegie Hall. It would start at midnight and go to two o'clock in the morning. This concert was legendary because it was so good. It sold out weeks before, even though it was so late on Christmas Eve. Each year, Schneider would audition and gather talented high school students from all over the country and form them into a string orchestra. Then he would put all of them up in New York City for two weeks over the Christmas holidays, work with them for eight hours a day, and get them ready to play on Christmas Eve at Carnegie Hall, on New Year's Eve at Kennedy Center in Washington, DC, and once more at Carnegie Hall the first week of January. Dad told me he thought this would be a good thing for me to audition for, so I found out about it and sent in my application.

A special holiday opportunity

I remember the auditions that year were being held somewhere in downtown New York City. I had no idea who the people were I auditioned for, but they were powerful in the New York classical music scene. Evidently, I played a good audition. They accepted me and even asked me to play in the first violin section for the 1978 Alexander Schneider Christmas String Seminar. I was really excited! I was going to play in Carnegie Hall on Christmas Eve! I was one of the younger participants, but not by too much. They had done auditions all over the country and hand-picked the best kids to be in the orchestra. This was to be a particularly special year because Isaac Stern was going to play and narrate a special documentary that PBS was making. They were going to film the whole seminar.

I went to Austin, Texas, for a few days at Thanksgiving. Susan's parents lived there, and Dad and Susan were there. It was a good break to get out of New York for a few days, that's for sure. I wasn't very happy where I was living, and I was struggling at Madison High School. Juilliard was exciting, overwhelming, and full of pressure for me all at the same time. I was getting high on marijuana two or three times a week to cope with the pressure. I was strung out and tired most of the time because of my schedule. As I look back at that time in my life, I am really amazed that I didn't fall apart completely under the pressure! So when I arrived at Susan's parents' spacious western home, I was glad to be there. Even to see Dad again was a welcome relief. New York was hard for me, even if I didn't want to admit it at the time.

On Thanksgiving evening, I went out for a walk after dinner. Suddenly I stopped and looked up at the sky. It was a bright, clear, cold night there in Texas, and the stars were amazing! It seemed like I could see every star in the Milky Way. It was breathtaking! I sensed right then that time seemed to stop. Suddenly there was that Presence again, and tongues started to flow out of me. I was praising the Lord from my heart. Peace came over me and flooded my whole being. Somehow I knew that everything was going to be all right.

I had often prayed to the Lord and asked for His help, but I didn't talk about it much because I didn't want anybody to think I was a fanatic or something. Very often, those tongues would just roll up out of my spirit. But that night when I prayed, I had the assurance that somehow I would make it through the rest of the school year. I had been experiencing a growing sense of panic because I felt I couldn't handle it. I didn't think I was good enough to make it on the violin. I was scared that I would fail in New York and have nowhere to go. That was all I had. I had to do good. But I felt the Lord minister to my heart that night and assure me that He was with me and that I would make it through somehow. All the stars in the sky seemed to sing that to me. Everything was going to be all right.

Something within me said, "Fear not, for I am with you. Do not anxiously look about you. Surely I will help you. Surely I will strengthen you. Surely I will uphold you with My righteous right hand." I walked back to the house full of peace, fell into bed, and slept like a baby.

I returned to Madison and finished out the fall semester. Then I packed my suitcase and took the train to New York City for the Christmas String Seminar.

Our practice schedule was very strenuous. We practiced mornings, afternoons, and evenings. In addition to orchestra rehearsals, I also had a string quartet rehearsal. Some of the teachers were very difficult. They would scream and curse at us if we didn't perform up to their expectations.

On the second day of my quartet rehearsal, a little, old man came into our room to coach us. His name was Felix Galimir. From the moment I saw him, I knew this was going to be another intense experience. I was so tired from the orchestra rehearsals that I kind of spaced out. As soon as we started to play, Mr. Galimir began jumping around and shouting, "Play the music! Don't just sit there like a bump on a log! SKLARRR! I am talking to you! STOP! WHAT ARE YOU DOING?"

Then he would put both hands over his ears and scream, "STOP PLAYING SO OUT OF TUNE!"

That was all I could take, and I started to cry. Mr. Galimir felt bad and said in his thick Viennese accent, "Oh, don't be so sensitive. You are acting like a little girl. Stop that! PLAY LIKE A MAN! You have to be tough to make it here in New York. Besides, I know who you are. You studied with little Fredell, bless her heart. Now, STOP PLAYING LIKE A LITTLE STUDENT AND PLAY THE WAY I HEARD YOU AT YOUR AUDITION!"

Then, under his breath, he said, "How can you play this way now and play the way you did in the audition? Dear God!"

Mr. Galimir jumped up and screamed, "One, Two, Three, Play!" And we crashed into the next part.

Finally our coaching session ended. I put away my violin and just sat there, stunned and deeply shaken. It took me some time to even be able to talk to the other players in the group. Stephanie, the second violinist, told me she thought I was playing really well and didn't understand why Mr. Galimir had gotten so upset.

"Don't worry about it," she told me. "Just forget it. Mr. Galimir gets frustrated sometimes for no reason at all, especially at younger students. He doesn't think they are concentrating or something." After she said that, I felt a little better, and I left and got on the bus to go get dinner. Fortunately, our group was never coached by him again.

That night, before orchestra rehearsal, I started feeling really low. I was tired and discouraged from the chamber music coaching. I walked around the school where we were practicing and found an alcove nobody was using. No one was around, and it was quiet in that part of the school.

Asking for help

Suddenly I fell to my knees and prayed, "Lord, please help me. I don't have enough strength to get through this. I know I haven't been living right before You. Please forgive me for all the times I have sinned against You. Please, Lord, is there someone here who could be my friend? Is there anyone who knows You who could be with me at this seminar? I know I haven't been very open about You to anyone, but no one seems to like it when I mention that I am a Christian. Why don't people like You, Jesus? Please help me through this Christmas Seminar and enable me to play well." Then I got up and went into that evening's rehearsal.

The next day we went to Carnegie Hall for our final rehearsal. When we all got out on the stage, we could feel the excitement in the air. It was scary out on that famous stage, especially with those big cameras rolling, microphones everywhere, and TV lights on. This was going to be a spectacular performance!

The rehearsal went great, and I was getting up to put my violin away when I noticed a girl who played first oboe. She seemed like such a quiet girl, but there was something really special about her. I went over and introduced myself and asked her if she had enjoyed the seminar so far.

She said, "Yes, but it is a tiring schedule, isn't it?" I agreed, and she introduced herself as Linda Strommen from Wisconsin.

We talked for a few minutes, and I couldn't take my eyes off of her. It wasn't that she was a raving beauty or anything, although she was attractive. There was just something radiating from her face and out of her eyes that absolutely captivated me. I asked her if she would like to have lunch with me, and she agreed, so we went to a nearby diner and ordered our meals. The waitress brought our food, and I began to eat. Then Linda said, "Excuse me, but I always pray before I eat and thank the Lord. Is that okay with you?"

I practically dropped my fork in amazement and embarrassment. I said, "Sure. I am sorry."

Then she bowed her head, closed her eyes, and prayed, "Dear Lord, thank You for this food and thank You for my new friend Maury. I ask You to bless our lunch and our time together. In Jesus' name. Amen."

At first I was embarrassed, and then I was dumbfounded. I had never met anyone who prayed before they ate. Something was jumping up and down inside of me. I didn't know what it was, but I asked Linda, "Are you a Christian?"

She said, "Yes, I am."

When she said that, I felt waves of pure love pour out of her eyes and go into me right there in that diner! Tears flooded my eyes, and I said, "You know, I may not look or act like a Christian, but I am one, too." I had a lit cigarette in my hand. Embarrassed and convicted, I quickly put it out.

Linda just smiled at me and said, Don't worry about that. God doesn't look at the outside anyway; He looks at your heart." As she said that, I saw her face light up again. She looked like an angel to me. We finished our meal and went back to the hotel. Linda invited me up to her room. She said she had a book she wanted to give to me. She said she had just finished reading it and felt that the Lord wanted her to give it to me.

When we got to her room, she invited me in. She found the book, lovingly opened it, and began to write on the flyleaf. Then she handed it to me. It was called *Knowing God* by J. I. Packer. Linda said it had helped her to understand the Lord so much better. I turned to the flyleaf and read what she had written. It said: "*To my brother Maury, May this book be as much of a blessing to you as it has been to me. Remember, God is able to keep you from falling and to pre-*

sent you blameless before the presence of His glory with exceedingly great joy! (Jude 24). I will rejoice with you on that great day when we will stand before His throne! Love always, In Jesus, Linda Strommen, Christmas 1978 - New York City."

When I read that, I was totally overcome. I began to weep. God's love and grace had completely overwhelmed me. I thanked her and God for how good He was to me. I told Linda, who also had tears in her eyes, that I wanted to live right for God, but I didn't know how. I prayed that God would help me to do so. I told her that I wished I was a better Christian. Linda said that she had felt that way many times herself and that the Lord was very merciful and patient with us. Then she read Psalm 139 to me. She told me that this Psalm meant so much to her, especially verses 7 and 8: *Where can I go from Your Spirit? Or where can I flee from Your presence? If I ascend into heaven, You are there; If I make my bed in hell, behold, You are there...* Then she read Romans 8:38-39: *For I am persuaded, that neither death, nor life, nor angels, nor principalities, nor powers, nor things present, nor things to come, nor height, nor depth, nor any other creature, shall be able to separate us from the love of God, which is in Christ Jesus our Lord.*

God's holy presence and peace had just saturated that room. We didn't want to move. We sat there in silence for some minutes. I'll never forget being with Linda in that hotel room that day and the expression that was on her face as she looked at me. Jesus was looking at me through her eyes and loving me through her kind words. I have prayed many times since that others could feel His love through me in the same manner that I felt through her that December 23rd in 1978.

God certainly had answered my prayer! Linda was an inspiration to me. I experienced God's grace and His unconditional love that day in a way I had never known before. God had not forgotten me nor had He left me alone without someone else who believed in Him. Linda and I became good friends for the rest of the seminar, and even though I still went to several parties that she would not attend (understandably), Linda was a tremendous support to me. During all of my teenage years, she was one of the few Christians who loved me unconditionally and really wanted to be my friend. Because of her, I could believe that God really loved and cared for me, in spite of my sinful lifestyle and my emotional and social insecurity. He would truly "never leave me or forsake me," no matter what I did or what I felt.

Chapter 12

The Curtis Institute
of Music

*T*he concerts were triumphant and glorious for me
and everyone who participated that year. The next day,
however, without any real vacation, I returned to school
and resumed my weekend commutes to New York City. I
felt more and more like I wasn't welcome any longer where
I was living, even though the family never told me I had to
be out by a certain date. It was just one of those unspoken
things I could feel very distinctly. I had grown very sensitive to it. I knew I had worn out my welcome and it was time
to leave. I called Dad and told him that things weren't going
so well where I was staying, and he told me to keep my eye
out for any families in or near the city that I might live with.
Fortunately, I wasn't forced to leave until I had somewhere
else to go, so I continued living there as January came and
went.

I finally found a place in Brooklyn with the family of
another student. I began attending the Professional
Children's School and continued with my training at
Juilliard. Things seemed to be going okay. I was still getting high on pot a lot during that time. I felt insecure about

my future and where to live, and pot provided a way to escape the pressure that seemed to surround me.

A part of me loved the freedom of New York, but I had never felt so alone before. I had no place to really call home. When I did get high on marijuana, I began to experience an overwhelming sense of hopelessness and paranoia. I knew it was wrong to get high, and I began to be bombarded with negative thoughts that didn't really seem like my own. What I thought would bring relief from pressure began to do just the opposite. I began to have trouble remembering details. I often slept too late and had to call in sick for school. Still, I enjoyed the party scene wherever I could find it. Of course, I was still practicing, but I knew that I could be doing far more.

I felt condemned because I knew I wasn't living the way the Lord wanted me to live. I was wasting far too much of my time. The original euphoria of getting high was not there anymore. Whenever I smoked marijuana, I felt a dark fog surround me. But at least it was better than the constantly growing pressure that I felt all the time. With the marijuana, I could shut it off for a while, even if I had to pay a price emotionally and physically to do so.

Even Mr. Galamian noticed that I was dragging into my lessons. He stopped me one day during a lesson and said, "You're like the absent-minded professor. You never remember a thing I tell you. I think New York is too much for you at your age. I think you should go to Curtis. Philadelphia is a better environment for someone young like you. I would like you to audition there this year."

I was amazed. He only invited the very best students to take lessons from him there. I was playing very well that day, so I could understand what prompted him to ask me, but I also saw concern in his eyes. He somehow knew that things weren't easy for me and that I was slipping personally.

I called Dad immediately and told him the news. He was thrilled and said that he would get an application and send it in right away. A few weeks later, I got a letter from the Curtis Institute of Music in Philadelphia, inviting me to come and audition in late April. This was what I had dreamed of doing since I was very young. I knew that if I made it into Curtis, I wouldn't have to worry about regular high school any more and I would be like the kids I had met at Meadowmount!

I started really practicing. I had a recital at about the same time this happened, so I chose a program that would include the required pieces for the audition. I practiced like I had never practiced before. I wanted this so much. It seemed like the only way out of a desperate situation for me in New York. I wasn't very happy, even though if you had met me at the time, you would never have thought that was the case. The world seemed much less appealing to me now that I had been living in New York for nearly a year. I wanted out. Curtis seemed like heaven in comparison! I had been told by my dad so many times that if I got in there, I would have it made. I could finally be happy because I would be one of the best and be with others who were the best. I would be in a happy "family" of great musicians, and we would live happily ever after.

The Curtis Institute of Music is housed in a old mansion that once belonged to a lady named Mary Louise Curtis Bok. Her family owned the Curtis Publishing Company, and she was worth millions of dollars. She was also a great lover of fine music and a philanthropist to the arts. In 1924, she had converted this mansion into a school that would teach only the most elite musical talents in the world. She brought together the greatest artists in the world at that time on every instrument and paid them handsomely to teach there. It was her vision to provide schooling free for every student who was good enough to go there. Curtis became legendary for producing the greatest classical musicians in the world from its inception. Such names as Leonard Bernstein, Samuel Barber, Jorge Bolet, Rudolph Serkin, the Guarnieri String Quartet, Oscar Shumsky, Leonard Rose, and hundreds of other famous artists were once students in those hallowed halls.

Auditioning at Curtis

When I arrived at Curtis for my audition, I began to feel nervous. I knew there were only a few openings—about four or five—for the next fall. When I saw the list of names of students who were also auditioning, I really felt nervous. It looked like over a hundred!

I had about an hour before my audition, so I got my violin out to warm up. As I did, fear gripped me so strong that

111

I could hardly tune my instrument. I heard a voice saying, "You'll never make it in here. Do you really think you're good enough? Ha! Ha! That's a joke. The violinists here can play you under the table. They've already filled every opening. Just forget it. You're going to go in there and blow it! You're going to fail to get in, and then what are you going to tell your father?"

On and on this voice screamed in my inner consciousness. The fear got so bad that I dropped my bow and staggered back until I couldn't even move. I could hardly breathe. I felt like I was suffocating...like something had its hand on my throat. Then I heard, "You'll never make it on the violin. You're a total failure! Do you really think your *Jesus* can help you now? You're a pathetic talent! You can't even begin to measure up here. *Jesus* can't get in here, and you can't either. I won't let you. *I'm* the one in charge here!"

I had never felt or heard a voice like that before, and I didn't know what to do. I hadn't thought about Jesus until that voice said His name. I had nearly passed out because I couldn't get my breath. I cried out, and all I could get out was, "Help me, Jesus! Help! Jesus! Jesus!" Suddenly, my throat opened and I could breathe again. The voice stopped screaming at me, and a warmth came over my body. I started speaking in that funny language again, and the words poured out of me for ten minutes straight like a machine gun.

Now I felt peace, like I was encased in a thick, heavy blanket. As I started to warm up on the violin, I was playing like I never had before. My body was on fire. I had to stop and get a drink of water. I was thinking clearly and feeling alert as a woman finally came to take me to my audition. That negative voice was still trying to speak to me, but it couldn't get through. I couldn't hear it. I heard another voice now that said, "I am with you. Do not be afraid. I am playing through you."

The fire that had heated me up so much began to intensify in my belly, and I felt a boldness and confidence come over me that I had never known before. As we reached the top of the stairs, I felt as though I could do anything on the violin. I literally felt the Lord by my side as I waited for the large, wood-paneled door to open. Even though I was overwhelmed at the pressure, I wasn't afraid. That blanket of the Lord's presence just surrounded me. The large door swung open, and a young Japanese girl with a very pale face left the room. Then I heard, "Next, please," and I entered.

There were seven or eight violin teachers sitting there, including Mr. Galamian. I started playing in a way that I had never played before. I felt like it was the easiest thing in the world as I played each passage with such a power that it startled me. That Presence filled the room like a mighty cloud. I felt as if I was standing over my body watching myself play. I couldn't even say it was me playing, even though I knew it was. It was a strange experience.

They let me play for some time and then stopped me and asked for a Bach fugue. As I played almost the entire fugue, what I know now as a "spirit of might" came on me. I felt like Samson picking up and carrying the city gate, bars and all, out of town. I played with such force and power that when I stopped, nobody moved for about twenty or thirty seconds. The fear of the Lord was in that place! When I put down my violin, that blanket of power instantly lifted off of me, and I felt like a little kid again as I stood there, fidgeting.

The teachers were all just staring at me as if they were stunned. Then they all started fumbling with the papers in front of them and rearranging them. They thanked me, and out the door I went. The lady who had brought me to the audition escorted me down the stairs and told me, "Maurice, you will receive a letter from us in two to three weeks, letting you know about the results. You are free to go now." I walked triumphantly down those stairs and out of Curtis. I knew that I had done my best, and I was very happy.

The letter came a few weeks later, telling me I had been accepted. I had made it! I could return to Louisiana now with my head held high. Since I had made it into Curtis, I knew that my time with Dad would be positive. I had done it! I thanked the Lord because I knew I couldn't have gotten through that audition without Him. I was really tired and stressed out from such an intense year, and my partying hadn't helped any. I was ready to go back to Baton Rouge for the month after school for some much needed rest and relaxation!

Continuing problems with Dad...and the devil!

When I got to Baton Rouge, however, I realized that Louisiana was clearly no longer my home. I felt really lonely there. I would sleep until noon most days and then just hang out and do whatever until Dad and Susan got off work. Most afternoons I smoked a joint and practiced. I was really bored. I wasn't so happy anymore, even though I was going to Curtis in the fall. Things were unsettled for me, and I felt like I didn't belong anywhere. I was feeling disillusioned about life and Dad in particular. It seemed that he really didn't care much about me. He spoke about my getting into Curtis like I was some kind of prize pony that had just won a trophy at the races. He didn't ask anything about how I was doing and didn't really seem to care that I might have problems. He just wanted to revel in my acceptance at Curtis. It was as if he had done it instead of me. It made me sick the way he carried on. I felt as if I was seeing him as he really was for the first time, and it was too much for me to accept. So I tried to put it out of my mind. I just couldn't figure out why I was so angry at him.

There was such a distance between us. I was really no longer a part of his life, except for my violin career. He fed off of my stories about New York, what I had seen in Philadelphia when I was there, reports of my lessons with Mr. Galamian, and my upcoming summer at Meadowmount. He relished my learning new pieces that were challenging and reacted negatively if I had been assigned anything that seemed to be easy or "student like." He was living in his own make-believe world. It was like feeding an animal that never got full. He would be so happy for a while, and then he would want to hear all about the same things again and again. I was an example of how *he* had been successful, but there was little real communication between us. He was totally caught up in my success and seemed oblivious to the fact that I needed a father at that time more than ever before. Sadly, our relationship remained that way for the rest of my teenage years.

I still had a big supply of enthusiasm and optimism about the music world, however, and about being on the East Coast "on my own." It was something the Lord graced me with from my summers at EMF and my childlike faith in the goodness of the outside world. I believed that my "salvation" lay in the music world. That was the "family" I would fit into. I tried to convince myself that Curtis *would* be all that Dad had told me it would be! I was going to be happy now! But inside, way back in my mind, I had a growing dread about returning back to Meadowmount. I was scared that I wasn't good enough. Worse than that, I was scared that I would be unhappy in the one place where I could "fit in," according to Dad.

I was beginning to realize that the world wasn't at all like Dad had described it. He was living in a fairy-tale world, but it took me many years to finally see that truth. Also, I knew that I couldn't play very well unless that special Presence took over. I knew it wasn't really me doing the playing—it was this "special ability." But I didn't understand it. The marijuana was beginning to affect me. I would get high, thinking I would feel better, and then I would fall into a foggy stupor of depression and anxiety that was worse than the pressure. Nevertheless, I always chose to get high anyway. I simply had to escape the pain and pressure, regardless of the side effects. But the pot was only making things worse for me.

The Holy Spirit in me became grieved when I got high, and then I would fall into condemnation. Then the devil—who had open season on my drugged and defenseless mind and emotions because of the door I had opened with the pot—would begin to accuse, condemn, and torment me hour after hour with his lies. Sometimes I would lie on my bed in agony. I simply believed that all those thoughts were my own...and that they were true. Such was my inner life for the next five to seven years. June of 1979 was the beginning of an emotional spiral downward into bondage and oppression. But whenever it got too bad, I would cry out to the Lord and He would come and help me. Praise His holy name!

Of course, I see all this now in hindsight. As a fifteen year old, I was just aware that things weren't very stable in my life. I was doing my best to cope and to pretend that I was on top of the world. After all, I was succeeding musically, wasn't I?

Meadowmount was a little better for me since I was a little older and going to be a student at Curtis. I received a new level of respect from "the elite" group of kids at Meadowmount. And that was important to me because I wanted their approval so desperately. Unfortunately, because I tried so hard to get them to like me, they really got tired of my hanging around them. I labored all the time under such a heavy load of either real or imagined rejection that seemingly my only recourse was to get high—which only made things worse. Nevertheless, I still was playing the violin quite well and improving.

In preparation to play in a concert that summer, I started practicing the *Tchaikovsky Violin Concerto*. I had never been asked to perform in a concert at Meadowmount before, so it was a great honor. But I had only been given three weeks to prepare. Of course, I prayed and asked the Lord to help me, as I always did. But I was suffering from such deep feelings of inferiority and rejection that when I got onto the stage, I was extremely nervous. For the first time, I didn't feel like I had any confidence at all when I played. My bow was shaking, and I felt like I was playing horribly during the whole piece! Actually, upon hearing the tape of my playing afterwards, it was quite good. But during my performance, I felt like machine gun bullets were hitting me as voices screamed, "You sound terrible! They hate you! You are going to be the laughingstock of the whole camp!"

I couldn't figure out where all these awful thoughts were coming from. I was being so tormented with fear that I almost had to stop playing about five minutes into the piece. Somehow I kept going. Then I noticed that by the end of the slow movement, many of the students were crying. When I finished the finale, the whole audience stood up and erupted in shouts of "Bravo." They must have given me seven curtain calls. They wouldn't quit! They kept clapping and clapping. I had to keep coming out on stage to bow awkwardly in front of them. Mr. Cerone, who was my assistant teacher that year, was beaming from ear to ear. It was a triumph!

I was shocked. How could I be so tormented and still play well when I thought I was playing so badly. I felt like I was in a torture chamber the whole concert. I didn't know where those thoughts were coming from, but I knew that somehow they couldn't be true. It wasn't until years later that I discovered those thoughts were demons trying to tear me apart with their lying words full of venomous hate. Their words were penetrating into my spirit and beginning to affect everything in my life.

Dad and Susan came to pick me up once again at the end of the summer. We headed to Philadelphia to visit with Dad's cousin, Tim Sklar, and his family. Tim was a prominent attorney, and his wife, Carol, was a counseling psychologist. Carol and I hit it off very well.

Finding a confidante in Philadelphia

One afternoon, Carol watched while Dad was practicing with me. She got quite alarmed as she saw how distressed I was getting because Dad kept pushing me and saying I wasn't good enough. She finally took Dad aside, and said, "For God's sake, Chuck, why don't you ease up on Maury? I'm really concerned for him. Let him have his own life. He's already in a bad way because of what you have done with him. I can tell just by being with him. He's showing signs of severe stress, anxiety, and neurosis. He can't continue to live that way. No one should be made to. I hope he makes it but, actually, with his level of stress, I'm not sure that he will. He could crack up if he doesn't get some help. It may have already gone too far. You've got to just let him be a boy before its too late. Stop living through him. It's dangerous!"

Even though Carol tried to be discreet, I had overheard what she said. And I also heard my dad's reply, "That's ridiculous, Carol! He's fine. I don't know what you're talking about. I'm not living through him. *He's* the one who wants to play the violin. I'm just *helping* him. Without me, he'd never have gotten to first base! *You're* the one who doesn't know what is going on. He wanted me to hear his piece. I can't help it if it wasn't good enough. I had to say something or Maury would keep playing it as out of tune as before. I resent your interruption. Don't you *ever* say that to me again!"

As he kept talking with her, Dad's voice continued to rise. He got angrier and angrier. Carol just looked at him and said, "You need help, Chuck."

That infuriated him even more, and he told her, "If I need your opinion or your help, I'll ask for it." And that was the end of the conversation.

As Carol walked out of the room, Dad shook his head and said to me, "She thinks she knows everything just because she's a "shrink." I don't plan on ever returning to this house as long as I live. I'll never take advice from some know-it-

117

all, condescending psychologist. How dare she try to preach to me about how I raise my own son. You turned out all right. Everything you ever got is because of me. You got into Curtis because of me. You'll be a world class violinist because I cared enough to make you into something more than just a mediocre violinist who rots in the back of some violin section in some podunk orchestra somewhere. She's got some nerve to tell *me* off!" With that, he stormed out of the room.

I just stood there, not knowing what to think. I just felt numb. I cleaned my violin and put it away for the night. Later we had dinner, and everyone acted as if nothing had happened. Dad chatted nicely with Tim and Carol, but to my knowledge he has never returned to that house or spoken kindly about Carol Sklar to me again.

An hour or so after dinner, Carol pulled me into her office, shut the door, and put her arm around my shoulders. She said, "Maury, I really like you and I care about you. I didn't mean to intrude today, but I just couldn't help it. I know your dad means well, but he can't help the way he is. If you would like to visit with me sometime, I would be happy to see you."

I said I would. Then I surprised myself and blurted out, "Could I visit with you some tonight? I have to leave tomorrow."

Carol said, "Sure, but let me finish up with your father and Susan first. They want to go to bed early. Let's meet in my office about ten o'clock, okay? Don't say anything to your dad about it, though." (As if she had to tell me that.) Then she smiled at me, gave me a quick hug and a kiss on the cheek, and said, "I'll see you later."

Just as Aunt Carol had said, Dad and Susan went to bed about 9:30 that evening. When I went to her office, I heard her talking on the telephone, so I knocked on the door. She opened the door and let me in. She said, "I'm glad you wanted to see me. I talk to people all the time, and I could tell you weren't very happy during your 'lesson' with your father."

I told her that was true and that it had been that way since I could remember but that things were better now because I wasn't living at home any more. She said she wanted me to be happy and to do well at Curtis, but she was concerned that I should have a normal life, too. Then

118

she asked me about girls and how I was doing socially. I explained to her that I liked girls very much, but they didn't ever seem to like me. I had never had a relationship that really worked out for me. I told her about how many times I had moved and mentioned that it was hard to keep friends for very long because of living in so many different places. But I told her I thought things would be better at Curtis because I would be with people like me.

Carol said, "There are people like you in a lot of places. You just have a special talent, but you are normal."

I told her I didn't feel normal. I told her about feeling bad about myself and not being able to fit in anywhere even though I did well on the violin. I told her that I got high on marijuana even though I knew it wasn't right. I also told her I was a Christian but that I didn't seem to be able to live like one. I just unloaded my heart to her. At the end of two hours, I was crying and saying I was scared that I wouldn't do well at Curtis and that no one would like me. I felt really bad about myself. She said that most likely, I would do fine at Curtis, as far as my music went.

She said, "It may be harder for you in your personal life, but just try not to put so much pressure on yourself to be perfect. No one is perfect. We all make mistakes. We just do our best to make it through in this life. I hope your religion will help you. I'm glad you've found something to hang on to, at least."

Then she said, "Your father has sheltered you from many things that you need developmentally and kept many other things from you that you should have had as a child. As a professional who has been trained to look at people, I see many warning signals that you aren't very happy and that you need relief from all the pressure. Maury, what will you do if you don't become a great violinist?"

I told her, "I don't know. I'll just do the best I can, I guess, at whatever else interests me."

She said, "Do you really want to go to Curtis?"

I said, "Yes. I love to play the violin, but I just hate all the other things that I have to do to learn to play well. I just wish I played better. I don't think I'm good enough."

Carol paused a minute and then said, "I don't think that's the problem. I think you don't believe you measure up as a person. You feel that no matter what you do or how you act, you aren't good enough. You seem to say to me in all of your words that you feel something is desperately wrong with you. You think it is impossible to change that, too. *That* is the thing your father has planted in you since you were a child. It isn't the music; it is who you are apart from the music. *You* are more important than how you play the violin. Maury, you have to be secure and know that you are okay and loved whether you play the violin or not."

I just sat there silently wiping the tears from my eyes. I heard the clock out in the hall ticking away. It seemed so quiet. I thought to myself, *This sounds so absurdly simple. I know that.* Yet, what she said had struck a chord deep within me.

I said, "Carol, I think you are right. I do need to feel better about myself. I don't know why I think so negatively and feel so insecure. I realize I haven't lived a normal life, but why is it getting so hard now? I used to feel much better when I was younger. I should be so happy that I got into Curtis. What's wrong with me?"

Carol said, "Maury, I don't know you well. It would take a lot of time with you to answer all those questions. But I do know that you need someone like me to help you sort through all of this. Your father has projected his dreams of a solo career on to you. He is living through you. You are doing what he always wanted to do. Certain parts of your personality haven't developed properly because you haven't been allowed to grow up normally. He has bound you up from the time you were very young.

Nevertheless, I believe you will make it through. You may have a rough time, but there is something in you that refuses to give up. I can hear it in your voice. I think that is an even greater gift than your music, if that is possible. If you can hold on to that and harness *that*, it will pull you through. Maybe your religion will eventually do that for you. I don't know. Anyway, it's getting late, and I've got to get up early in the morning, so I'll see you then. Maury, here is my card. You'll be starting school soon here in town, and I want you to call me if you want to talk or you need any help. My fees are expensive, and I'm sure your father wouldn't want to pay for my help, but you ought to have *someone* to talk to. Maybe there is a way we can work it out financially. I'll do my best to work you in if I have time."

Her words were to prove prophetic, although I didn't know it at the time.

Chapter 13

My Introduction to Mormonism

*B*efore he left Philadelphia, Dad found me a place to live. Then he and Susan returned to Baton Rouge. As I always did when Dad would leave for the year, I felt a strange mixture of regret, sadness, disappointment, excitement, relief, and freedom all at the same time. On the one hand, I felt bad because I couldn't really connect with Dad in any deep or significant way apart from the violin. I had wanted our times together to be times when we could enjoy being father and son, or at least to share together something other than music, but it never happened. I just had to live with it. On the other hand, it was such a relief to be out from under the anxiety and control of his obsessive and overbearing personality. When he left, I felt free again, even though that freedom was mixed with the disappointment of not having a dad I could really share things with. However, I just shrugged it off, as I always had done.

I felt like I had won some unseen battle and had found a place of refuge in Philadelphia. I was probably the most hopeful I have ever been as I approached my first year at Curtis. Maybe life was going to work out for me after all, and I would find my place in life. I thanked God for what He had done for me. I knew that it was a great act of His grace that had gotten me in to Curtis. I took that as a clear sign that He had answered my prayer and that I was to be a great violin soloist.

I was very excited when I awoke for my first day at Curtis. It was a beautiful, warm, and sunny day, and I whistled as I walked across the grounds. It seemed like a dream that I was actually there. Curtis was indeed a magnificent place. Here I felt that I was part of an exclusive, chosen elite. Each of the practice rooms had a Steinway studio grand piano in it that was in top condition. In many of the rooms, students were practicing, and it sounded glorious to hear such awesome playing from such young kids! I kept thinking, *This can't be happening to me! I'm actually in Curtis!*

Shocking reality

Later that week, there was an orientation day for all the new students. We met in Curtis Hall, and the Director of Curtis addressed us. He said, "New students, I want you to know that during your entire stay at Curtis, you are on probation. There are no guarantees that you will remain here. Just remember: There are a hundred others waiting to take your place if you do not meet the standards of either your private teacher or the faculty as a whole. Since your tuition has been so graciously donated by the benevolence of others, you are to be exemplary of the high standards associated with Curtis."

I don't remember anything else he said. His first words shook me up quite a bit. What if I blew it? I could be kicked out. Then what would my dad say? I was filled with dread, fear, and intimidation. I was overwhelmed in spite of myself.

As soon as it was over, I ran downstairs to the basement. There was a tiny bathroom there behind the elevator, and I went in and locked the door. My heart was beating fast. My palms were sweating. I could hardly breathe. I hadn't felt that afraid since the day I had auditioned when the same completely irrational fear had gripped my heart. My head was spinning, and I almost passed out. I fell on my knees and said, "Jesus, help me! Please! I don't know what is wrong with me. I'm scared I will fail here. Right now, I commit myself and my entire time at Curtis to You. Please keep me from getting into trouble and getting kicked out. I ask You to be with me and to enable me to make it through this school since You wanted me to go here."

As I prayed, whatever had caused me to panic just seemed to lift away from me, and I felt peace again. I sensed that God was with me and that somehow He would keep me through my time there. I got up off my knees and left that bathroom thinking, "Jesus sure is real. I feel like a different person now."

I felt Him whisper back to me, "I love you, and I am with you."

I began my time at Curtis with great hope, but it didn't last too long. Don't get me wrong—I had a great many rich musical experiences at Curtis. My academic classes were easy, and I enjoyed my musical training. On a social level, however, I somehow managed to hang out with people who weren't very happy. Most of the older kids didn't want me around, it seemed. I reminded them of the way they were when they were in that "prodigy stage." So I stopped trying to be with them much.

I had some fun times with other students my age, but overall I became discouraged. If I went to a party after a concert, I ended up feeling left out—like there was something wrong with me. People didn't want to talk with me, and I couldn't figure out why. I liked some of the girls, but they seemed so out of reach because they were older. Every once in a while, one of the college kids would make friends with me and invite me over for an evening, but I always felt as if I was on the outside of every social gathering, trying to get in. When I was bold enough to say something, many times people would laugh or just walk away. I felt like I had put my foot in my mouth—but I didn't know why. I don't know to this day why I had such a hard time. I just know that I became more and more depressed because I felt so lonely. Curtis seemed to be such a cold, harsh place.

I found some relief when I hung out with my high school class. But some of the kids had been at Curtis from the time they were eleven or twelve and they only came to school long enough for their classes. They never practiced there or stayed longer than they had to. They just took the first train out.

For me, however, it was different. School was the only place I could go. If I went home to my little attic room, I felt lonely and depressed. Besides, it took so long to commute to where I was living. If I had an evening rehearsal, it was better to stay at Curtis than to have to turn right around and come back. Most days, after my classes and practicing were over, I would hunt for someone to hang out with. If that didn't work out, I would stay and practice until eleven o'clock in the evening when the school closed. Sometimes I hung out at a nearby diner that was open twenty-four hours a day.

One day I met a violinist named Alison. She was from Provo, Utah, and she stood out because she always smiled and was sweet and friendly. Even though she was a senior, I was really attracted to her. She had a kind and gentle demeanor. I invited her out to supper one night, and during the course of dinner, Alison began to tell me that she was a Mormon. I had no idea what a Mormon was. It sounded like some kind of an alien from outer space or something.

Alison took two hours to tell me all about it. I was troubled, confused, and fascinated at the same time. She told me she was a "Christian," and that there was another Bible in addition to the one I had. An angel had appeared to a man named Joseph Smith in America about a hundred years ago and told him about these golden tablets that recorded more of the Bible. It sounds so absurd and ridiculous to me now that I recall it, but at the time when I was staring into those big, brown eyes in the candlelight, she could have told me that she believed in pink elephants that flew, and I would probably have believed it.

It became clear to me after an hour or so that Alison wasn't going to quit, so I just sat and listened. After a while, I become more and more fascinated by this "new revelation of Jesus" as she put it. She seemed so sweet and sincere, almost too sincere. Something kept bothering me and leaving a bad taste in my mouth, but I tried to ignore it. At least Alison took a genuine interest in me, which is more than I can say for most of the others I met my first year at Curtis. She told me there were two other Curtis students who were Mormons. Yet, something kept nagging me on the inside. Something was wrong with what she was telling me. I felt like alarm bells were going off inside, but I did my best to override those impressions. Like a whirlpool, I was being drawn into this strange faith of hers. She actually had me convinced that she was right by the end of the evening.

I told her of my experiences as a Christian, but I said that church people seemed strange from what I had seen and I didn't like the idea of "church" very much. She said that was because the churches I had attended weren't "the true Church of Jesus." I was pretty blown away by that time. I paid the check, and she invited me to her apartment. She gave me this blue book. It had a picture on the outside of it of a gold angel statue blowing a trumpet and said, "The Book of Mormon." When she put it into my hands, I felt sick to my stomach, but I took it anyway. I felt like I wanted to get out of there as fast as I could.

On the train home, I took the book out and began to read it. It was written like the Bible in King James English. I had read some of the Bible from time to time, but this was strange. Nevertheless, something got a hold of me. I began to be drawn into the stories, and I would take the book out and read it every day as I rode the train to and from Philadelphia. I began to believe that what Alison had said was true. Maybe these absurd stories of Jesus appearing to the South American Indians after His resurrection had really happened. It made a certain kind of sense to me at times.

Alison had also put her two Mormon friends on my trail. I saw them at lunch time frequently. They began to tell me that I had to quit smoking, drinking alcohol, and even drinking coffee if I really wanted to be pleasing to God. It was nice to have a few friends, even if all they talked about was this different "Jesus," but I felt really badgered at times. It seemed like I wasn't in control of my thoughts like I used to be.

Then one day, Alison and her two friends ganged up on me and said some of their other friends wanted to give me a "presentation." These three guys dressed in suits and ties came and gave me a recitation of the story of Joseph Smith and the Mormon Church. I still remember that flip-chart they used with the poorly drawn pictures. I agreed to attend their church with them the following Sunday. I went, but I was so uncomfortable during the service that I got up and left halfway through the service. I felt like I was being smothered by a wet blanket. Even so, I began to believe that what they were saying was right.

About a month later, they wanted me to be baptized into the Mormon Church, but they said in order to do that I would have to quit smoking. I tried, but I couldn't quit. I have thanked God many times since then that I couldn't quit smoking at that time. Because of it, I was saved from joining that horrible cult that twists the Bible so badly. Even so, I was reading the Bible more, and some of it was getting through to me. I began to really live better than I had been. I believe the Lord used my Mormon friends to get me into some systematic reading and studying of the Bible, however twisted their doctrine is.

Home for the holidays

Before I knew it, Christmas came, and I went home to Baton Rouge. Dad had arranged for me to play at the Unitarian church he and Susan attended. Everyone seemed to enjoy my music, but I felt like I played poorly. I hated performing because I was hit so hard by fear, condemnation, and doubt. I had to play at least fifteen minutes before the negative feelings would go away, and then the most incredible peace would come. It was always the same every time, but those first few minutes were a living hell. Somehow I always got through it, but I was glad when it was over and I could put the violin away for a few days.

Dad had married Susan that fall and bought a large two-story home. I felt much more comfortable being at home now that Dad was married and had moved out of the apartment.

One day Dad asked me, "Maury, what would you like for a Christmas present?"

Before I could even think, I answered, "I would like a King James Bible, please."

He was very surprised when I said that, but I had been telling him on the phone during the year all about Alison and how nice she was and how I had found the true church in the Mormon Church. I had begun to be very vocal about my faith. Unfortunately, my Christianity had been swallowed up in the Mormon doctrine. It was the first time I really talked much about any of my beliefs with Dad and Susan. The other tragic thing was that I was not living a very clean life either. The combination of the cult doctrine and my partying really set Dad and Susan at odds with me.

I remember Dad's first words to me when I told him. He said, "You can believe any way you want to, Maury. You have your way, and I have mine. We all have to decide what's best for us. If it makes you happy and helps you live a better life—fine. Just don't put this Jesus garbage on me! That Mormon stuff is a bunch of bunk as far as I am concerned. You'd better get away from those 'friends' of yours before they totally mess you up! I don't care what you believe as long as you believe in your music enough to practice. Let that be your religion and you will be a lot happier. You'll get over this, I am sure. You'd better, for your own good."

I really believe Dad was genuinely trying to understand where I was coming from. Now that I was a Curtis student and had played such a good performance for all of his friends, I could have said I was a Hare Krishna and he probably wouldn't have been too upset as long as I kept going along nicely on the violin. I overheard him telling Susan, "Aw, this is just some adolescent phase he's going through. He'll grow out of it. He's got more sense than to stay involved with that crazy religion. Can you imagine that there are actually Curtis students who are involved in this cult?"

Surprisingly, he wasn't too overbearing about it. He even bought the Bible for me, and that really amazed me. It was wrapped and under the tree on Christmas.

When I opened it, he just said, "I have always given you everything I could to make you happy. If a Bible will make you happy, I'll get one for you. It's a free country. You can believe anything you want, I suppose. But if you ask me, that is one outdated book of nonsense."

Susan had grown up as an Episcopalian. She said, "Chuck, it can't hurt him to read it. It may do him some good."

Dad mumbled, "Yeah, it probably would, if Maury would get a little morality or something. Just so he doesn't become some kind of religious nut. I know there is a lot of pressure at Curtis. Maybe that Bible will help him to handle it better, although I can't see how it could."

A close call

Soon the holidays were over, and 1980 dawned. I returned to Philadelphia with a renewed sense of purpose and joy. This was Curtis after all, and I was going to get the best I could out of it. I was still having lessons up in New York City with Mr. Galamian every two weeks, but now they were on Sunday mornings instead of Saturday mornings. For the most part, Mr. Galamian's prediction had been correct. I was better off in Philadelphia than I had been the year before at Juilliard. I wasn't quite as wild that year. My lessons were going well, and I was better prepared. Nevertheless, I didn't stop getting high, and I certainly wasn't living a very holy life. I spent as many weekends as possible partying and hanging out with my friends. For me, being with someone—anyone—was far better than going home alone, so I stayed at different people's apartments a lot, even on weekdays.

As a result, I wasn't getting enough sleep. More and more often, I called in sick and didn't go to school. I was so exhausted from the night before that I couldn't get up. By the time February came, I had missed too much school—especially in my high school classes—and I was in trouble. It was serious, but for me it seemed very sudden. I hadn't realized how much school I'd missed. The school contacted Dad, and he was flying in to have an interview with the director. I was in danger of getting kicked out of Curtis!

Dad was very concerned when he came to see me. He said, "What have you been doing? You've cut too many classes. I thought you were doing better with things, now that you have religion and all, but I see you're up to the same shenanigans as last year. Don't you realize that you may have thrown away your whole music career because of this? When are you going to grow up and learn?"

I sat outside of the director's office as Dad talked with him for almost a half hour! As I sat there, I prayed, "Oh Lord, I know I have blown it. I probably don't deserve to be here anymore. But please help me now. I ask You to keep me from being thrown out of this school. Dad would never let me live it down. Please help me, Jesus."

I was so nervous that I was sweating profusely, and my heart was pounding! As I finished those words, the big double doors swung open, and the director motioned for me to come into his office. I felt extremely small and insignificant as I sunk into the chair in front of him, especially with Dad glaring angrily at me. I couldn't remember ever seeing him that angry at me.

The director said, "Maury, your father and I have been discussing your situation at some length. I am very concerned about how many times you have been absent from school. You have gone way beyond the limit of absences. Furthermore, you have taken advantage of our policy of calling in sick way too much and have also been tardy to a number of your classes. Also, there have been reports of you staying out late and not returning to your home at night as you should. That is both dangerous and delinquent. You are still a minor, and we cannot abide by this and take responsibility for your 'shenanigans,' as your father calls them, anymore. On these grounds, I should dismiss you from Curtis immediately. However, your private teacher, Mr. Cerone, has spoken to me on your behalf and has asked me to be as lenient as possible due to the fact that you are doing well in your lessons. I have a genuine concern that you may be too young to be as unsupervised as you are. We realize how difficult it is sometimes to adjust to the high standards of this fine institution.

"I had every intention of dismissing you if your father could not convince me that you could change. However, because I like him and because of his assurance that you will not continue in the way you have been going, I have decided to give you another chance. Young man, you came very close to being thrown out of Curtis. If it weren't for your father coming up here and speaking to me personally, I wouldn't have thought twice about it. But we believe you have a great gift, and we think you will grow out of this foolishness and immaturity. You must not miss any more classes. IS THAT PERFECTLY CLEAR?"

I had started crying, and I faintly said, "Yes, sir."

"Very well!" he thundered. "I am extending mercy to you and giving you a warning this time, but if I hear that you are continuing in this behavior, there will be no next time. DO YOU UNDERSTAND?"

Once again I mumbled that I did.

We all stood up, he shook Dad's hand and then put his arm around me as he walked us to the door. He said, "We want you to have every opportunity to develop into the artist that we believe you can be. Don't let your father and yourself down, all right? Let's see you rise to this challenge and meet it." Then he turned to Dad and shook his hand. "Chuck," he said, "you've got a talented son, and we want him to make it. I'm impressed that you came all this way to speak to me on his behalf, so we will give him another chance to prove himself."

The doors clicked shut with a soft thud. We were standing out in the hallway once again, and I was shaking with fear. I was crying almost uncontrollably and couldn't speak. We just walked down the hall, through the lobby, and out to the street. Dad was so angry he couldn't even speak. Finally, after about twenty minutes or so, he calmed down and began to talk with me as we took the train back to my apartment. All he could say for about five minutes was, "You could have thrown it all away! You almost lost it all!"

Finally he looked at me and said, "How could you do this after all I've done for you? Well, at least David Cerone stepped in on your behalf. If he hadn't, I could have talked to the director until I was blue in the face and it wouldn't have done any good. At least your lessons are going well. If I hadn't left my law practice to come up here to meet with him, you'd be finished. Do you understand? It's a good thing you have me. When I was your age, my father could have cared less about what I did. But I never would have pulled the stunts you have. Don't ever forget how much I do for you and how much I love you. Because of me, you're getting all the very best handed to you on a silver platter, and you still have the nerve to pull these kind of stunts!"

He had again worked himself into such a state that he couldn't talk, so we didn't say much more that evening. The next morning he told me good-bye and went back to Baton Rouge.

Needless to say, my attendance was much better for the remainder of the year. I was pretty shaken up by that incident, and I vowed not to let it happen again. The director had had every intention of throwing me out of school, and I am sure that I deserved it. But God had certainly intervened by once again showing mercy to me. Sometimes I've wondered, however, if it might have been easier for me in the long run if I had been expelled. The next three years were very hard for me in many ways.

I finished the year with no further incidents and passed all of my classes. I packed my things, took a cab to the airport, and left for Baton Rouge to begin my summer.

I had my birthday in June and turned seventeen. My seventeenth year was a dark one. There were a few bright spots, of course, but overall it was painful and sad. It began to dawn on me what it was really like in "the real world." My "rose-colored-glasses" view of reality and the romantic optimism that had framed my early life began to crumble. I was happy to be at Curtis, which brought me a sense of security, but the weight of life became heavier upon me. I had no idea how to fight against the torrent of evil thoughts and condemnation that bombarded my mind and heart all the time. There was no guard over my spirit, and I began to reap the fruit of the negative words I had spoken over myself. I see this so clearly now as I am writing. If only I had known the revelation I now walk in, I could have probably saved myself much misery. But as it says in Hosea 4:6, *My people are destroyed for lack of knowledge.* Because no one was there to disciple me in God's Word, I went through this dark time with almost no compass or light.

Of course, I returned once again to Meadowmount for my fifth summer in a row. Meadowmount was a secure and steady place for me. I had been there for a longer consecutive period than anywhere else. It was like a home to me, even though it was filled with great pressure. I enjoyed the familiarity of it, in spite of the fact that I was no longer one of the younger ones there.

Mr. Cerone was bearing down on me pretty hard. Most of the time he wasn't very happy with my lessons because they were very inconsistent. I would play one lesson so well that he would just listen in amazement. The next week I would barely be able to get through the piece. This was frustrating to him and to me. I didn't understand it. He just concluded that I wasn't practicing enough, which really wasn't the case. Actually, I was practicing about the same each week. For some strange reason I would just freeze up during some of my lessons. Because of that, I wasn't asked to play in any concerts that summer.

One evening I was trying to read the Book of Mormon, and I got so angry that I tore it up and threw it in the garbage. I said, "I will never read you again as long as I live. If that is God, then I want nothing to do with Him." I kept my Bibles and read them occasionally, but I quit trying to be a Christian, largely due to the Mormon teaching I had experienced. I just couldn't handle all the condemnation I felt. Whenever I read in the Bible about the righteous being blessed and the wicked being cursed, I thought to myself, *If only I were righteous like this says, instead of so full of sins, I would be so happy!* I knew I couldn't even begin to meet its standards, so I turned away from God and closed the door on all of it.

The Mormon doctrine had so infected my spiritual life and my relationship with Jesus that I just completely shut it all down. I closed the door on God entirely and had very little fellowship with the Lord for many months. That's when the light went out and the enemy really moved in on me. Fear began to grip my heart whenever I played. I was even more insecure than before, although I did my best not to show it.

Chapter 14

Meeting
Steve Strumbeck

I returned to Curtis in the fall. Dad had gone up earlier and found me a really nice apartment close to the school. It was a studio apartment on the twenty-ninth floor of a high-rise building just across from Curtis. I remember that the apartment had a new smell to it, like it had just been painted. It had gorgeous wooden parquet floors throughout, except for the kitchen and bathroom. It wasn't very large, but I liked it very much.

I remember the bathroom was on the right as you entered. A fifteen-foot, narrow hallway led into a large room that had windows looking out onto a building next to it. It wasn't much of a view, unfortunately, but if you stood way over to the left, you could see a tiny bit of Curtis. It had an adequate kitchen, and Dad had brought up some of his old dishes and a card table and chairs that he had bought before I was even born. It was falling apart, but it worked as a place to eat. It didn't look so bad when I covered it with a tablecloth. We went out and bought a twin bed and got some used furniture from a thrift store, including a lamp, a dresser, and a small night table. Dad drew up a design for a desk with a small bookcase that he could cut out of one large piece of plywood. Then he and I spent two days building it, and it was really nice. We bought a large area carpet to go over the whole living area, and finally everything was set.

I was so excited about having my own apartment, and fixing it up was a nice experience to share with Dad. He had wanted a place like that of his own when he'd been going to school in New York, so he was proud to be able to provide it for me. I kept it for three years until I graduated from Curtis. Whenever friends from school came over, they were amazed at how nice the building was and how fine my apartment was.

I did pretty well in school that year, particularly with my music. I began to take the violin pretty seriously because I realized I could no longer hide behind my youth. I was beginning to feel really overwhelmed about my future. Somehow, deep inside, I felt completely inadequate to deal with life as an adult. This feeling would intensify more and more during the next six years as I had to face adult life. But for now it was something I could put out of my mind. Facing life as an adult still seemed a long way off. After all, I was still only finishing high school.

I was also doing better spiritually after I returned to Philly. I even attended a few services at a Presbyterian church a few blocks from my apartment. It seemed really dull to me, but at least the minister seemed to believe in the Bible. For the most part, his preaching was clear and forthright, but I just couldn't get into it somehow. Somehow, Jesus seemed to get lost in this man's sermons, as well-meaning, sincere, and precise as they were. On the few Sundays that I went to church, I left feeling that I would have been better off just staying in bed. Soon after, I drifted away from nearly all church-going activity because it seemed so false to me. Nevertheless, I did start reading the Bible again and the few Christian books I had.

That fall I auditioned for the Schneider Seminar and was accepted. I spent the Christmas and New Year holidays in New York City once again, but I wasn't very happy. I felt depressed most of the time and stayed in my room when I wasn't playing in the orchestra. It wasn't nearly as exciting for me this time. I was feeling so inferior and neurotic about myself that I didn't talk to anyone very much. I didn't enjoy the party scene, either. It just wasn't the same anymore—it seemed so empty. I was exhausted from the long hours of rehearsing. As Hamlet once said, everything felt "stale, flat and unprofitable" (Act I, Scene II). Life for me was beginning to lose its luster.

I tried to pray, as I had at other times, but God seemed far away. The music was really great, but I didn't feel the same thrill that I'd had two years before when the world seemed so much fresher and the music was so new and inviting. Nevertheless, I still had moments when the music really touched me. Then it was over.

The hardest night of all was the night when we took the bus back to New York from Kennedy Center where we had played. I slumped over in my seat, and through my tears, I watched the street lights go by. I felt so lonely and sad. Depression seemed to rest on me like a heavy cloud. I began to realize that the music world was nothing like what I had believed it was. Arriving back at our dingy hotel, I went upstairs and went to sleep. It was over, and I had to go back to Philadelphia.

Well, I thought, at least I can rest for a while before school starts up again. I have a week or so. I almost missed not having gone home to Baton Rouge for the holidays.

Losing Mr. Galamian

In the spring of 1981, life at Curtis changed forever for all of us. I had just arrived back from a lesson with Mr. Galamian in New York. I had played the Bach Chaconne for him, and it was a triumph of a lesson for me. I had never seen him as pleased with me as he was at the end of that lesson. Three days later, we received word that Mr. Galamian had died of a heart attack. I was struck speechless. This couldn't be possible! How could he die? He was everything to his young violin students. He seemed immortal, even though he was nearly eighty years old.

When we heard the news, most of his students burst into tears. I wandered around center city in the rain for two days. I felt totally lost. For about two weeks, all I could do was play pinball at an arcade on Chestnut Street. The whole school seemed like a funeral home. Two weeks before Mr. Galamian died, the great viola teacher Max Aronoff had also passed away. All of the violin and viola students were going through this horrible time together. It wasn't just our violin teacher who had died—it was the greatest violin teacher of the twentieth century. The world would never be the same, it seemed.

I somehow managed to regroup after several weeks, and things began to return to normal. Mr. Cerone took over Mr. Galamian's best students for the remainder of my time at Curtis. He did a good job, but it never was the same after Mr. Galamian's death. We all just did the best we could to adapt to the tragic circumstances. Mr. Cerone had a tremendous affect upon me that made me work really hard, and I dramatically improved during that period of time.

The year finally ended, and I held my high school diploma in my hand. I had graduated! I was going to be a college student at Curtis in the fall. I had made it through one of the darkest years of my life, by God's grace.

As always, I returned "home" to Baton Rouge in late May after my school year was finished. My relationship with Dad was beginning to change. He was treating me with more respect. I was playing well on the violin, and he was really pleased to hear my progress. He reveled in my descriptions of the musical life at Curtis and my experiences there.

I struggled with a very low self-image, and I constantly berated myself. I would tell Dad, "I don't think I'm good enough on the violin. Everyone else seems so much better." I felt terrible about myself, and I didn't know why. I felt as if I was a misfit in the deepest existential sense of the word. I didn't feel as if I belonged anywhere. I felt as if I was some kind of neurotic accident. I tried to feel better by reading self-help books. I remember immersing myself in science fiction novels, and trying to escape the horrible feelings of rejection and loneliness that seemed to engulf me at times.

Life in the large two-story house with Dad and Susan seemed awkward to me. They were nice enough, but even though Susan did her best to accept me and make me feel a part of their lives, I could sense that she was looking forward to me dominating less of Dad's life. Even though I was with him very little in comparison to previous years, I still dominated his thinking and consciousness to a great extent. He spoke of little else other than my accomplishments at Curtis and my future violin career. He was proud of me, which made my time at home that early summer much easier.

Once again I left Baton Rouge and headed up to Meadowmount. When I arrived, I immediately realized that it wasn't the same anymore now that Mr. Galamian was gone. Nevertheless, I practiced very hard that summer. I began to realize that I couldn't rest on the laurels of being a young prodigy anymore. I knew it would take a whole lot of blood, sweat, and tears for me to play the violin at my best. I started to really cry out to the Lord again. I was scared at the prospect of growing up. I didn't feel prepared for life as an adult, and this began to loom over me more and more.

I was a sad sight. I felt so inadequate and was still tormented in my thoughts and emotions by voices that told me what a failure I was and that I was never going to make it. I still smoked like a chimney and hung out with some of my friends, but I was more reclusive this summer than before.

Dad had planned a recital tour for me in Louisiana that August, so I left camp early and went to do a week of concert recitals. I guess I played well, but I had such a difficult program that I didn't enjoy it very much. Soon after, I returned to Philadelphia to begin my first year of college.

During this time, I began to see some steady growth in my life as a Christian. I began to really pray a great deal, and even though my life was still full of darkness and blatant, outward sin, in my heart I was growing closer to the Lord. I began to read and study my Bible a little more, even though I still felt condemned when I did.

I'm not proud of this in the least, but during that time, I turned my walk-in closet into a hydroponics garden. I had found a book on growing pot, so I decided to try it. I went out and bought a special fluorescent plant light, dirt, and pots. I did quite well, unfortunately. I planted about twenty marijuana plants, and they grew! Over the Christmas break, however, the custodian who agreed to water them forgot about them and they died. When I came back in January of 1982, they were all dead, so I just smoked them. I admit that I was a very paradoxical person, but somehow the Lord had patience with me and saved me from those compulsive ways of sin.

A new friend and new experiences

One day in the spring, I happened to be down in the basement and passed by an office located off the stairwell. I glanced in and saw a tall young man with curly brown hair and glasses sitting behind a desk. I waved and said "Hi," and he responded immediately with a friendly wave. I passed that way often, so after about a week, I decided to go in and meet this smiling man. He seemed to be one of the few people who ever smiled much, so I was curious and decided to talk with him. He introduced himself by saying, "Hi! I'm Steve Strumbeck. I work as an assistant for the Admissions Department. It sure gets quiet down here! You're one of the first to ever stop in and say hello. I live in South Jersey and commute in every day." I told him my name, that I played the violin, and that I was in my third year.

I glanced at his desk and saw a Bible. "Is that a Bible?" I asked him.

Steve said, "Yeah. I read it during my breaks and in the morning before work. I'm a Christian." When he said that, the word Christian went through me like a jolt of electricity.

I said, "I am, too. Well, I am sort of. I don't live as good as I ought to, I know. But I read the Bible, too, and I believe in Jesus. I just don't talk about it much here because they don't seem to understand or appreciate it. I get into trouble if I say too much about it. Besides, I don't seem to be able to live that kind of life anyway, even though I want to."

Steve just put his hands behind his head, leaned back in his chair, and laughed. "I thought I was the only one in this place who had even heard of the Bible, much less believed it. I think all of you Curtis kids worship your music, not God." And so began a friendship that would prove to be far more providential than I ever could have thought at the time.

I would go down to his office every once in a while when I could get up the courage. His very presence convicted me of the sin in my life and made me very uncomfortable, but at the same time I was drawn to him. He never spoke condescendingly to me or preached at me, so after a few quick visits, I began to be a little more comfortable with him. I had so many questions about the Bible, and Steve seemed to be able to answer them all in such a beautiful and simple way that made total sense.

One late afternoon, I came into his office as he was getting ready to leave. It was a Friday, and Steve was heading home for the weekend. We talked for a few minutes, and then I had a burning question for him. I asked him, "Is it wrong to speak in tongues? I have been listening to this radio teacher who really hates it and says that it's from the devil. But whenever I am going through a tough time, I sometimes seem to speak that way. It just rolls out of me in spite of myself. Is that in the Bible? Every Christian I have talked to seems to think I should stay away from it. Actually, most of the Christians I've met don't stay around me very much either. I don't blame them, seeing that I don't seem to live right or anything."

Steve spent a long time showing me passages from the Bible and telling me, "Maury, I know that you have been taught against tongues, but they are for us today. I speak in tongues all the time."

Then he said something that branded itself to my insides: "PRAY IN TONGUES AS MUCH AS YOU POSSIBLY CAN, AND IT WILL ACTIVATE GOD TO WORK IN YOUR LIFE IN A GREAT WAY."

Steve talked to me about all the condemnation I felt. He said, "You have been alone in your Christian walk—that's all. And from what I can gather, the devil has really beat your brains out. You just need to sit under good teaching and be a part of a good, Spirit-filled church. I am amazed that anyone could survive spiritually in this place. Listen, would you like to come and spend the weekend with me and my family?"

A weekend in New Jersey

I happened to be free that particular weekend, so I said I would go. I went back to my apartment and got some clothes, and we took the high-speed train to New Jersey. Then we got in his car and drove all the way to Pennsville, which is about as far south in New Jersey as you can go before you cross the bridge into Delaware. It was very rural. Finally we turned off the county road onto a little street called "Plow Point Road" and made our way toward a little tiny house across from a farm. It had a sweet, quaint look to it, but it seemed very far from civilization.

Steve told me that his mother-in-law, Anita Jacobs, lived there and that she was a very special lady. She loved Jesus a whole lot and spent many hours praying each day. When Steve had called about my coming, she had been happy to have me. So I was to stay in her guest bedroom. When we knocked, a short, heavyset lady in her fifties with a dark, Italian complexion and the most beautiful smile I had ever seen came to the door and fairly enveloped the entryway. She put out a stubby hand and said, "Hi! I'm 'Nita Jacobs!" She welcomed me into her home, and I remember feeling such tremendous peace there like I had never felt before.

We ate supper and talked, and afterward, I went outside to smoke. Again I was overwhelmed with peace. I was so used to the strife and confusion of the environment of my life that I had never experienced the level of peace I felt on her property and in her house. All along Anita's property, I could feel that unearthly sense of God's presence, but as soon as I walked past her property line into the next field, it went away like a wispy vapor. As soon as I turned around and walked into her yard, that peace returned. I was so amazed that I mentioned this to Steve and Anita.

Anita said, "Well, of course. Jesus is my husband now that he is gone." She pointed rather sadly toward the picture of her late husband. "You know," she told me, "God establishes the border of the widow. The Lord owns my house and all of this property. He LIVES here."

I somehow knew exactly what she meant when she said LIVES. I marveled at her faith. She spoke like Jesus was her best friend. He was obviously as real to Anita as any "real" person might have been. In fact, He seemed to be more real to me that night than He had ever been before. I felt His wonderful love as she spoke. It just seemed to ooze out of Anita through her eyes and through each word she uttered. For Anita, even doing the dishes wasn't a chore. She sang praise and worship songs the whole time she stood in front of the sink. I had never met anyone who seemed to be so openly in love with Jesus as Anita.

Steve's wife, Natalie, came over, and we all talked for a while. Suddenly I blurted out, "Can Jesus help me stop smoking? I know it isn't right to smoke, but I just can't stop."

Steve immediately responded, "Sure, He can. Let's pray and ask Him to take smoking away from you."

I reluctantly agreed. I wasn't too confident that I could quit.

Anita said, "Maury, nothing is impossible with God. I've seen Him answer my prayers over and over. He'll deliver you of that nasty habit."

New spiritual experiences

Then they all came over to me and put their hands on me. I was extremely uncomfortable at that point, and I thought to myself, *What in the world are they doing?* I just wanted them to pray—and did they ever pray! All three of them at once—in tongues! I had never seen this before.

I had my eyes closed pretty tightly, and when I opened them, it felt like there was an unseen blanket of power around us. I felt "high," and my body was just pulsating with that awesome energy. It was amazing. When Steve, Anita, and Natalie went back to their chairs, I just stared at them in total shock. I had never seen anyone pray that way before. They were so bold and open about their faith in Christ. It seemed that was all they thought about, talked about, and lived twenty-four hours a day. A deep hunger began inside my spirit that night that has never left me. I have it to this day.

I ended up attending their church on Sunday, and I realized very quickly that their church was the center of their lives. Everyone was very friendly, but I was suspicious and in a bad mood that Sunday morning, so I didn't like it very much. When the music started, I liked it even less. It was the worst music I had ever heard. Then everyone got to their feet and began to clap, dance, shout, lift their hands, and sing together. I just sat there. I couldn't believe anyone could get so happy over such horrible-sounding music. I walked out after about five minutes and smoked a cigarette outside.

This is ridiculous, I thought. *What are they doing in there, anyway? They've lost their minds or something.* I was embarrassed to be in there with such things going on. These were really strange people, even though they seemed to love Jesus very much. One thing was for sure: they weren't pretending. I knew that this was the way they really were. There was no hypocrisy there. I came to the conclusion that they were emotionally unbalanced and needed help, but I felt they were certainly harmless enough. Even though I hated to admit it at the time because of my pride, I actually envied them for being so free in the Lord. Way down deep inside, I wished that I could be like them, foolishness and all.

I wish I could say that I loved my visit with Steve and his family, but at the time I was just relieved to get away from them. (Little did I know, that my visit there would pave the way to my deliverance and victory only a few years later.) Still, something had gotten a hold of me. I was different in a good way. I began to pray in tongues all the time as Steve had told me to do. I would whisper in tongues when I was walking to and from school. I would pray out loud when I took a shower, when I was alone in my apartment, and even when I was in bed at night before I went to sleep. The Lord really impacted me through that visit. He began to answer my prayers and the cry of my heart. From all that praying in the Spirit, I began to have an increased hunger for God and His Word.

School ended even more quickly that year than I had expected. It just kind of snuck up on me. Before I knew it, the year was over and I was headed back to Baton Rouge and Meadowmount. The summer of 1982 was my final one at Meadowmount. I had definitely changed. I felt like I was too old. I was sad because I knew somehow that I would never return there as a student again. So many dreams I had dreamed there never happened. I never had a time when I was able to do what those violinists did in "the glory days" when Mr. Galamian was alive. The camp had kind of fizzled out, and the great talents were not there like they had been. Sure, I had experienced a limited time of success, but it was bittersweet for me. Before I left Meadowmount that summer, I remember saying, "I will never return here as a student again." My days at the Meadowmount Summer Camp were finished forever.

Chapter 15

Graduation From Curtis

Dad and Susan had planned a vacation in Florida that August, and I flew down and joined them there after I finished the summer program at Meadowmount. Dad was really making an effort to build a better relationship with me, and I was trying to do the same. But it was a great effort for either one of us to get out of the only inevitable topic of conversation—my music career. I really wanted a solo career now, and I was eager to show Dad that I was right on track. He was thrilled at my progress and admired my focus.

I would swing from thinking I was a great artist and feeling on top of the world to thinking I was a terrible player and could never make it. My emotions ruled over me, and I had a hard time staying on an even keel. Dad and I walked along the beach together and talked to each other in a way that we never had before. He now was treating me like the young adult I had become. It seemed that if I could play the violin at a top level, nothing else seemed to matter. In fact, if I expressed an insecurity or emotional instability, he ignored it and chalked it up to the fact that I was "an artist...and artists tend to suffer more than the rest of us." Dad's view was that my suffering would make me a better violinist and a better person.

"It's all a part of growing up, Maury," he told me. "You have to deal with things in a different way now. But you'll turn out all right. Don't worry so much and stop analyzing yourself all the time."

There was one thing that he didn't like very much, and that was "my religion." This was the one area where he felt he had failed because I was so "extreme" in my belief in Jesus and the Bible. Dad felt that maybe he had failed to give me the support I had needed in that area and consequently I had compensated by being so extreme. He saw this as a tragic outcome. It was probably the only place that he felt he had not been a perfect father for me. It was, in his opinion, the only flaw in my representation of all he wanted in me as his son. It troubled him, and he always tried to get me away from it and to focus my attention on what he felt really mattered. Dad expressed this in a gentle way, however. He was scared that it would ruin all that "we" had worked for all these years. My faith in Jesus was an embarrassment to him. I think he thought I would just somehow grow out of it.

After about a week or so in Florida, we said good-bye, and I flew back to Philadelphia. I was always excited to begin school in the fall. I felt so free when I got back to my apartment.

As the school year started, Mr. Cerone announced that he was taking a select group of his students to Indianapolis, Indiana, to observe the first-ever International Violin Competition of Indianapolis, which would take place in late September of 1982. This was a creation of Joseph Gingold—a European-style grand competition in the genre of the Tchaikovsky Competition in Moscow. He had assembled a huge jury of soloists and teachers from around the world and made the first prize so large that it would launch a major career for whoever won it.

We arrived in time for the second round and then heard the finals with orchestra. It seemed like torture to me. Another Curtis student was having an even worse time than I was. She hated being there and kept saying, "I wish I could just go home to Philly. I hate this. It's like some kind of public crucifixion of violinists or something." I understood her point. The music world seemed like an awful place. The violin jury was so pompous and arrogant. It seemed like a very sophisticated way of feeding these precious talents to "the lions." If they failed to make it to the final round—which all but just a very few would—it would take them months and maybe years to get over it. At least that is the way I would have been if I'd had to play there.

I thought to myself, *Is this what you have to go through to have a solo career?* Even though I heard some violin playing that was greater than I had ever heard in my life, I still left there feeling extremely depressed and low. All of us were silent in the van as we drove back East. We were thinking, *If all the violinists I heard didn't make it, where does that leave me?*

I was going through more and more emotional turmoil. When it got to be too much, I would start to pray in tongues and cry out to the Lord, and I would feel better for a while. I had made one decision for sure. I was going to graduate from Curtis, and this would be my final year there. I had taken enough credits to graduate with an Artist's Diploma in May of 1983. It wasn't a bachelor's degree, but I had taken all the music classes, and I just needed a couple more hours of academics to receive my Bachelor of Music degree the following year. It seemed perfect to me. I had it all planned out.

I was becoming more and more distraught about being at Curtis. I wanted a chance to just be a "normal" student in a college somewhere. I thought that perhaps then I wouldn't feel so insecure and overwhelmed with life. I had an almost constant feeling of torment. I couldn't seem to get away from it except for a few brief seasons of time when I would pray and it would go away for a while, or late at night when I would listen to a Christian radio station I had found. I listened to it every night, and it brought me peace.

An incredible spiritual experience

One night I was up late because I couldn't sleep. I had the classical radio station on my stereo, and this amazing piece of music came on. It was a tone poem by Richard Strauss called "An Alpine Symphony." I was enthralled with this piece. It felt like I was way up in the Swiss Alps or something. What a magnificent symphony that is. The end is so triumphant!

When it ended, I was so moved that I fell on my knees and lifted my hands straight up in the air before I could even think what I was doing. I began to praise God, and tears started pouring out of my eyes. I must have stayed that way for about ten minutes or so when suddenly something just hit me. I fell backward, flat on my back on the floor. I didn't faint or anything, but for some reason I just couldn't move. Then I began to see something. It was like the room wasn't there, even though I could see it with my natural eyes. I perceived that I was at the bottom of this narrow ravine. There were huge cliff walls on either side of me that stretched up as far as I could see. At the top of this ravine, there was a bright light, brighter than I had ever seen before. It was blinding, it was so bright. Then I began to see angels going up the walls and disappearing out of sight into the light and then coming back again and descending down toward me.

I began to tremble and shake. I was so afraid of the bright light at the top. I knew that God was there and that He was looking directly down at me. That light was so pure and clean, and it showed how wretched I was as it shone down on me. And it kept getting brighter and brighter until all I could sense was that I was being pulled up into it. One thing was absolutely clear to me: God Almighty was so AWESOME! He was greater than anything I had ever known. I was crying out for mercy and pleading with Him to forgive me for all of my sins. I was so desperate and depraved before Him. I couldn't even look into that brightness. I knew that I was experiencing the holiness of Almighty God.

For a long time, not a word was spoken. I just laid there flat on my back and shook and trembled. I was afraid. I know now that the fear of God was upon me. It wasn't a terror like being frightened but a searing awareness of my own desperate, sinful condition and my utter hopelessness and moral failure before Him, the Lord who loved me so much. It was more than I could bear. I cried and cried for mercy. The glory kept increasing until the whole room was lit up.

Then a voice spoke, and I knew it was the Lord. He said: "My son, I love you! I have heard the cry of your heart. I have answered your prayer and forgiven and cleansed you. I CALL YOU FAITHFUL! I am able to keep that which is committed to Me. YOU ARE MINE! FEAR NOT! I AM WITH YOU. I WILL NEVER LEAVE YOU, AND I WILL NEVER FORSAKE YOU. And ten years from now, you will be a great man of God. I have called you. I have chosen you. I have ordained you, and I will use you in ways you cannot imagine or comprehend at this time. I am big enough to save you to the uttermost. You shall fulfill My high calling on your life. I CALL YOU FAITHFUL! I CALL YOU FAITHFUL! I CALL YOU FAITHFUL!"

Then I heard the Lord say these words, "But when I bless you, will you turn from Me?"

After a while, the brightness lifted, and the room returned to normal. I was stuck with my back pinned to the floor—right where I was when the music had ended. The radio station had signed off the air, and only static was coming from the speakers now. I couldn't move for about thirty minutes. Finally I was able to get off the floor. I didn't understand what had happened to me, but there was no doubt at all that this was God talking to me. I was amazed.

I prayed, "Lord, You can look into the future and see my life in its entirety right now. If I would turn from You and forget You, I pray that You would kill me right now this night. I would rather die now than to grieve Your heart by turning away from You after You have blessed me. If I would cause others to stumble, then slay me now. It would be a far greater blessing than to bring reproach on Your holy name."

Those words just came out of me. I didn't really understand them at the time. The Holy Spirit helped me to pray them. But I meant every word that came out of my spirit, and I still mean those words and would pray them again now. Like an anthem with bells pealing over and over, as I fell asleep that night I heard the Lord say those words over and over, "I CALL YOU FAITHFUL! I CALL YOU FAITHFUL! I CALL YOU FAITHFUL!"

The next day when I awakened, that special Presence was still there. There was a holy peace in my apartment, but I hardly noticed it since I was late for a class. I just rushed and put my clothes on and dashed across the park to school.

Spring had come to Philadelphia, and even though I was in a hurry, I enjoyed feeling the warmth of the sun and seeing the colorful flowers in bloom as I walked quickly through Rittenhouse Square. My favorite times of the year in Philadelphia were April and May in the spring and the month of September in the fall. It was really nice weather then. The rest of the year was either too cold or too hot.

After my class that morning, I stopped in to visit for a few minutes with Steve Strumbeck. He was always friendly and warm when I talked with him, and today was no different. I didn't mention anything about what had happened to me the night before. I just asked him if it was possible for God to give visions to us today. He said that it was indeed possible, and he showed me several passages in the Book of Acts where Peter, Paul, Ananias, and others experienced supernatural visitations inspired by the Holy Spirit. He asked me why I wanted to know and how I had been doing. I said I was just curious and was doing just fine. I quickly left his office, saying that I had to practice. I really marveled at the speed with which Steve had found those passages in the Bible. He really knew "The Word," as he called it.

After that visit, I went down and visited him several times a week. I was so hungry for God and the Bible, and Steve seemed to give me so much from the Lord. He really fed my spirit. He encouraged me to start reading the Bible every day. He told me, "Even if you don't understand what you are reading, just spend time in the Word, and God will help you and strengthen you. I read every morning before work for at least an hour. It's a habit now."

I was astonished that anyone had the discipline to read that much of the Bible every day, and I told Steve so. He just laughed and said, "Maury, if you can have the discipline to practice your instrument every day like you do, reading the Bible like this is a piece of cake. I'm the one who is amazed at how you guys practice so much. Just put some of the same discipline toward seeking God that you do toward your violin, and your whole life will change. Don't just pray in tongues and that's it. Spend time in God's Word, and it will come alive inside of you and give you supernatural strength and abundant life. I can't live without my time in the Word anymore. It's more important to me than having breakfast. It is my spiritual breakfast, actually."

I just sat back in my chair and stared at him. What he had said made perfect sense, but I had never seen it before.

I said, "Steve, is this why you know so much about the Bible and why you seem to be so happy all the time?"

He said, "Of course—although I also am a part of a strong church, which helps a lot. None of us is very strong on our own, but together as a body of believers, the devil can't touch us. Overall, I'd say that without my time in the Word every day, I'd be pretty dried up, defeated, and starved spiritually—kind of like you are."

When he said that, it stung a little, and I got defensive and offended for a while. I know he said it in love, and I understood that he meant well by it. Besides, Steve was right. I wasn't exactly reigning in life as a king. The devil had beaten me up my whole life. It finally dawned on me that Satan was my problem and that I had neglected the Bible for years. I decided I would begin to do some of those things that Steve suggested. What did I have to lose?

The school year was rapidly drawing to a close. I was surprised at how fast April was going. I got a notice in my mailbox at school to give the Registrar my sizes for a cap and a gown. I was going to graduate! I had been practicing and working so hard that I had entirely forgotten about it. I spent a lot of time talking to Dad about it. He contacted Audrey, my real mother, and she was planning to come for the graduation. Of course, Dad was also going to be there. Before I knew it, they were both in town. Audrey called and wanted to see me, so she, Dad, and I got together and went out for dinner together. Dad was very amiable as he deftly tried to help the two of us communicate in a positive way. He was an expert at pretending that nothing was wrong, no matter how difficult a situation might be. The night went okay as I just told them what I was doing and all about Curtis.

My long-awaited graduation day!

Finally the miracle happened, and graduation day dawned. As I received my diploma, Audrey took lots of pictures and cried. I was relieved and happy. I had made it! Suddenly I excused myself and went down to the basement to that little bathroom again. I closed the door, and like it was a holy altar, I knelt before the Lord on my knees in front of the commode—with my gown on and everything—and thanked God for His faithfulness in enabling me to graduate. Then I went back upstairs and we celebrated. I was kind of dazed in a very happy way. I had done what Dad had always dreamed of—I had gone to Curtis and graduated. He was very happy.

I had been talking with Dad about what I should do the following year. Of course, he would have loved for me to stay at Curtis for two more years—and I could have since I had come in my third year of high school. But when Dad realized how miserable I was and that I would not stay, we began talking about other options. The only place I wanted to go to finish my degree was the University of Houston. I could return to Fredell Lack and study with her. I just couldn't take another year of pressure on the East Coast. I wanted a break, and I wanted to be with "real, normal" people for a change.

So Dad and Miss Lack arranged for me to go to the University of Houston to study and to attend summer school right after I left Philadelphia. Not only that, I had been accepted to audition for the Houston Symphony National Young Artist's Competition, which was held at the end of May. I took first prize in that competition, which meant I would play solo with the Houston Symphony a short time later.

I thought, *Thank God I am getting out of Curtis. I just can't stand it here any more. Maybe Houston will be better for me, where I can be with normal kids in a college.*

I felt overwhelmed by the thought of being out of Curtis and wondered what I would do now that I wasn't a little "whiz-bang" prodigy violinist anymore. I was praying quite a bit, and I began to really read my Bible more than I ever had before, even though it made almost no sense to me. I just plowed through much of the New Testament, asking God what it meant as I went. I knew way down inside that I was passing out of a phase of my life that would never return again. I regretted that I had not done better at Curtis. I realized I hadn't really succeeded in the way some others had in starting their careers, meeting their marriage partners, or just simply passing into adult life. I felt totally unprepared for the world in front of me. I could hear a time bomb ticking away on the inside of me. I knew that unless I did something soon, it would blow up. The problem was, I didn't know what to do other than to just get out of the pressure cooker I had been in on the East Coast.

I thought, *At least I can be in Houston for a while and just practice and learn under Miss Lack again without all of the pressure. And she is such an artist that I can't go wrong musically.* Still, I was deeply troubled inside, and I didn't know why. I blamed it on the weird Curtis environment and just immersed myself in preparation for the competition in Houston, which was only two weeks away.

Chapter 16

The Faith Message

*M*y time in Houston turned out to be the most productive two years I have ever had as an artist. I really flourished under Miss Lack, and I learned a great deal of repertoire. She was still very motherly toward me and gave me more attention than I had ever had from any teacher. I am thankful for all that I learned under her teaching from 1983 to 1985.

I really enjoyed being at the University of Houston. It was nice to live in the dorms and to have my meals at the cafeteria instead of having to eat out all the time like I had in Philadelphia. I liked talking with the other students I met, and I felt an almost immediate relief from the intense pressure I had lived in every summer since I could remember. It was so nice just to be free to attend my classes, practice, take my lessons with Miss Lack (which were wonderful), and just live in the most normal environment I'd had since my summers at Meadowmount.

One night when I was walking back to my dorm after a long practice session, something happened that changed my life. As I walked past one of the small lecture halls, I heard singing, shouting, and clapping coming through its open doors. I wondered to myself, *What in the world is this?* So I stopped and went inside. I felt drawn into that building by some strange compulsion. I soon discovered that it was a church service! A small group of people was on the stage singing with a guitar, a keyboard, and tambourines. They were really lively! It reminded me of the service I had seen at Steve Strumbeck's church in New Jersey. Everyone was standing up, with their hands up in the air, singing praises to God, shouting, and talking in tongues! I was really excited and sat down in the back under the balcony, where it was dark and no one could see me.

There were only about fifty people in the auditorium, but they made so much racket that it sounded like five hundred! I had never seen anyone so enthusiastic and excited before! They were all jumping around and shouting "Praise the Lord!...Hallelujah!...Glory to God!" They acted as if they had just won the World Series or something. I got stirred up, just listening to them!

After a little while, an evangelist named Rice Brooks got up and began to speak. I was riveted—I couldn't take my eyes off of him. He started shouting and going from one end of the stage to the other with his right arm going up and down, and it seemed like his index finger was pointing directly at me. He kept shouting, "Get right with God!... Repent!...Sell out one-hundred percent to Jesus." Then he calmed down a little and began to read from the Bible. He told us to turn to Deuteronomy 28, and proceeded to read every curse from the law listed there. He stared right at me and shouted, "If you don't repent, get the sin out of your life, and give your life to God completely, every one of these curses from the devil can come on YOU, and you will quickly perish from off the earth. Then the devil will DRAG YOU INTO HELL, WHERE YOU WILL BURN FOREVER AND EVER!"

The more I listened to him, the angrier I got! How dare he preach like that! He seemed like the most arrogant human being I had ever heard! But it was getting to me. Something in my mind kept shouting at me, "Get out of here! These are a bunch of crazy fanatics! They are brainwashed! This is a cult! Get out quick!" But something just kept me glued to the seat. I couldn't move. I could hardly breathe. I knew that what he was saying was in the Bible, but I had never heard anyone preach it so boldly before.

Soon my anger melted away, and I was weeping and asking God to forgive me.

Another spiritual experience

When the evangelist gave an altar call, I went forward. I was under such conviction that I was weeping and shaking under the power of the Holy Spirit. I had never been so overcome by the power of the Holy Spirit as I was that night. Rice Brooks led me in a prayer of salvation and rededication to the Lord.

A young man with fiery eyes approached me and said, "Brother, what is your name?" I told him, and he asked, "Do you want to be free from that nasty habit of smoking?" He must have smelled it on my breath.

I mumbled, "Yes, I would."

He shouted, "You foul devil of nicotine and addiction, loose him and let him go FREE, in Jesus' name!"

I shuddered and felt something break inside of me. I just stood there. I didn't know what to say. The boldness and brash behavior of these people had completely disarmed me. Yet there was an authority in their eyes that I had never seen before. About four of the leaders of this group came and introduced themselves. The young one who had just prayed over me was the pastor of this group called "Maranatha Campus Ministries."

Rice Brooks started grilling me about what church I went to and what I did. I told him I didn't attend any church but was a Christian. I told him I was a concert violinist, and that I was a graduate student there at the university. He grunted and shook his head at me. He said, "Brother, you'd better get serious about your commitment to Christ. God sent you here tonight, and you should join this church." Then he motioned to the leader of the group to come over and talk with me. He said to him, "Get this brother hooked in to your church." And then he walked away.

The pastor introduced himself to me and said, "We meet here every Wednesday night and on Sunday mornings. You need to come and get in fellowship. Will we be seeing you?"

I said I would try to come as I was able to.

Then he said, "You'd better. You look like you need a lot of help. Don't forget! We meet at ten o'clock this Sunday morning!" Then he walked away, too. Everyone was talking among themselves after the service, so I slipped out and went to my dorm.

I was so angry at them! How dare they act so insolent and arrogant in the way they spoke to me. Who did they think they were, anyway? What right did they have to tell me what to do when they didn't even know me? And yet there was something in that church I had never experienced before. There was an authority, a strength of character and holiness, and a radical conviction about their faith in God—no apologies, just raw power from the Bible and God. Deep down I was attracted to them, but I refused to admit it for a long time.

I returned to their service the next Sunday morning, but I was so offended at the people and the message that I decided it wasn't for me. The next week I went to their mid-week home group because one of the other college students invited me. That was a really exciting service. About twelve to fifteen of us gathered in a circle. We sang worship and praise songs, accompanied by a guitar, and several people gave wonderful teaching from the Bible. Then they asked if anyone had any prayer requests.

I spoke up and said I was playing a concert next week in Hermann Park with the Houston Symphony Orchestra and would they please pray that I would play well. I thought they would just pray quietly about it in that circle. Instead, they all gathered around me, put their hands on me, and prayed in tongues very loudly for about five minutes!

Finally the leader spoke up and said, "Lord, we pray and ask You to anoint our brother Maury as he plays and to touch all of the people who come. We ask You for an outpouring of the Holy Spirit, and we ask You to help him prepare and play the best he ever has for Your glory. In Jesus' name."

Then everyone who had surrounded me shouted at the same time, "Amen!" and took their hands off of me. I felt as if I had been lifted off the floor and was floating in midair. I felt that prayer, that's for sure! They all wanted to know where my concert was and when, and I told them. One of the men hollered, "That's our home group night. Let's go hear Maury's concert that night." Everyone agreed. Then he winked at me and said, "We'll be there to hear you! You'll bring great glory to the Lord, and this concert will be a testimony. God's going to anoint you in a powerful way! Get ready, brother. We'll be there, lifting you up in prayer."

At the time, I didn't understand all of their lingo. I had never heard of "anoint," "testimony," or "lay hands on them and pray"—but I knew that they knew God in a way I didn't. I felt very inferior to them and wanted to be like them. But when I left the group that night, I was so consumed with getting ready for the concert that I completely forgot about them.

I couldn't sleep the night before the concert, and I was really attacked with fear. But the next evening, I played the *Mendelssohn Violin Concerto* with a sweetness and an ease that I had never had before. It was a thrilling performance.

Bringing church to my concert

Afterwards, as I went out to greet those who had come by to see me, I heard several people shouting, "Praise the Lord! Glory to God!" I looked and saw that whole Maranatha group. I was embarrassed because the conductor was there as well as the other musicians...not to mention Miss Lack and my parents. But it didn't faze that fanatical bunch. When the group finally got to me, the leader shook my hand briskly and squeezed it so hard that it hurt.

He said extremely loud, "Praise the Lord, brother! God anointed you tonight! The glory fell all over us! We were praying for you! God's hand is on you, and He is going to use you and your violin mightily for His glory. Don't be ashamed of Jesus! He's helping you! Praise the Lord! HALLELUJAH!"

The last hallelujah was shouted so loudly that Dad turned red in the face and scowled at him. Miss Lack and several of her students who were standing there tried to pretend the group wasn't there.

Dad said to them, "I would appreciate it if you would keep your religious enthusiasm to yourself. If you want to shout and carry on, do it in your own church—not here!" Then he angrily asked me, "Do you know this group?"

I said, "Not very well. I just attended a service they had in my dorm."

Dad said, "Well, stay away from them. They're bad news. If you stay around people like that, they'll ruin your career. If you ever get like *that*, it won't matter how well you play—

you'll be finished as far as a solo career is concerned." When he said the word "that," he practically spit it out.

There were a lot of others waiting to congratulate me, and Dad suddenly turned all smiles. I said a lot of "thank-you's" until all of the well-wishers had left. Dad and Miss Lack were so thrilled with the concert that they forgot about the little incident with the Maranatha group...but I didn't. I was mortified at the thought of what they had done to me. Why did they act that way? I decided that I would never return to their church again.

Throughout the fall, Miss Lack encouraged me to enter competitions. We chose four different ones to enter in the spring of '84, and I began to prepare for them.

One day she said to me, "Maury, you are the only student I've ever had who has a real chance for a solo career. You can make it. You've got everything it takes for a major career, but it is so much harder nowadays than it was when I was young. There are a lot of politics, and you have to be prepared to deal with that aspect of it. Now, Maury, you have something special in your playing, in your sound. You move people when you play, which most fiddle players can't do nowadays. I think that with the right breaks, you can be one of the great violinists of your generation—but there are no guarantees...remember that. You've got to be as tough as nails and want it very badly to be a soloist. It's not easy for anyone, no matter how great their talent is."

As I listened, I was amazed at her wisdom. In fact, I felt as if another voice was speaking to me through her. The Lord was actually warning me of what was to come. I realize now that the Lord told me much about my future through Miss Lack. At the time, I simply said, "I don't know about all of that, but I'll do my best to enter some competitions if you think that would be good for me."

Competitions—a blessing and a curse

She said, "Competitions are both a blessing and a curse. If you have the temperament to handle the pressure, they can be a shortcut to launching a career and can put you with a manager and get you concerts. On the other hand, they are very difficult to go through. I know—I've been in several big ones, and there is so much pressure. You must have nerves of steel to endure them and win, but you seem to do well under pressure. I think you should enter some competitions during the next three years or so. You'll never know what you can do until you try."

I told her, "I don't think I need any more pressure than I've already been through in the last five years, but I'll do it if you think I'm really good enough." So I agreed to enter the competitions, although I felt dread and reluctance to do so.

I began to train and practice during the next three years like I had never done before—and will probably never do again! I practiced on my violin for hours every day. I saw some limitations in my technique that seemed impossible to overcome, but I pressed on and saw breakthroughs as I learned pieces that I had previously thought I could never play because they were so difficult. Miss Lack was so motivating and encouraging that I really wanted to please her. I didn't want to let her down. I began to believe that the Lord wanted me to enter and to win all of these competitions for Him. During the spring of 1984, I entered four national music competitions.

For about two weeks before each competition, I would get so nervous that it interfered with my sleep. During my practice each day, I would be attacked by such high levels of fear, intimidation, and anxiety that at times it almost felt like panic attacks. I would have to put my violin down and wait for it to pass. I would be shaking and my heart would be racing. Going through the competitions was even worse. It was agonizing to wait backstage, go out and play my audition, and then hear them say, "Thank you very much." Then I would walk off, put my violin away, go back to the hotel room, and wait for the verdict of the judges as to whether I was good enough to go on to the next round or not. I was miserable and stressed out from all the preparation, practicing, and the disappointment of seeing it all go down the drain if I didn't win.

Dad, of course, was very interested in my doing these competitions and wanted me to enter all that I could. It was a consolation to him that I was at least taking steps toward a solo career, even if I wasn't on the East Coast, studying and "getting in with the right people" in the music world. When I was discouraged because of not winning, Miss Lack reminded me that you could never tell what was going to happen in competitions. It just depended on what the judges liked that day, what mood they were in, and how well I might do at that particular audition.

I entered the Music Teachers National Young Artist Competition and won at the state, regional, and national levels. I also went to North Carolina to play in a symphony competition there, but was eliminated in the preliminary round. My biggest challenge was the Naumberg competition in New York City. It was a huge undertaking to prepare for, and I had to learn two entire recital programs, in addition to two violin concertos for it. Although I had practiced six hours a day for a month to prepare for it, I was eliminated in the first round.

I really felt that my worth as a person hinged on how well I did in those competitions. I was getting scared that time was running out on me. I wasn't a teenager anymore. I was competing against players my age who were really amazing.

Nevertheless, I would pray and read my Bible and soon some semblance of peace would return. I even went to a different Christian campus group and met a few friends. I attended church on an occasional Sunday morning with one of them. On February 18, 1984, at about 6:30 in the evening, God answered a prayer for me and completely delivered me from smoking cigarettes. I threw them in a garbage can, walked away, and never smoked again. Praise the Lord!

The Lord was becoming more real to me, and I was beginning to witness to the other students. As always, I was praying in tongues a lot—a habit I had gotten into since my Philly days. I began to see some big changes taking place in my life as I got stronger spiritually. The problem was, I got frustrated in nearly every church service I attended. They seemed so superficial, hypocritical, and dead that I didn't want to attend anymore. I couldn't figure it out. The only place where I'd seen Christians who were totally sold out was in that Maranatha group. I had been warned that they were a cult, however, so I did not return to their meetings that spring. Besides, I was so consumed with practicing for competition that I didn't have much time for fellowship or church.

In the spring of 1984, Miss Lack talked to me at length about going to study with a teacher named Dorothy DeLay. Of course, I had heard of her. She reigned as the "Queen of

Violin Teacher Land," and was the most sought-after violin teacher in the world after Mr. Galamian's death. Miss DeLay was also the most powerful monarch over solo careers. One word from her and the wheels necessary to launch a new solo career would begin to turn, and the powers that be would cause the right doors to open at the right time. Miss Lack had spoken to me about her a number of times, but in one particular lesson, she put her violin down and motioned for me to sit next to her.

She said, "Maury dear, I've been thinking. I believe it would be very good for you to go and study with Dorothy DeLay out in Aspen, Colorado, this summer. She is not an easy teacher to get lessons with these days, but she might take a liking to you. I don't think she'll give you the attention I do, but I don't have the connections she has. She knows how to package young violinists and help them launch their careers. You know, there is a whole lot more to 'making it' than just playing the violin well."

As she spoke, I began to feel sick to my stomach. I hated the thought of having to play the politics game she was talking about.

"Sweetie," she continued, "you have everything it takes for a major solo career. It's time for you to begin taking that step now, and she is the one who can help you get there. Dottie is a very good psychologist, you know. She can help you with your confidence and can help improve your technique further, I believe." Then she looked at me over her little reading glasses and said in her matronly way, "Maury dear, I think it would be very good for you to go there. Maybe you'll even meet a nice girl or something—you seem so lonely. You could go hiking in the mountains and go fishing...or you could just relax. All the New York musicians go there in the summer. They call it Juilliard West. Maury, I haven't heard many violinists in my life who can play as expressively as you do, but there are a lot of kids studying with Dottie who can play to a standard of perfection that will probably astound you. One thing for sure, you won't be the king of the roost like you are here in Houston. She has more students than she can handle, but would you like to go to Aspen this summer?"

The chance of a lifetime!

I said, "Sure, I suppose so."

She said, "All right then. I'll write a letter about you to Dottie and see what she says."

Several weeks later, the great Dorothy DeLay and Miss Lack spoke by telephone, and "Dottie" said she would do her best to fit me into her teaching schedule that summer.

When I told Dad, he quickly went into high gear. He submitted the application, and I was accepted shortly thereafter. He even paid for it. I was very anxious about it because I knew the level of violin playing was extremely high. Miss DeLay was almost a legend because her students played with such ease and perfection and won so many competitions.

The departure date finally came, and I left to go to the Aspen Music Festival. When I arrived, I suddenly realized what a huge festival it was. I was just one among hundreds of great players. I was destined for one of the biggest shocks of my life. When I heard the level of violin playing going on there, it absolutely knocked all the wind out of my sails. I had never heard such a level of playing before. Miss Lack was right—these were the best! They didn't even play this well at Curtis. Although most of the violin playing had no real musicality in it, it was an amazing thing to hear such technical perfection. Some of the violinists were only eight or nine years of age, and they were playing things I hadn't even studied yet.

Two important things happened to me that summer. Under Miss DeLay's teaching, I learned how to practice to get my playing to a much higher technical level than I ever had before. By the end of the summer, I had completely changed the way I practiced. She heard me three or four times that summer, and each time I was really impressed with her teaching. She is a genius, for sure. I practiced the way she told me, and my technical ability greatly increased, and I began to have more confidence in my playing.

The other change was in my spiritual life. I had begun the practice of getting on my knees every morning and praying in tongues for an hour. I somehow knew I needed that in order to make it at Aspen. Because of that, I was becoming very keen and sharp in my spirit. In fact, many of the giftings I now experience in my prophetic ministry were beginning to manifest at that time in an extremely vivid way. I was so tuned-in spiritually that I could tell as soon as I met a person what was happening in his life. Sometimes I would even see demons in people. That was entirely new to me, and I didn't understand at all what was happening. I would get in front of people, and demons would manifest out of them. Of course, I didn't mention this to anyone, but I noticed that many people were uncomfortable around me.

I also got involved in a Bible study led by a violinist from the Dominican Republic named Caonex Peguero-Camillo. Another Christian violinist I had met in Aspen invited me to attend Caonex's Bible study one evening. When I arrived at his room, I saw several students sitting around the bed, listening to a tall, dark-skinned young man with big-rimmed glasses who was speaking very excitedly and fast. He was holding a big Bible that was written all over and underlined in three or four different colors. He was so animated that he had totally captivated his listeners. I slipped in and sat on the edge of the other bed and listened. He was sharing a "revelation" he had just received that afternoon. I didn't understand most of it, but I saw his violin in the corner and surmised that this must be the right place.

After about ten minutes, Caonex announced that it was time to pray. To my astonishment, everyone started praying in tongues at the same time. They were praying so fervently it seemed like they had forgotten that anyone else was there. It was the loudest praying session I had ever been in.

I began to enter in, and as I did, it felt as if a flood of liquid power began to flow out of me, and I began to pray louder and louder. As I continued to yield to the Holy Spirit, I felt as if I was lifted up higher than I had ever been into the Spirit. It was awesome!

At seven o'clock, Caonex stopped us, and we got the room ready for the Bible study. Soon a steady stream of people began arriving until the room was nearly full. Caonex had a small blackboard on which he had drawn three separate circles, one inside the other. The one furthest out said "Body," the next one said "Soul," and the one at the center was labeled "Spirit." He told us that we are made up of three parts, not two. Man is not just soul and body, but he is spirit, soul, and body. He said when we are born again, God recreates our inner man or our spirit in His image—taking us out of sin into righteousness. He said we have to present our bodies as living sacrifices and that our souls are the part of us that houses our minds, emotions, and intellects. That part of us needs to be renewed by the Word of God.

On and on he went. I was like a starving man dying of hunger and thirst in the desert. I drank in his words like water into my parched being. I was rejoicing and crying at the same time. I don't remember everything he said, but I do remember that I didn't want to leave. I felt as if I floated all the way home as I prayed in the Spirit. I fell asleep with more peace than I had ever known in my life.

After that I spent nearly all my free time with Caonex and the others in our Charismatic Bible group. I became so "on fire" that I could witness and preach to anything that moved...and some things that didn't move! We saw miracles happen, and a lot of people received the Lord that summer from our preaching. I hung around with Caonex so much that I began to have quite a reputation. We became really good friends.

The second time I had a lesson with Miss DeLay, she said, "You know, Maury, I believe in God, too. I don't think He is as narrow as some people say, and I think He can speak to us in many ways. I am concerned about this Bible group you're involved with, however. I don't think it is healthy to be as extreme as that Hispanic fellow. Do you believe the way he does?"

I said, "Well, yes, I suppose so. I am a Christian and I believe the Bible is true. I have greatly enjoyed his Bible studies."

When she saw that I answered with such boldness and conviction, she didn't say anything for a moment. I could tell she was thinking very profoundly about what to say. Finally she said, "I think you've had a rough time, considering your background. Didn't you say you spent seven years in a row at Meadowmount? Dear me! That's enough to scar the healthiest psyche for the rest of his life. I know. I spent thirty years there as Mr. Galamian's assistant. I know far more than you might realize. You have an exceptional gifting that I don't think I've ever heard before in all my years of teaching. I can't explain it, but when you play, I see light all around you that seems to come from inside you. You seem to enter into another world, and then a force that I don't understand seems to take over. Whatever it is, it makes you play far greater than you ever could by yourself."

She continued, "I think you've had more pressure on you in your life than any human being should ever have to go through. I am so sorry that you have had such a hard time." She wiped away some tears from her eyes.

I still don't know to this day why she said those things to me or how she could have known so much about me after just having met me. I was embarrassed and said, "Well, I have had some rough days, but Jesus has taken me through everything so far, and I know He will never leave me or forsake me."

Miss DeLay was still crying a little. She said, "I admire your courage and your keen faith, even though I think it is too extreme and harsh and has some aspects that could be bad for you. Even so, not many have the kind of strong spiritual anchor that you seem to have. Who knows, maybe one day you'll find a way to combine your music and your faith in a way that will bring joy and hope to many. What makes me so sad is that I realize you've had to pay such a price for it. I hope you'll make it through the next few years."

I wondered, *What in the world does she mean?* Then my lesson started, and she was very professional again.

During my summer in Aspen, I also learned a great deal about the Bible, particularly about the faith message. I read books and listened to teaching tapes about faith. One book in particular completely changed my life. It was written by Charles Capps, and it is entitled *The Tongue, A Creative Force*. It told about how the words we speak have great power. I decided after reading the book that I would never speak anything negative about myself or others again. Instead, I began to speak the promises of God over my life from that summer on.

I had found the truth I'd been seeking for so many years. I "knew that I knew that I knew" that this was true, and it set me totally free...at least for the summer. I felt for the first time that I had a fighting chance to overcome and be happy in my life. I didn't care anymore about anything except Jesus, the Word, and this wonderful, newfound oasis of joy and love I had discovered in my new life in Christ. For the first time, it didn't matter to me whether I ever made it as a soloist. I had been set free from the controlling spirits that had plagued me all of my life.

Sadly, I couldn't hold on to this freedom after that summer. Without a proper foundation, the enemy of our souls will come in like a flood, steal the Word away from us, and destroy much of what the Lord plants in our hearts—especially when we are young in Christ.

Chapter 17

My Violin is Confiscated

*W*hen the summer was over, I returned to Houston and the university. I now had my bachelor's degree from Curtis and lived in the graduate student's dorm. I was charged up! I had learned not to speak anything that was a negative confession, so I began to believe and set my faith on becoming a great violin soloist for the Lord. I was going to do it. "Nothing is impossible for those who believe," I constantly affirmed. I was determined never to speak anything that I did not want to come to pass in my life. I spent all of my time either practicing on the violin, reading the Word, or listening to sermon tapes of great faith teachers and preachers.

Deep down, however, I was becoming more and more troubled about my future. I just insulated myself from it by immersing myself in the word of faith. If I was overcome by anxiety or fear or if I felt bad, I got on my knees and prayed in tongues until I felt better. As long as I stayed with other Christians, I felt wonderful, so my first priority was to find a good church to attend.

I decided that I needed to go back to the Maranatha church I had visited. The people didn't seem so unbalanced and fanatical anymore. In fact, I was just like them now. I grew more spiritually that year than I ever had before. I learned about water baptism and was baptized one Sunday afternoon in the pool of an apartment complex, and I was never the same after that. Something was removed from my life that had caused me to draw back, and I began to grow spiritually in a way I never had before. Previously, I had always taken two steps forward and one or two steps back in my walk with God. But after my baptism, my path seemed to be much clearer, and I wasn't hindered by all the stumbling blocks Satan had been putting in my way. Seeds were planted in my life that have shaped me into the man I am today.

I also had an extremely fruitful year on the violin. My lessons were wonderful, and I had a lot of free time to practice and learn new repertoire.

Revival in Dallas

One day I ran into a friend who told me about an awesome revival meeting that was going on in a church in Dallas, Texas. She said, "It is amazing what is going on there! Hundreds of people are coming every night to hear a man named Norvel Hayes speak. I just wept all the way through the service last night."

I had heard Norvel Hayes on a tape series, so when my friend told me about the revival, I got really stirred up. She gave me directions to the church, and I decided to go see what was happening. I packed my suitcase for a three-day weekend, got my ticket, and took the first flight to Dallas.

The service that night was awesome. The whole time Brother Norvel was preaching, it looked like he was staring right at me. After he had preached for a while, he called for anyone who wanted to be touched with the anointing of the Holy Spirit to come forward. I went to the front, and he put his hand on my head as he passed by. When he did, I fell backwards onto the floor. I don't know how long I was on the floor, but when I got up, I felt totally different. Whatever was upon Brother Norvel went out of him and into me, and it stayed for days. I felt waves of pure love pour over me all that night.

For the next three nights, I sat in his services and basked in the Lord's wonderful presence. Then I flew home, repacked my suitcase, and flew to West Palm Beach, Florida, for a competition. I won second place. When I called Dad and Miss Lack with the news, they were very happy. I was just glad it was over. Every time I played, fear and dread came over me.

All I wanted to do at that point was to return to Dallas and get back to the revival. I had won quite a bit of prize money, so I decided to go for a couple of weeks since school was over. I phoned Dad, and he told me not to go, but I told him I was going anyway.

After a week in those meetings every day, something began to break in me. I began to get freedom from the controlling spirit that had bound me so tightly to my father. Then one night I had a vision and the Lord spoke to me. He said, "My son, I have a call on your life to minister for Me. I want to prepare you and heal you of all that you've been through. Call Anita Jacobs in Pennsville, New Jersey. I want you to go there. If you will, I can set you free from the terrible yoke of bondage your father has placed over your life. You no longer have to serve him in slavery. I am your Father now, and I have a better life for you."

More control games

I immediately started thinking about getting in touch with Anita, but later as I was coming out of the service, a man stopped me in the parking lot. He said, "You're Maury Sklar, aren't you?"

I was startled, but told him I was. He said, "I am a private investigator who specializes in getting people out of cults. Your father contacted me after he secretly came here to see what you were doing. He was at the services the last two nights. I have been authorized by him to seize your violin, your bows, and your case. You have to give them to me now, or I will call the police and have you arrested."

I was shocked and just stared at him in stunned silence for a minute. Then I asked, "Why does he want my violin?"

The man said, "Your father is scared you will give it away under the mind-control tactics of this church. Actually, I want you to know that I am a Christian myself, and I don't necessarily think you are brainwashed, like he does. Nevertheless, I think you are rather unstable at this time, although I can't say I blame you too much. Your dad wants you to leave these meetings immediately. Will you come back to Baton Rouge now? I will take you to the airport if you like."

I said, "No, and I don't want to give you my violin, either. Just leave me alone." As I turned to walk away from him, he swung me around and said, "I am required to seize your instrument and bows, and you're not going anywhere until I have them." I was stunned and close to tears at that point, so I yielded to him. He drove me back to my hotel room, took my violin and bows, and drove away.

I called home, and Dad answered. I asked him why he'd had my violin seized and taken from me by force. He said it wasn't really my violin—he owned it. And he thought I might give it away to "that crazy, money-hungry preacher" he had seen the other night. He said if I didn't return home, I would never see my violin again.

I was furious and hung up. How dare he do such a thing! After I calmed down, I remembered that the Lord had asked me to call Anita Jacobs, but I had disobeyed. I hadn't done it. I realized that if I stayed in Dallas any longer, I might lose my violin. I didn't know how to survive on my own, and my prize money from the competition was nearly gone. So I left a few days later and flew back to Houston. Dad met me there and helped me pack up and move back home to Baton Rouge.

Surprisingly, he wasn't critical of me the way he usually was. He seemed genuinely concerned about my welfare and kept saying how proud he was that I had done so well in Palm Beach. He thought I just needed a break for a while. He arranged for me to see a Lutheran priest who was a counseling psychologist. The priest gave me a personality test and was very concerned when he got the results. That was probably because I answered every question "in faith" instead of honestly. I refused to disclose very much about my life to him at first, although I finally confided in him that I had been very unhappy and felt that I'd been forced to play the violin for years. I told him, "I'm not sure that playing the violin would really be the best thing for me." He folded his hands, nodded his head, and said, "Well, I am sure it hasn't been easy for you to have lived the kind of life you've lived." After several weeks, we shook hands and I never saw him again.

Dad was very concerned about me—especially about my questioning and challenging him that I didn't have to play violin if I didn't want to. I had thrown down the gauntlet, so to speak, but I wasn't strong enough to break out from under his years of control. He had gotten me back when he seized my violin, and he knew it.

Nevertheless, I had many tapes and books from the revival, and I locked myself up in my room and studied many hours every day. My faith was soaring as a result of the time I'd spent in the Word, in those services, and in praying in the Holy Spirit. Something had broken inside of me, and I was never the same after those meetings. But I had to return to the violin. I had actually had a minor emotional breakdown after one of my competitions, and Dad had to "patch me up" emotionally and convince me once again that "the show must go on." Now I locked in with my faith and decided that I was going to be a great violinist for Jesus and that I would once and for all prove to my father that *I can do all things through Christ which strengtheneth me* (Philippians 4:13).

Dad felt sincerely sorry that our relationship had deteriorated to such a state. He had hoped I would put this radical, born-again business behind me. But I think he finally began to realize that I was serious about it and that it probably wouldn't go away...at least not any time soon. All I had done for a solid month, other than practicing on the violin, was to study the Bible and listen to my faith tapes. Dad even took me to a church in Baker, Louisiana, called "Bethany World Prayer Center," pastored by Larry Stockstill. I had been there several times and enjoyed it immensely. It was almost a sacred duty on Dad's part never to be "totally intolerant" of my religious views. He wanted to show me that he was accepting of it—"If it makes you happy and you lead a better life and are able to help a lot of people." But that statement would be immediately followed by, "But don't force your views and your Jesus on me. You have your way and I have mine." And that was the end of the conversation.

I had been invited by Dorothy DeLay to return to Juilliard in New York that fall after another summer in Aspen. Dad said it was the only course that would be right for me to take. Then he wanted me to sign a student loan agreement so I would pay for the next two years of graduate school. I flew up and took my entrance audition at Juilliard for the 1985-86 year and was accepted. I didn't receive a scholarship because Dad made too much money for me to qualify for one.

After that, I left Baton Rouge and returned once again to Aspen for my second summer at the Music Festival. Looking back, I marvel at how I was able to get back up and go on after such an ordeal. I believe I may have missed God at that point. Maybe if I had obeyed God and gone to New Jersey, I would have been better off. But I didn't heed the warning, and I wasn't strong enough to break free from my dad at that time...for whatever reason.

Chapter 18

Dark and Difficult Days

As I prepared to leave for Aspen in late June, I knew that I would never be welcome at my dad's house for more than a short visit ever again. I also realized that all of my game playing at being a violinist was over. I could no longer pretend and play the role of student prodigy violinist. I turned twenty-two in 1985. I was a young adult now, like it or not. Gone was the glamour of being a Curtis student, gone was the security of being in Houston at the university, and gone was the sense of well-being that had supported my inner life—the hope that in "making it" I would find myself and become happy. In fact, even in my life with the Lord, I had no sense of direction. All I knew to do was to just keep going forward and go for the career! Like an old bottle of pop with all the fizz gone out of it, the glamour of that old dream had vanished. I felt more like a prisoner going to the gallows than a budding concert violinist going toward the rising sun of a major solo career.

The day before I left, Dad told me, "Maury, I just don't understand you. I have never seen anyone with as much talent and ability on the violin as you have. Most violinists dream of being able to play like you, but you can't seem to accept or embrace it. Why don't you ask your Jesus to make you happy with yourself and your music? You sure seem miserable in the midst of all of that Bible preaching you listen to every day. Surely with all of that time in your religion, if Jesus is real, He would at least make you happy with yourself.

"It's all Deanna's fault! It's too bad she fed you all of those lies about yourself when you were young. I would have been thrilled to have had half of what you have been given. My father could have cared less whether I ever played my instrument or not. I had to fight and scratch for everything I ever got. I hardly got a hundred dollars out of him in ten years of schooling. But because of me, you have been given the best training possible. You've had me to pay for it all, and all you can do is tell me constantly that I am going to hell because I'm not your brand of reborn Christian. A lot of thanks I get!

"Well, wake up to the real world, buddy! You are going to have to do some things for yourself now. I can't coddle and shelter you forever. I've got a new family now, and they need me. I am not made of money, you know! It is time for you to learn to accept some responsibility for yourself. Since you are so consumed with your fantasy "Jesus," let Him take care of you now. Yeah! We'll see how real He is! I will never do to you what my father did to me. I'll support you as much as I can through school, but I have a limit. The shenanigans you pulled in Dallas stretched me about as far as I am able to go. Things are changing, and you may as well get used to it. Reality is reality, and you cannot escape from it." And with that, he walked out of my room.

The summer of 1985 in Aspen was okay for me. I tried my best to get along with everybody, and I found that I related quite easily to almost everyone. I had learned that I couldn't preach to everyone all the time if I wanted to make any friends, so I didn't. For the most part, I stopped blasting people with the gospel. I had no problem finding people to be with socially, but I had almost no close friends. I was very lonely. All of life seemed very plastic and super-ficial to me. Where were the "on fire" Christians I had remembered from the previous summer? They seemed to have disappeared and departed forever. I finally realized that if I was going to relate to people, I had to quit acting so super-spiritual all the time and try to be as normal as possible.

I went to Juilliard that fall to get my master's degree. I was excited about being back in New York City. I had brought a whole suitcase full of books and teaching tapes that I had gotten from my last two years in Houston and my trips to Dallas. I listened to tapes and read books and my Bible, which I carried with me everywhere. I was staying in the YMCA, and a lot of Juilliard students were there, so I hung out with them. We ate together, went to school together, and just plain lived together there.

When I practiced in my room, the anointing would come on me. The sound of my violin would fill the courtyard and echo through it and down the hall. I have a really big-sounding violin anyway, and the anointing would just blast that sound throughout the building. After a while, people who knew me would say, "Was that you practicing the violin the other day? It sounded awesome!"

I made some new friends, and they began to really respect my playing after hearing me practice, which probably fed my ego more than I needed. God gave me grace to flow into the school routine that first year, and in spite of all of my insecurities and problems, I was able to do quite well and to really progress under Dorothy DeLay's superb teaching. I knew quite a few people from Aspen, so I wasn't without friends or really even alone that much, which was very good for me. It was great to be in an environment where I could be with others if I needed to, and no one would look too deeply at me. We would go have a slice of pizza or a quick breakfast at the diner across from school. We would play a game of cards in someone's room or attend one of the many concerts that were going on.

Miss Lack called me one night and wanted to know how I was doing. I hadn't really said much of a good-bye to her in Houston since I had left so abruptly for Dallas. She had heard about what happened with me and my father and was concerned about me. She was enormously relieved to hear that I was in New York, had returned to my senses, and was with Miss DeLay. She then got to the reason she had called.

Auditioning for Susan Wadsworth

She said, "Maury dear, I know of a lady named Susan Wadsworth. She is the head of a group called Young Concert Artists, and she helps young emerging talents like you to launch into a solo career by setting up concerts and a New York debut for them. She has auditions every year, and I think you would be perfect for her. I wrote her a lengthy letter about you last week. I think it would be so good for you to try out for that. I think she would love your playing. Why don't you find out about her competition? I think you should enter it."

It was kind of funny that she had written to this lady who headed up Young Concert Artists because I had just heard about YCA from several of Miss DeLay's students. In fact, I had even gotten the application the day before and begun to fill it out! I sent it in the mail the next day, and about a week later, I got a form letter from this Susan Wadsworth, saying that she would like to hear me play in the preliminary auditions the first week of December.

I began to practice more than ever. I was excited and nervous at the same time. I decided that once again I would set my faith upon this competition. I did little else that fall other than to prepare for it. I felt like an Olympic athlete in intensive training. Even Miss DeLay took notice, and she helped me put my repertoire together in her uncanny, simple way. Other than feeling scared about my chances, I had enormous purpose and momentum building up to this audition that gave me a sense of security. I didn't have to think much beyond December at that point—I just had to train for the competition...and that was all.

I ate all of my meals out, which was very expensive in Manhattan, let me tell you! But I had no choice. Dad obliged me by sending a check for about $100 each week to cover the costs. When I spoke to him about all of my successes with Juilliard, Miss DeLay, and the upcoming YCA auditions, he seemed relieved and proud. He probably thought to himself, "Maury has finally gotten over this religious phase, and now he's back on track." So he gladly gave me what I needed for food each month.

Of course, my massive student loan covered most of the rest. (It took me over twelve years to pay it off!) I knew I had to do my best not to let God (or me) down. I had internalized this vision of a big solo career and had switched it over from being my dad's vision for me to being God's vision. I had prayed in tongues through this portion of my life, and I was just living it out in the natural, so to speak. I decided that if being busy would get the job done and find me a place in this awful world, then work I would. So I did little else but eat, sleep, go to the few classes I was required to attend, and practice, PRACTICE, PRACTICE!

I passed my audition in December and the semi-finals in January. I was only one of four violinists chosen for the finals. I prayed and prayed, and the night of the finals, I felt God's glory pouring into the auditorium as I played. It was the best I could have done, and I was really pleased. After about two hours of deliberations, the jury announced the winners, and I had been chosen as the only violinist. For that night at least, I felt I had reached heaven. I had won!

Unfortunately, my euphoria didn't last that long. In spite of winning, as the spring months began, I became more and more distressed. I hid it very well, however, even from myself. I signed the contract with YCA for three years and started preparing for the concerts in the fall. This music world I was seeing was making me sick to my stomach. I felt like it was sucking me into its powerful vortex more every day. What I had thought would bring me the greatest happiness was now beginning to feel like slavery—not an outward slavery but an inward passive allegiance to idols I couldn't submit to. The business of music became crystal clear to me. I saw it for what it was for the first time, and I became more anxious, distressed, and confused each day.

Losing control

Now I was a "somebody" in the eyes of the other students and even the faculty. I felt an enormous pressure that I had to be better than any of the others or I would be the laughingstock of the other violin students. Fear began to grip my heart more and more throughout that spring semester. Although I stood against it the best I could, I couldn't seem to stop the mounting pressure and consuming fear and anxiety. I could only alleviate it by reading my Bible or singing worship songs to the Lord. I went though an inner torture for the next six months that kept growing worse and worse with each passing day. Once or twice a week, I would start crying for no apparent reason. I would just break down and cry. I got to where I didn't want to be with people at all. I was scared that they were looking through me and that I was transparent or something. I would go to my lessons and classes and then leave as quickly as possible so I wouldn't have to talk to anyone.

Of course, I tried to stand against these things. I prayed as I had during the times in Houston and Philadelphia when I was overwhelmed and distressed, but it took longer and longer to get to a place of peace. Then the anxiety and fear would return again after only a few minutes. I was beginning to lose perspective on things. At times I overreacted emotionally and responded in an imbalanced way. I couldn't figure out what was going on, and that scared me even more. *What's wrong with me?* I asked myself. I had no answer.

Miss DeLay began to pick up on it. She was very concerned about me and told me to make sure I ate right and slept enough. I explained what was happening to me, but she didn't have much to say, except that I shouldn't worry so much about my future. But it wasn't that. I simply couldn't get free from this suffocating and tormenting fear and anxiety. Day and night it hounded me until my faith began to break under it. It only went away for very short seasons when I prayed or worshipped or confessed the Word. Inch by inch, this horrible condition was wrapping itself around me and squeezing the life out of me.

As March turned into April in 1986, I began to feel a despair that would not go away no matter what I did. I was in trouble and I knew it. The heavens were brass over me. I heard nothing from God. All I felt was the constant torment of fear and despair. At times, the pain was unbearable. I called Dad and told him. He said, "You're just nervous about the concerts ahead, but you always do fine when you play. Stop worrying so much. You can begin to enjoy the fruits of all that you've worked for now."

I tried to call old friends and ask them to pray for me—like some of those from the Maranatha church in Houston—but they didn't seem to be able to help me much. There didn't seem to be an answer to whatever this was that was afflicting me. When I tried to read the Bible, I couldn't even focus on the words. They just blurred. I felt so alone in New York...like the whole world had abandoned me and gone on without me.

I heard a voice saying, "What's the use of living anymore? No one wants you. There is something WRONG with you. You'll never make it in life."

At first, I resisted those thoughts. I knew they weren't true, but as the school year came to an end, I realized that I didn't know who I was anymore. I felt like an empty shell. I couldn't find any joy in my life. My music was fine, of course. I had trained myself so that it didn't matter how I felt—I could play nearly flawlessly. But I came to the shocking conclusion that IT DIDN'T MATTER. *So this is making it,* I thought. *I am in torment. I am in misery. I feel like I am in hell. I am losing my mind.*

So what, that I could play the violin well and impress everyone? It didn't seem to bring much satisfaction to me anymore. Oh yes, there was the momentary thrill of accomplishment when I achieved a new level in my technique or conquered a difficult Paganini Caprice. But afterwards the feeling would vanish into this awful fog of anxiety. I would just sit and look at the walls in my room or crawl into bed to take a nap and hope that this hopelessness and despair would lift when I awoke.

The school year finally ended, and I went home to Baton Rouge. It seemed as if I wasn't really very welcome any more in Dad and Susan's home. They were having some real problems communicating. Susan was very sullen, and Dad was feeling very frustrated with his marriage. He seemed moody and caught up in his own sad world. He was pleased and proud of me, of course, for I was now well on my way to fulfilling his lifelong dreams for me. He talked excitedly about my bright future in music, but his words seemed so hollow. All of my life seemed to be hollow. I had so little satisfaction in the music world. I was chained to the intense pressure-filled world of the concert artist, and I thought even God wanted me to do this. There was no way out. The only other thing for me was the Bible and my faith. Sometimes I would dream about what it must be like to be a minister and to be free to preach and teach about Jesus any time I wanted. It must be nice to be able to just live somewhere and to be a Christian and have a job and to be happy.

I was grieving deep inside of my spirit, like I had lost something and would never get it back. The grief just wouldn't go away. Even Dad noticed it. He said, "I just

179

don't understand why you can't be happy. Everything is going well for you now. The hard days are behind you." I just looked at him and didn't even try to respond.

Most afternoons I practiced and then slept for several hours. When it was morning, I wanted it to be evening. When it was evening, I wanted it to be morning. I got relief when I slept, so I slept quite a bit. Susan was a little concerned about it, but she dismissed it by saying, "Maury, you've had a hard year, and I guess you need to rest a lot right now."

By the time I left for Aspen, I was out of control. I was getting to where I wouldn't go outside of my room unless I had to. I hid in my room or in a practice room, or I went for long walks by myself far away from any people. I felt that something was terribly wrong with me as a person. I was afraid I would embarrass myself and say things that would make people look at me like I was a weirdo.

About halfway through my summer session, when I knew I had to go back to New York and start my concerts with YCA, a paralyzing fear gripped me. It never went away. Day and night, I was tormented by it. What was I going to do in the fall? I couldn't pretend that everything was all right anymore. I was suddenly breaking down and crying in front of people for no reason.

Thinking about suicide

By late July, I couldn't get free no matter what I did. Praying didn't work. Reading the Bible was useless. Listening to tapes on faith teaching or praise and worship did nothing. I was doomed. It was all over. The pain inside got so unbearable that I decided I would find a way to kill myself. I wanted to go to heaven. This earth no longer had anything for me anymore. I couldn't break free from this horrible state. So I made up my mind that when I returned to New York, I would kill myself. I was determined to find a way. Thoughts of suicide were the only things that consoled me. I knew that somehow, if I could just kill myself, I would be free from this horrible world and would be happy in a place where I belonged. So I began to dwell on suicide day and night.

I cried out to God, but to no avail. It was worse if I tried to pray. Then I felt like my mind was in a vise, and I would just collapse on the floor, shaking in convulsions and weeping uncontrollably. So I gave up trying to pray. I heard these words constantly, "I've got you now, you useless, deranged mess of a person. You'll never get out of my grip now. I'm going to kill you, and there is nothing you can do about it. Ha! Some Christian you are! It looks like Jesus has abandoned you, doesn't it? I'm going to tear your heart out, rip your music to shreds, and consume you, you wretch! By the time I'm through with you, you'll never touch your violin again. I'll tear your mind apart until you perish! We'll see what becomes of you then!"

The devil didn't even try to hide anymore. I saw and heard him in my consciousness day and night. I was alone. No Christians were with me there in Aspen. What little was left of my resistance shattered. I fell into this evil force, and its chains were wrapped around my spirit. I couldn't fight it any more. My faith finally gave out, and I caved in to this awful tormenting spirit.

The summer ended, and somehow I managed to return to New York City. I prayed, "Oh, God, please make this thing pass, whatever it is, so I can complete my schooling and make it past this year."

For a while, I got a little better. The fear seemed to subside somewhat, and I was able to attend my classes. Just as I thought I was getting over my depression, however, one morning in mid-September of 1986, as I was preparing to go to school, I froze. I couldn't get out of bed. All I could do was lie there. I couldn't move. I couldn't get dressed. I couldn't even call anyone on the phone for several hours. Then the pain got so bad inside that I began to think again of how to kill myself.

Finally I called Dad and told him I was in real trouble. I told him about all that had been happening during the summer. He listened and said, "You're going to be all right, but I think we need to get you a psychologist up there in New York who can help you. I'll come up on the first flight I can get." And sure enough, Dad came up to New York a few days later. He had found a "Christian" psychologist through a friend of his in Louisiana. His name was Dr. Davis.

Dad told me, "I'm sure he can help you. It's too bad that you can't pull yourself together. You're on the verge of a major career. For God's sake, Maury, you are going to give your New York debut next spring. You are playing great. NOTHING IS WRONG! It's all that garbage Deanna fed you growing up—I know it is. You are just going to have to accept life the way it is! This is reality! Life isn't easy, you know. Can't your Jesus-religion comfort you now? WHERE IS YOUR JESUS NOW? You sure preached Him strong to me—that He has made you happy and all. At least He could keep you from this if He is as real as you say!"

I had no strength to respond to him. I just burst into tears and went into the bathroom and closed the door. In a few minutes, he knocked on the door and said he didn't mean anything by what he had said and was sorry. So I unlocked the door and came out.

Starting therapy

A few days later, we went to see Dr. Davis. Dad gave a crisp synopsis of the symptoms I had described and said, "I want Maury to get all the help he can so he can get over this, whatever it is."

Dr. Davis said, "It sounds to me as if you are experiencing what is called 'clinical depression.' Don't worry. It's treatable and far more common than you might think. One thing worries me, however. I am concerned about this desire to kill yourself. How long have you been thinking about suicide, Maury?"

I told him I'd been thinking about it for about three or four months, off and on. I could tell that Dr. Davis was a warm and good-hearted man. I liked him. He seemed trustworthy.

Then he said, "I would like to see you two or three times a week right now, if that is okay. I think you need some intensive counseling. This didn't just happen overnight." Then he asked Dad to leave the room for a little while, and he asked me about some of my background, my musical training, and what I was doing now at Juilliard. After a while, he really zeroed in on me and asked me pointblank if I was planning to kill myself.

I said, "Yes, I would if I could find a way. I want to go to heaven. I have had enough of this life. It's too much." Then I started crying again before I even realized that I had.

He gave me his card and said, "I want you to call me if you need help anytime, and I will get back to you." Then he called Dad back in and said, "I want you to go and see a friend of mine who is a psychiatrist. His name is Henri Weisman. I cannot prescribe any medication for Maury, but he can. It is very likely that a large part of this is chemically oriented and can be helped by some new medications that are now available. I will call him, and I believe he can see you this afternoon."

We went to see Dr. Weisman later that day, and he gave me two prescriptions and made arrangements to meet with me once a week. Dad went to the drugstore and got my prescriptions filled, and the next morning he returned to Baton Rouge. I was alone again.

Before long, I began to have suicidal thoughts once again. I decided that I would go to the George Washington Bridge, which was only a few blocks from my apartment, and see if I could jump off of it. For the next week, I went every day to that bridge and climbed up the ramp until I reached the middle of it. Cars and trucks would speed by as people drove to their homes up the Hudson River in the suburbs. I thought to myself, *How wonderful it must be to have a family and a place to belong. I don't have anyplace to belong on this earth anymore. It's all over.*

Then I would start toward the railing to climb over it. On the first day, I couldn't get near it. My feet got stuck to the ground, and I couldn't move forwards, only backwards. I got so mad. I knew that angels were standing on my feet and wouldn't let me move them. By the fifth day, however, I managed to get close enough to the edge to get a leg over the railing. Suddenly a wind came and blew me backwards, and I fell to the pavement. I was stuck to the ground on that bridge for about twenty minutes. I was sobbing because I couldn't go through with it. God wouldn't let me die, but to live in that unbearable pain was worse than death. I couldn't stand it.

Finally I walked back down the bridge and onto Broadway again and headed back toward my apartment. I hadn't eaten anything at all that day. I couldn't remember the last time I had eaten a meal. I found some spaghetti noodles and a bottle of Ragu sauce in the kitchen cupboard, so I ate and then fell into bed and went to sleep.

When I awoke the next day, I couldn't move. I just sat in the bed for about three hours. Finally I got to the phone and called Dr. Davis. I told him, "I have tried every day for the past week to jump off the George Washington Bridge. I got pretty close, but the angels came each time and stuck my feet to the ground and I couldn't move them. Then yesterday, I got one leg over the railing and almost made it, but a gust of wind blew me so hard that I fell back onto the bridge. I was stuck to the pavement for a long time until the angels let me go. Then I had to come back down again. I just wanted you to know that I have set my faith to die, and I am going to do everything in my power to kill myself."

Naturally, Dr. Davis was alarmed. He told me to come to his office immediately. Deep down, I wanted to live and not die, but the pain inside was so great that I couldn't stand it. I obeyed and took a cab to his office. He said to me, "It is very dangerous for you to be going to the George Washington Bridge. I am thankful that you didn't go through with your plan to jump, but I don't want you to keep practicing that behavior. You might end up doing it eventually. I have decided that you must be hospitalized until you can control yourself. I have arranged with Dr. Weisman for you to be admitted to the psychiatric ward of the hospital tonight. I will drive you there myself. I have no choice but to do this."

I just sat there and stared at him. I didn't know what to say. I knew I needed help, so I agreed. I told him I had spent that morning trying to find a way to purchase a gun. I didn't know how to go about getting a gun, so I gave up on that idea. Then I had taken a carving knife out of the kitchen and held it to my wrist. But my hand froze, and I couldn't get it to make a cut no matter how hard I tried. I got so angry that I started screaming at God because I knew that an angel was stopping me. I told the angel to let go, but he wouldn't let go. That's when I realized it was no use trying to kill myself and finally called Dr. Davis. When Dr. Davis heard that, he was even more convinced that I had to be hospitalized right away, so we got into his car, and he drove me over to the hospital.

It was a horrible, dingy, devil-infested place. I had to sign all kinds of papers, and they put me in a light-blue hospital gown and gave me some kind of tranquilizer. I fell asleep on a cold, blue, plastic pillow. When I awoke the next day, it all came flooding back to me. I was in the psychiatric ward in a New York City hospital! I heard moans and screams from some of the other patients. I saw several people walking around in a stupor, talking to themselves. One old lady kept trying to tear out her hair, and I saw demons going in and out of her. It was a horrible place. I stayed there for a week, and Dr. Davis and Dr. Weisman both visited me once a day. I had brought my Bible and tried to read it, but it did me little good.

This was the beginning of October, and I was scheduled to play my first recital with YCA the following week. I called Miss DeLay and told her where I was. She said she would contact Susan Wadsworth and let her know. I had no choice. Of course, Dr. Davis notified my father. I was stuck. I was locked in this place, and I couldn't get out.

After a week in the hospital, Dad arranged for me to fly down to Baton Rouge. At first it was such a relief to get out of the hospital that I was happy to be there, but after a couple of days at home, I was miserable. All I could do was eat and sleep. When I couldn't sleep anymore, I would read. Dad had found a psychiatrist whom I saw every day, but it seemed like it did me no good at all. Everything was in a daze from all the medication I was taking.

A visit from God

Early one morning at about 3:40, I woke up with a start and sat straight up in bed like I had been hit with a bolt of lightning! Suddenly I was wide awake and felt completely sober. I didn't feel the least bit drugged or even tired. I was as clear in my mind as I had felt in a long time. Something was in my room. I could feel it. Then down on the inside of me, a voice spoke to me and said, "Get down on your knees and pray in tongues for one hour. Do not stop until that clock says 4:40."

I knew it was the Lord, but I said, "Why should I do that? Look where all that praying in tongues got me in the past. Forget it. I'm through with that mess. How can it help me now?"

The silence in the room got deafening, and the room began to light up like there was a light coming from everywhere and nowhere at the same time. I got scared—yet I knew it was all right. Jesus was in my room, and there were angels with Him. I was so angry at Him that I didn't want to see or talk to Him. Nevertheless, the desire to pray became so overpowering that I found myself falling on my knees, and I began to pray in tongues.

That hour went by so fast. As I prayed, I knew exactly what the Holy Spirit was praying through me. I was praying for a way of escape out of this horrible inner torture I was in. It seemed inescapable. It seemed hopeless. But the words just poured out of my spirit in such a torrent that I knew somehow Jesus was going to help me. It wasn't me praying because I didn't even have the strength to pray. Jesus in me rose up and prayed through me.

Then, as suddenly as He came, He left. The light left the room. The glorious angels seemed to fade away out of my perception, and the room became dark again. When I looked up, the clock showed precisely 4:40. I got back into bed and went back to sleep. Even miraculous events didn't do much for me. I was hurting too bad. The disappointment went too deep. The torment had gone on for too long. I just tried to forget it had ever happened. Still, I knew that I had prayed for a place to live and somewhere to go and that God would provide for me. Thank God for His answer to my prayers that night!

Amazingly, even in the condition I was in, a week later Dad and Susan put me on a plane to New York City! I was still suicidal, but since that late night incident, I had found some small shred of faith and hope to cling to. Maybe God was still with me. It was abundantly clear that I was not wanted in Baton Rouge...that staying and getting help "at home" was not even going to be considered by Dad, no matter how sick I was. He was determined that I wasn't going to miss my chance to "make it." In my father's mind, I was somehow "putting this on." I just had to snap out of it and I would be fine. For the last time, Dad tried patching me up and putting me back on a plane. Breakdown or no breakdown, suicide or no suicide, the show must go on! I must finish my last year at Juilliard and play my concerts. Once I got through this "phase" of my life, I would be fine.

Once again he gave me the usual pep talk: "You've gone too far to quit now!" This time, however, it could not even begin to do anything for me. As I boarded the plane, I remember thinking, *What in the world am I going to do when I get off the plane in New York?* I knew that no miracle had occurred as far as my mental and emotional state was concerned. I still wanted to kill myself.

After I got back to my apartment, I called Dorothy DeLay. I told her where I had been, what had happened to me, and why I hadn't been in school. She said she understood and asked for my phone number. She said she would call me right back. About fifteen minutes later, the phone rang, and

Miss DeLay's calm and pleasant voice was on the other end. She said, "Maury dear, I just called and spoke with Susan Wadsworth down at the YCA office. I told her about your situation, and she is going to call you in a few minutes. I know this isn't easy for you right now, but you'll be all right. I hope she can help you. I think you should take a break from school for a while. I will be in touch. Bye for now."

An answer to prayer

I sat there in stunned silence. Why did I call Miss DeLay? What a stupid thing to do. Maybe I would get over this and get back into class and no one would know. Now what was going to happen? Before I could think or reproach myself any more, the phone rang again. This time, Susan Wadsworth, the head of Young Concert Artists, was on the phone!

She said, "Maury, I just spoke to Dorothy DeLay. Are you okay?"

I said, "Well, not really. I've had a rough time for the past several weeks. I don't know what to do."

Then Susan said, "Come down to the office right now. I will be done in about an hour. Will you please come? I want to help you—that's all."

I felt a strange sense that she really did care, even though she didn't know me well at all. It was strange, coming from such a strong, tough businesswoman like she was.

When I met her later at her office, Susan invited me to go home with her and to stay with her and her family for the weekend. She asked me a lot of questions about my life, and I was able to speak to her freely. I knew that she really took a special interest in my situation, and she gave me her full attention as I answered her probing questions.

Susan and I went to her apartment, and I met Susan's husband, Charles. He was in his final year as the Director of the Chamber Music Society of Lincoln Center, which is one of the finest chamber music groups in the world. We had supper together and talked for a long time. Around eleven o'clock, it was time for bed, and Susan showed me how to open the couch in the study into a fold-out bed.

She told me, "Charles and I are glad that you could come here this weekend. We want you to know that you are welcome here until we can decide what's the best place for you. We want to help you through this dark and difficult time. You are going to make it, I am sure. There is something in you that I admire greatly. You are a fighter and a delightful person...and one of the greatest talents on the violin I have ever heard. And I have heard a few, believe me. We'll talk some more tomorrow. Just sleep until you wake up, okay?" Then she gave me one of the sweetest hugs and kisses I had received in a long time, shut the door, and turned out the light.

As I got into bed, I was overcome with emotion. I cried for some time. Susan was being so nice to me. I really loved her for her kindness.

How in the world did I get into this home? I wondered.

Then I thought I heard the Lord say, "This is what I had you pray for a few nights ago. I have provided a haven for you. I have put a special love in Susan and Charles' hearts for you, even though they don't even know Me yet. This will be a place of refuge for you. I love you, My son. I will surely heal you and bring you up from this place. Your healing from this will bring many souls to Me as you shall testify of My glory and grace poured out on your behalf. Know that I have heard your cries and seen all of your afflictions. I will rescue you, and you shall play your violin for My glory and for no other."

As I fell asleep, I felt God's presence flood that room...and I felt the Father's arms around me, holding me tightly. He hadn't left me in all of my pain and suffering. He was there. Maybe I could live...maybe I would actually get better and find a way out of this bitter and horrible bondage.

"Jesus," I prayed, "are You still there, really? Why did You let this happen to me? Why am I hurting so bad? Help me, Jesus! Hold me, Jesus! Please don't ever let me go! You are all I've got."

Chapter 19

At Home With the Wadsworths

*W*hen I awoke the next morning, I couldn't remember where I was. Then the memories of the night before flooded back into my mind. I was so amazed to be in this place, of all places. Susan and Charles Wadsworth seemed to belong to that magic, fairy-tale world that my parents always referred to as "the musical elite." They seemed larger than life to me, especially under the influence of my breakdown.

As I got out of bed, I was feeling very bad, which was normal for me in the morning. It took me about twenty-five minutes just to get out of my pajamas, brush my teeth, and put my clothes on. I was a little frightened to be in this fancy apartment. I sensed that somehow the Wadsworths would quickly grow tired of me and throw me out, and I would just go right back to the George Washington Bridge. After I got dressed, I fell back on the bed in despair and just laid there. I was hurting too bad to even cry. I would cry in floods of tears several times a day, but most of the time I just felt numb—like I had been tortured past the point of feeling it any more. I was shut down in my soul, and I felt like I was falling into a bottomless emotional abyss and nothing could stop it.

Susan came into the room after a while and immediately realized that I was really feeling bad. She asked about my parents, about the South, and Louisiana in particular. She asked about Dorothy DeLay and what I thought about her teaching. After talking for about twenty minutes, I began to sink into a hole again. I started saying that I would never get to have a solo career.

"I came so close," I lamented, "but I know it's over! It's finished. I can never live this way. I have failed!" On and on I went.

Susan kept saying, "Maury, that's ridiculous! You've got everything going for you. You're playing great. Of course you can do it. That's nonsense!"

I got into such a place of emotional anguish that I finally dropped my head down and shut my eyes as tightly as I could and didn't move. This happened frequently during those first months. Susan called it "getting squinched." That was exactly what I felt like on the inside—like I was being put through a steam roller and squashed like a bug. It was horrible.

She didn't know what to do, so she just sat next to me and stroked my hair. She said, "You'll get better. Don't worry. You are going to be all right. It's not your fault that this has happened to you. I think you are a very strong person to have lasted as long as you have. Like I said, you are a fighter. Maury, you are going to make it out of this."

In the coming months, she spoke this over me again and again. Looking back, I marvel at how strong her natural faith was. She always said something positive. Because of my illness and hopeless despair, I would argue with her, but she always remained positive.

After about an hour, I did pull out of it once again, at least enough to get ready to go to my appointment with Dr. Davis. Surprisingly, his office was within walking distance of the apartment. On this Saturday, Susan went with me to my appointment, and Dr. Davis met her. Of course, he had heard all about YCA from my previous appointments, and he was glad to learn that she had taken me under her wing, so to speak.

It was very obvious to Susan and Charles after that first weekend that I was in no shape to be on my own. To my utter astonishment, they said I could live with them until I got well enough to do something else, and Susan worked out financial arrangements with my father. I had a very hard time believing they really wanted me there. I was sure that the bottom would drop out at any moment and they would tell me I had to leave. But I could not hide from my own devastating pain any longer. Like an avalanche, years of pain from the past that I had refused to acknowledge or experience began to flood into my consciousness. I felt it was more than I could take, but I had to go through it anyway. There was no escaping it.

At the end of my rope
For years and years, I had pretended that I was okay. I had gone through life like there was nothing wrong with me. But now I realized that something was terribly wrong with me on the inside. I felt like I had been through a shredder or a meat grinder. I was through playing any more roles or trying to live up to what everyone else wanted me to be. I was exhausted. I was mentally and emotionally battered and bruised. I finally just quit and let Susan take care of me.

For the next several months, I stayed at the Wadsworths. I don't remember much of what happened, except that Susan helped me in a way I had never been helped before. I suppose when Susan entered my life at that point, I completely collapsed for a time. I had fought with every ounce of my faith and strength to keep going, until finally I had nothing left to fight with. I was at the end of my rope. When Susan offered to support me and help me, I just fell into her arms like a small child who had been emotionally battered beyond his ability to cope.

I was seeing Dr. Davis five times a week and Dr. Weisman once a week. So every day except Sunday, I went to my appointments. And each day I would lose it. The pain, anger, hopelessness, tears, and terrible sorrow I felt seemed to be overwhelming. Dr. Davis would look at me with such compassion. I felt like Job. Why was this happening to me now, of all times in my life? I was on the verge of doing what I had dreamed of doing.

The irony of living at the Wadsworths was a bitter cup for me at times. I felt that I would never recover, and yet I had to see what it was like to be a successful concert artist like Charles. The Wadsworths seemed to live a charmed life. I felt guilty because I felt that I was a burden on them. Most of all, I felt deeply embarrassed and mortified at myself because of the condition I was in.

Each morning, Charles and Susan would leave for work. Susan would set my breakfast out and put a note in my cereal bowl telling me that she loved me and to call her at work as soon as I was finished with breakfast. The notes were always handwritten in bright and beautiful colors of ink. And morning after morning, it never failed to touch me the way she seemed to care.

My adult mind told me not to give in to the strong pull of her "mothering," but I was in such bad shape that I had no choice. I had emotionally regressed until I was like a little child, and I let her mother me in a way that I'd never been mothered before. I became deeply dependent upon her. I called the YCA office several times a day to talk with her, and she always took my calls, even if I called during an important meeting. Every night before bed, Susan came in and spent at least an hour with me before tucking me into bed. Even when she was tired, she would stay up and talk with me until I had some sense of peace. She helped me remember to take my pills at the right times, to eat regularly, and to do many practical things that were difficult for me.

Tagging along with Charles and Susan

Susan never allowed me to be alone in the evenings, so I accompanied her to all of her social and concert events. I went to Charles' concerts at Alice Tully Hall. I went out to movies with them, or we watched video movies together. I went to a lot of fancy restaurants with them. I met famous artists night after night as a steady stream of the "who's who" of the music world flowed in and out of their lives. The Wadsworths were obviously reigning in this small but very elite world in an extraordinary way.

All through the fall of 1986, I tagged along with Susan in her strange and amazing New York music business world like a wounded puppy she was nursing back to health. And I still played my concerts! With her constant input and positive prodding, I managed to get through all of my recitals that year. Susan Wadsworth just wouldn't let me stay down. At the same time, I was able to rest in a way that I'd never been able to before. I had burned out from so many years of non-stop training on the violin.

I slept until at least 10:30 every morning, then went into the kitchen for my note, my breakfast, and the New York Times that Charles had ransacked for the music reviews. Then I called Susan at the office and talked to her for a while. When I began to feel a little better, I could practice a little. When I was feeling bad, which was most mornings, I got back on the couch and slept for a couple more hours. When I felt really distraught, I joined Susan at her office, met her for lunch, or joined her at some of the YCA auditions.

She was everything to me, and yet I felt tormented about my dependence on her. I became obsessed with her. Her attention was something I constantly sought after, at least whenever I was strong or coherent enough to do so. In one sense, I felt very loved and comforted. But I was so embarrassed to be in such a helpless condition that it made me ashamed to be with her most of the time, especially when I had to be out in public with her.

Day followed day and week followed week, until Thanksgiving rolled around. By that time, I had been to many concerts with Susan, had attended several fund raisers, and had met many of the elite in the New York classical music scene—but what a way to do it! Many times when I had to be at one of these events, I would find an empty room where I could hide. I would put my head down between my legs and just sit on the floor for long periods of time. When Susan would discover that I'd left the event, she would come and find me. She had a way of getting me to accompany her back out "in public," even though it was so painful to be with other people that I tried to avoid it whenever possible. Susan was convinced that it was better for me to be with other people, so she made me participate. The really amazing thing about my condition was that I *could* socialize and appear to be quite normal. I could even joke and laugh to some extent for short periods of time in the more comfortable situations.

For the most part, however, I was a miserable human being during that time. I was so scared to be with people that I still dreamed of a time when I could end my life and it would all be over. I thought about little else during those first few months. The worst thing was the condemnation I felt for being sick. I felt that I had failed spiritually and had fallen into the devil's hands. I truly believed I would never be happy again. It was horrible to feel as helpless and condemned as I did. I was convinced that my condition was somehow my fault. My thoughts were tormented and very dark for the most part, and yet I still managed to appreciate the rich musical environment I had fallen into.

I had given up on trying to pray or do anything spiritual. I just adopted Susan's persona and tried to be like her as much as possible. She enjoyed movies, so I did. She had fun just living when she wasn't working, so I tried to be the same way. I tried to live "in the natural" and ride out this horrible storm. I couldn't fight anymore, so I just gave up. And in every session with the doctors, more and more searing pain from my past came pouring out of me. When I talked, I felt as if I was listening to somebody else instead of me. I would wail, cry, and lament over how hopeless my life was. Then, as if someone threw a switch somewhere, it would be over. I would walk out of the doctor's office, go back to my room, and sleep until Susan and Charles got home for dinner. I felt like I was practicing "living" and being "normal," whatever that was. I am so thankful that I had Susan's stubborn and persistent attention. She just made me keep going and doing things with her.

As we moved into winter, I went through my days and nights in torment. The only relief I found seemed to come when I slept, so I slept a lot. I always hoped that maybe when I woke up, I would be better—but that never happened. Susan worked with me every night and was doing her best to train me to think in more constructive ways. I was slowly getting better, and I wasn't entertaining thoughts of suicide quite as much, although I still didn't think I was going to live much longer. It didn't seem possible that I would ever be able to survive without Susan and her constant support. I really loved her and needed her. How I wished I could go back in time and change my life so that I could be happy again, but I seemed trapped in this horrible state. Only Susan's stubborn and constant prodding and affirmations that I was going to get better kept the flickering candle of hope alive in me. Night after night, she would sit with me for at least an hour, as she spoke faith and love into my broken heart and shredded soul.

Meeting David

A few days before Christmas that year, the Wadsworths took me with them to visit Charles' son from a previous marriage. His name was David, and he was functionally retarded and lived in a special community in upstate New York for mentally and emotionally disabled adults.

I was feeling a little better and was trying to enjoy being out of New York City and in the country. We took David with us to a local restaurant, and there was a beautiful view of a mountain where people were skiing. As we sat down at the table, David just stared at me for the longest time. Then he shouted out, "Jesus! Jesus!" so loud that people turned and stared. I was embarrassed and so were the Wadsworths. But then the Lord spoke to me so clearly and said, "He sees Me in you. You see, I haven't left you." I bowed my head and started crying.

Of course, Susan immediately tried to pull me out of it, but I couldn't talk for a long time. I was glad the Lord had told me He hadn't left me.

I liked David Wadsworth very much. He was quite retarded, but he had a childlikeness about him that was beautiful to behold. I envied him because I knew that he was unaware that anything was wrong with him. Also, I knew that he was born again and knew Jesus. I hadn't seen or been with a Christian for so long that it was refreshing to have David with us that afternoon. Even though he had the emotional and intellectual capacity of a five year old, it was wonderful to have fellowship with him. He kept staring at me and nodding his head and making comments about Jesus. I thought, even then, how ironic and grim it was that a retarded boy could see more about me in the spiritual realm after only five minutes than Charles and Susan had ever perceived during all the time I had been with them.

Susan had admitted on numerous occasions that there was something about me that never seemed to give up, even when I was the most depressed or distraught. That was the closest she ever came to recognizing the Holy Spirit at work in me during the whole time I lived with her. But it didn't matter. I loved her anyway. I actually wished that I could change and just live in the natural world like she did. In fact, I did my best to do that for many weeks. I just couldn't fight the oppression of hell that was coming against me anymore. Still, that afternoon reminded me that Jesus' light shines through, even in the greatest seasons of darkness in our lives.

At Christmas, Susan made arrangements for me to go home to Baton Rouge. I was so dependent upon her by this time that the thought of being away from her for two weeks was devastating! I went into a tailspin for a couple of days, until I finally accepted that I had to go home to Baton Rouge and do the best I could.

Dad had been keeping up with me through Susan, but he had hardly spoken to me at all for several months. I knew one thing for certain, however—my father had hurt me very deeply by trying to live his life through me. This had become very clear in the sessions with my therapists and with Susan. Because of the hurt, I had never been able to develop emotionally when I was growing up.

Surprisingly, this was very hard for me to see or admit. I had denied that anything was wrong for so long that I disassociated my feelings from my "real life." I just burned out. I couldn't keep going with only the goal of pleasing Dad. My own life had been lost in this desperate attempt to "make it." I was in a terrible bind.

Dr. Weisman explained it to me this way: "Maury, I think you have been a victim of what I call a 'double bind,' and you broke down because of it. It's like this: If you succeed and become a great violinist, then you fail because your father can't have it and you can. But if you fail to become a great violinist, then you also fail because not only do you let him down, but your own life becomes meaningless. Your whole identity was swallowed up in your childhood relationship with your dad. You have been like Siamese twins attached at the hip, if you will.

"Sooner or later, this terrible pattern of behavior had to be broken. When it was, it caused severe emotional problems. Actually, however, the anger and depression had been there for a long time. I think you have been suffering with this for at least seven years, and maybe more."

Then he paused and looked at me very pensively and said, "You are a very strong person to have lasted as long as you did while accomplishing so much. Most people would have been institutionalized long ago if they'd had to endure what you've been subjected to in your life. But I believe you are going to get better. I have two reasons for thinking this way. First, you have a deep abiding faith in

God and in the Bible, and that has somehow sustained you through all of the hell you've endured in your inner life. Second, you have such a great gift in your music. You really do love to play for yourself or you never would have gone as far as you have. When you finally unravel yourself from the controlling menace of your father, I think ultimately you will find your way through this and be able to integrate your religion and your music in a powerful way."

Then his eyes twinkled a little as he smiled at me and said, "It's going to be very interesting to see what form that integration will take, but I am sure you are going to make it. In fact, I am awed at the strength of your faith in God. I don't think I have ever encountered anything like it before."

I just moaned and said, "If I had such great faith in God, it seems to me I wouldn't have fallen apart. I hope you are right."

An "up and down" existence

It was a very dark time for me during the two weeks of Christmas and New Year 1986-87. I called Susan every day and talked to her and sobbed over the phone. I called Dr. Davis and had a telephone appointment with him for an hour every day. Dad and his wife didn't know what to do with me. Dad had been paying for everything while I was in New York, and he made sure I didn't forget it. But he wasn't too vindictive about it. He saw that I was in deep trouble, and he was glad Susan was taking care of me. He was especially thrilled with my involvement in the New York music scene and was hoping that Susan and Charles would promote me. But I was in no condition to talk about all of that, so he just tried to be as nice as he could and went to work and stayed out of my way. I was absolutely miserable in that house and couldn't wait to get back to New York City.

During January and February of 1987, I became more and more attached to Susan. I was starting to be less depressed, at least when I could be with her. I began to think that somehow this could last forever. I took what little hope I had and wrapped it all up in the fantasy that Susan was going to make everything all right. I decided that I was somehow going to live and not die. All that mattered to me was that Susan liked me. Maybe it would be different this time, and this person wouldn't let me down. She always said, "Maury, I'm not going away. I will always be here and I'll always be your friend no matter what." She would say that to me nearly every night. I finally put my trust in that. I was going to be safe with Susan. She was going to take care of me. At that point, I began to believe with all my heart that Susan was everything. Of course, that wasn't real, but for me at that time, it was the only bit of hope I had, and I grabbed on to it.

Maybe Dad was right all along. I would find my way. Susan seemed to be treating me better than ever. Maybe she was going to really take me under her wing. I might get better, or at least be able to function as time went on. Maybe Susan would promote me, and I would become the next Young Concert Artist's real big artist. After all, I was meeting all these big artists by being with her. She always said what a great talent she thought I was. Maybe she really did have designs on making me into a great artist. It seemed almost like a fairy tale.

When I began to show some signs of improvement—however slight—Susan began to talk to me about my debut recital coming up on April 7. It became her whole focus, and she began to prod me into practicing and preparing. She had great confidence and faith in me, and I didn't want to let her down. She had my heart.

Then something else began to happen. Susan began to withdraw from me. She wouldn't spend as long at night talking to me. In fact, sometimes she just didn't come in at all to say good night. Then one day she told me I would have to find another place to live after my debut. When she said that, I freaked out. I couldn't handle it. I went into such a state of fear. I couldn't live my life without Susan. God wasn't there for me any more. Susan had told me it wasn't a healthy thing for me to be so religious, so I had abandoned my faith. When she saw how I really fell apart when she talked about my leaving and being on my own, she stopped talking about it. After all, the important thing was the big concert on April 7th. That was all that mattered.

Turning back to Jesus

About a week after this, Susan and her family left for a two-week vacation and I was alone. One night after returning from dinner, I turned on the television before going to bed. As I clicked through the channels, I stumbled upon a broadcast of an evangelist who was having a crusade in Baton Rouge. I was glued to the set—I couldn't move. The evangelist was pacing like a madman back and forth on the platform and shaking his finger at the television screen. He screamed, "You've got to get right with God! REPENT! Get that sin out of your life!" Then he started crying and said, "Oh Jesus! Have mercy on me! Have mercy on these precious souls who are watching me right now! Rescue them from their bondage and sin!"

He turned and looked into the camera, pointed his finger right at me, and said, "Rescue that one who is trapped in suicide and despair! There's hope for you! God will make a way out for you! Come back to Jesus right NOW!"

When he said the word, "NOW!" I felt as if a bolt of lightening had come through that TV set and hit me right in my chest. I went flying backwards out of the bed and hit my head against the wall in the far corner of the room near the window. I couldn't move. I was crying and sobbing and calling out to Jesus to rescue me like the preacher had said. I don't know how long I remained there. I kept thinking to myself, *I don't even like that preacher. What in the world is going on? How was I so overcome? I still believe in you, Jesus, and I'm asking You to get me out of this! HELP!*

As if in answer to my cry, I began to feel a bubbling rise out of me from somewhere deep inside, and I began to speak in tongues again. I hadn't done it for so many months that it felt really strange to me. The devil had lied to me through my doctors and Susan and told me that it was damaging for me to pray in tongues and that I should not do it. But in spite of all that, the words were rolling out of me in big waves.

Finally I stopped and crawled back into bed. I slept like a baby that night because I had such peace. At four o'clock that morning, I suddenly woke up and sat straight up in bed. I heard a voice that seemed almost audible say, "I want you to call Anita Jacobs in Pennsville, New Jersey! Call her right away!"

I said, "Lord, I don't know her phone number."

The Lord told me the number, and He kept repeating it until I wrote it down.

Then I fell asleep. The next day I called that number, and sure enough, Mrs. Jacobs answered the phone! I explained my situation, and she quickly wrote down my number. She said, "I'm going to call Steve right away. He is at church right now, but he'll call you right back."

Five minutes later, the phone rang. I picked it up, and there was Steve on the other end. He asked me what was going on, and I explained as well as I could what had happened to me.

He immediately said, "Maury, get down here right away! You've got to get out of that apartment and come down here."

I told him I would try to come, but I wasn't sure if I could manage to get there on my own. He explained how to get there, and I said I would try. Then he told me he would pray for me and hung up.

I had dreaded calling him because I didn't want to have to deal with his mindset. He was convinced that I was overcome by the devil, and I figured that if I went down there, he would just tell me to "snap out of it." That was why I hadn't called him in the first place. I was convinced that I couldn't break free from my depression through spiritual means because I had tried to do so and had failed. The enemy really pounded at my mind and screamed at me that I never should have called Steve. But I had felt so desperate and alone that calling him was my only hope.

The pressure was beginning to mount. I knew that April 7th was coming closer and closer with each passing day, and it felt like an appointment with the guillotine. When the Wadsworths returned from their spring vacation, I knew that my days in their home were numbered. Susan was speaking to me more and more about how important it was for me to be in my top form for my debut concert. Ironically, my playing had not suffered through any of this. I was still playing very well, and through Susan's persistence and with the doctors' help, I had managed to get out of my suicidal pattern of thinking.

I was now in the habit of "shutting down" when things got too hard for me. I realized that if I felt awful, it would pass in a little while and I would be better if I could simply disengage my emotions in some way by distracting myself. Most of the time that involved taking a long nap, so I slept a lot. There was no escaping the fact, however, that Susan wasn't going to be there for me like she had been.

A trip to New Jersey

When Susan returned, she was very kind to me and really encouraged me. I told her about Steve and his invitation to come visit him for a few days. Surprisingly, she wasn't too upset about this and encouraged me to go, but she said, "Just be sure you don't let him put a big guilt trip on you with his religion." So I packed enough clothes for several days and took the train to Wilmington, Delaware.

I still remember the day. It was March 23, 1987. I was familiar with the train I needed to take because it was the same train I had ridden when I'd lived in Philadelphia and traveled back and forth for my lessons with Mr. Galamian. This time, however, it was very difficult for me to board the train because the oppression I felt was so great. I forgot my wallet and left it at the ticket counter. I dropped my ticket, misplaced my knapsack for a few minutes, and encountered countless other torturous short-term memory tasks that seemed too difficult to perform. I felt as if there was a hole in my stomach because the pain was so intense! Fortunately, I arrived at the station early enough to get on the right train with the right ticket...and with all of my belongings. It was an act of God's grace!

Steve met me at the station in Delaware and took me to Anita's house. I couldn't help but notice how peaceful it seemed. That night Steve took me to a special meeting at his church. I felt numb, but the people were kind to me and helped me the best they could.

The next night, however, was very significant. We went to a prayer meeting that a lady named Charlotte was leading. She called me to the front and had everyone gather around me and lay hands on me. Then they prayed over me in tongues for about ten minutes.

As Charlotte put her hands on my head, she shouted, "I command every curse to be broken off of you in the name of Jesus! Every generational curse of depression, I BREAK YOU NOW! Satan, LOOSE HIM AND SET HIM FREE! I break every chain and every word that has held you in bondage. Set him free, Jesus, by Your miracle power RIGHT NOW! HEAL HIM AND DELIVER HIM FOR YOUR GLORY!"

After she had prayed those words, I fell flat on the floor. From that moment on, I began a process of healing. That was the turning point right there. That prayer was the start of a long process of recovery. I didn't get better instantly,

He Restoreth My Soul

but something that had me bound was broken. Suddenly I had a will of my own again and could begin to fight back. That service was the turning point in my life.

202

Chapter 20

Gradual Recovery
and Spiritual Growth

*F*or the next few days, Steve got me up every morning and we walked over to the church where he was a full-time associate pastor. Steve would go through the Lord's Prayer with me step by step, and we would pray in tongues over each part of the prayer. He also showed me a set of tapes on prayer by a minister named Larry Lea, entitled "Could You Not Tarry One Hour?" In it, Larry has a prayer outline taken from the Lord's Prayer as recorded in the Book of Matthew. Steve would go through the prayer with me step by step, and we would pray in tongues over each part of the outline. Each time we prayed, I could tell that I felt different. I felt stronger. I felt hope inside of me for the first time since I could remember.

Praying through each part of the Lord's Prayer really helped me. When I would come to the part *Forgive us our debts, as we forgive our debtors,* I began to forgive those who had hurt me. Slowly, I started to experience some breakthroughs emotionally, and there were times when I was free from the torment and hopelessness.

When I got back to New York City, everything was different. I was back in fellowship with the Lord. I was still weak and vulnerable emotionally, but I had received something in church and through the prayer outline Steve had given me that had fortified me deep inside. Susan noticed it immediately, but instead of feeling positive about my improvement, she seemed to feel the opposite. She didn't say much, however, because my New York debut was only a week away, and it was going to be a night that would be remembered.

My debut recital—a spiritual breakthrough

The big day came, and I felt ready. I had played the music so many times in little recitals throughout the country all year that it wasn't going to be difficult for me. Still, I had asked Steve's church to pray and intercede for me that God's glory would fall that night. I was so excited. I knew that God was going to help me.

I was quiet and a little nervous before the concert. At about six o'clock, I felt a blanket of peace come over me. The Lord spoke to my heart as I taxied up to the hall. He said, "I will play through you tonight in a mighty way, and many shall see My hand upon you as you play. I will be glorified, and tonight shall be a moment that shall always be remembered before Me."

Wave after wave of God's anointing swept over me. I felt I was being painted with one coat after another of His presence and anointing. I could hardly stand up as I walked through the backstage entrance and into my dressing room. I fell into a chair and closed my eyes, and I thanked the Lord for the covering of prayer that was coming from Pennsville, New Jersey. I could feel their prayers in a wonderful way.

At precisely eight o'clock, I took a deep breath and briskly walked out onto the stage. A thunderous sound of applause greeted me! I glanced out and every seat looked full. It looked like there were at least 1,500 people there, although I am not sure how many seats there are in Kaufmann Hall. As soon as my accompanist hit the first low pedal note of the *Bach Sonata*, I felt like my body was on fire! A boldness and a strength came on me, and it felt like liquid power was flowing through me. For the first piece, the feeling grew and grew until all fear left me. I felt like this would be the time when I would pass through and never be the same. As I was playing, I realized that this debut was a milestone in my life that I would pass and never return to again.

I began to feel like Samson while I was playing. I had been robbed and plundered. My "hair" had been removed from me. The devil had put out my eyes and had paraded me around in chains, mocking and laughing at me for that whole year, and I had been helpless to overcome him. I had been at his mercy. I had been the slave of demons and controlling spirits. They had put me to work pushing around the grinding stone of oppression in their prison.

As I played the *Prokofiev Sonata*, however, I felt a holy anger rise up inside of me from the Holy Spirit. I cried out in my heart as I prayed like Samson, "Oh Lord, just this once, avenge me for my two eyes and let me die with the Philistines!"

Then I played as if this would be the last time I would ever play. A scream began to rise up out of me from the inside as the anointing began to come out of me like water gushing out of a fire hydrant. No one in that concert hall could deny it. Everyone felt it. I knew they did. It was a witness. By the end of the recital, I just "knew that I knew that I knew" that thousands and thousands of demonic spirits had been slain and were lying dead all around me. The devil paid dearly that night when that Spirit of might and power came on me, and his power was broken from all of those people. I knew they wouldn't notice, since almost all were lost in darkness. Nevertheless, I knew for sure that the hosts of hell were diminished that night considerably and the kingdom of God had advanced in a way that only eternity will tell.

When I finished that night and walked off the stage, I knew I had conquered the enemy and Jesus' power had been demonstrated in a way that no one in attendance would ever forget. The enemy lay around me like a bunch of dead corpses, and the smell of victory was in the air.

After the recital and a nice reception, I went to Susan's and fell into bed exhausted and drained but feeling very fulfilled. I thought, *Maybe I am going to make it in this music world after all. If only I could be happy in life.*

Like some unseen door closing, my life and my relationship with Susan changed dramatically after my recital. She began to talk to me about what I was going to do in the fall and thought it would be a good idea for me to go to Boston to study at the New England Conservatory there. I dreaded going back to school, and I dreaded leaving the Wadsworths most of all. Susan was quickly withdrawing her emotional support from me, and it was hitting me very hard. I began to fall into a slump and went into a terrible time of fear and torment. I turned to the Lord more than ever. He was my only hope. Somehow, I didn't feel welcome in Susan's home any more. Most of all, I knew I was never going to have what I had thought I would—that Susan would promote me into a major career and provide for me.

I started spending the weekends with Steve and then coming back on Monday mornings in time for my appointments with Dr. Davis and Dr. Weisman. I began to experience a terrible conflict between my faith and the therapy. I began to see that I would build my faith in God's Word and His promises and then I would go into those sessions and tear it all down by my confessions of defeat and heartache. Of course, the doctors, who knew me quite well by then, would try to talk me out of that way of thinking, but it didn't work.

Important lessons on prayer

Steve was having a great affect on me as he kept putting the Word into me and encouraging me to pray through the Lord's Prayer every day. In some ways, the inner pain of rejection and hurt I was experiencing at that point was far worse than the actual depression I had experienced. When it finally dawned on me that it was all over for me at the Wadsworths, I was almost overcome with grief. I didn't know what to do. Thank God for Larry Lea's prayer outline. If it hadn't been for praying through it every day, I wouldn't have made it.

I began a habit of praying each morning for several hours—going through each part of Larry Lea's outline of the Lord's Prayer and praying in tongues over each section until the Holy Spirit released me. There were three revelations that really impacted me at that time. The first was the power in daily forgiveness, both in giving it and receiving it. The second was the power of putting on the whole armor of God as I prayed from Psalm 91 for daily protection. And the third was the importance of being committed and faithful to a local church and of being submitted in a proper way to a pastor. These truths went down very deep into my spirit during that time. I have been active in a local church ever since. Steve showed me that I would be cared for and protected when I was in the right body of believers. Because of Steve's patience and loving discipline during that summer in 1987, I pulled out of my depression in less than two years.

In spite of the positive changes I had experienced, however, I was still a broken human being on the inside. My soul had been so shattered that I wondered if I ever would be able to really live life again. But at least when I went to see Steve, I had moments of relief, and I enjoyed the services at his church.

One of the first things Steve told me to do after my first visit to see him was to find a good church in Manhattan so I could attend there. He said I should go whenever the doors were open because I wasn't protected spiritually until I found a good local church. It was then that I remembered a church called Living Word Christian Center that I had heard about a few years before when I was at Juilliard. So I located it and started attending.

Oh, what services they had! The Holy Spirit moved so strong in the praise and worship that it lifted me into another realm. Jesus was so real there! I met several friends at the church who were a real blessing to me, and I was ministered to deeply in the services, particularly when one of the pastors would teach and minister on emotional healing during Wednesday night Bible studies. I will never forget what they did for me and how the Lord began to use them to help me as I began a long and painful recovery and healing process. If it hadn't been for the spiritual support I received there, I never would have made it. But the Lord was indeed carrying me in an awesome way, like a loving daddy would carry a son who had been beaten up and left by the side of the road, nearly at death's door.

That summer I continued to commute back and forth from New York to Delaware, but mostly I stayed in Pennsville with Anita Jacobs. I prayed, practiced, and listened to hours and hours of teaching tapes of Bible teachers. I was praying in tongues every moment of the day when I wasn't speaking to someone—from the time I awakened in the morning until I went to sleep at night. I was still taking antidepressant medication, and there were many times when I would slump into depression, but gradually it began to lessen both in frequency and duration. I was still seeing the doctors when I went to New York, but not as often as before, since I wasn't there as much. It was really good to be with strong, believing, Spirit-filled, faith-filled Christians all the time! Even in my weakened condition, I began to really thrive spiritually in that greenhouse environment of faith.

Best of all, my life was now totally surrendered into Jesus' hands, and He was free to restore me and to put me into His plan for my life. By daily releasing forgiveness toward my dad and others, the horrible bondage began to break and joy began to come back into my life little by little. At first it was very hard to detect, but by the end of the summer, I began to see a new freedom emerging.

The hardest thing of all was to relearn how to live and to function as an adult. I had trouble remembering things because of emotional overload, and everyday life was extremely difficult. But God's grace was there, and I somehow managed to even negotiate the New York City trips by myself. That was a real miracle! For the first time in my life, I was actually living my own life! No one was telling me what I had to do or living through me.

I could feel Jesus' presence with me all the time, and because of my desperation, hardly five minutes would go by without me thinking about Him and praying. I literally couldn't make it through my days without His constant support. It became very clear to me that I was in no condition to go to Boston to study, and I really had no desire to go anyway. I knew that I would never go back to school to study music ever again. I had paid my dues to my dad and to everyone else. I had made up my mind that I was going to go God's way even if I had to turn my back on everything I had ever worked for in classical music. I had joined a charismatic church and that was that! If Jesus didn't help me now, I would just perish or be willing to live the rest of my life in a little church somewhere and get along the best I could.

Learning to live again—God's way!

In August I moved out of the Wadsworths' home, and it was one of the hardest and saddest days I've ever experienced. I moved in with another musician and began doing freelance jobs to survive financially. I also changed doctors—going to a woman psychotherapist who was very skillful in putting my shattered soul back together. I would come out of my sessions with her rather drained and would immediately pray this prayer: "Father, in Jesus' name, I renounce, reject, repent of, and negate every word that I have spoken out of my mouth that is contrary to Your Word and Your will for my life. I take authority over them now and pray for crop failure on every bad confession I have made out of my mouth. Amen."

If you are not familiar with what the Bible says about the power of the words we speak, that prayer would make little sense to you. But I noticed that as I started doing that, I wasn't staying torn-up as much. I was able to go right on with my day and began to function quite a bit better. I also started working out at a gym three times a week and would schedule this around my appointments with the psychotherapist.

I was an adult now, whether I felt like one or was equipped to be one or not. Somehow, I was able to get through each day of terrible pain, and I was supporting myself as a violinist in New York City! My father was still paying for my therapy but little else. Because of all of the practice at daily living that Susan had done with me for the entire year before, I had developed habits of coping and doing the practical things of daily life in a way that kept me from falling apart. Nevertheless, it was a terrible blow to me when I finally realized that I might never become the solo artist I'd dreamed of becoming. Real life was a wrenching disappointment. Thankfully, I was able to attend church several times a week and develop some good friendships there, which made life a little easier. Gradually, I became less and less tormented, and the terrible inner pain began to go away. It was only in tiny increments at first, but I could tell I was feeling better in general as the fall of 1987 gave way to winter and the air began to get chilled.

I survived another trip to Baton Rouge during Christmas and made it through without too much suffering, thanks to all of the teaching tapes I took with me and listened to. Life was going on. Time has a way of healing even the worst of wounds. Life in New York City—Bible tapes or no Bible tapes...depression or no depression—is just plain hard, especially if you have as little money as I did. But I seemed to always have enough money to get by. I gave away so much money and took friends from church out to dinner and still ate out three meals a day! In fact, when I took my tax return in, the accountant who helped me with it said I was lying about how much I gave in deductions.

She said, "It's impossible to live on the little that you made."

I not only lived on it, I ate out in New York City—three meals a day—and did quite well. Money would just come to me in all kinds of ways—through different playing gigs, the few YCA concerts I played, or just "Pentecostal handshakes" at church that left me holding that green stuff.

I immersed myself in my church. I even started playing in their praise and worship team. My whole identity now was in the church.

Learning about ORU

One afternoon I stayed at church after everyone else had gone home. I took a nap on the couch in one of the offices in the back and waited for the evening service. When I woke up, I happened to glance at one of the tables in the room. There on top of it was a large Bible. It was an Oral Roberts Edition Bible. I went over, picked it up, sat back down on the couch, and opened it. In the front of the Bible, there were pictures and the story of Oral Roberts' testimony and ministry. I didn't know much about him, but I had been listening to a lot of tapes by Kenneth Copeland, who had gone to school there, and he always talked about when he attended Oral Roberts University and how he flew Oral's airplane.

As I flipped through the Bible, I came to some color pictures of Oral Roberts University being built and the amazing story of how God had called Oral to "build Me a University based upon the Holy Spirit's authority to train up students to go into every man's world with the message of healing evangelism." It showed the massive "City of Faith" hospital that had been completed and opened only eight years before. I had been so affected by Brother Copeland through his tapes, and he had spoken so highly of Oral Roberts and how his life had been totally changed at ORU. I had seen some of these buildings in a television show called "Richard Roberts Live," which was hosted by Oral's son. My heart was gripped as I kept reading. I started getting really excited in my spirit, and I didn't know why. I just knew that I would go there one day! God had some kind of connection for me with that school, but I didn't know what it was!

Another wonderful thing happened that day—I met a young lady named Deborah Salatti. She was volunteering that night in the church's lending library, when I went to turn in my latest tape series and borrow another one.

She said, "I think you use this library more than anyone else. Do you actually listen to all those tapes?" She had a pretty thick New York accent.

I said, "Yeah, I listen to them day and night, whenever I don't have something else I need to do. These tapes have been my lifeline for almost a year. I'm very thankful they are here."

She looked at me and smiled. "Enjoy!" she said.

I had to occupy myself when I was alone during the day, so rather than being depressed and moping around, I just clicked on my tape player first thing in the morning when I awoke and listened to tapes as I got dressed and headed out for breakfast. I always had a cup of coffee, a large orange juice, and a blueberry muffin every morning at Zabar's on the upper west side. It was my ritual. Most of the time I was listening to Kenneth Copeland blasting away about faith, righteousness, the authority of the believer, healing, or whatever. That was my life—those tapes.

I no longer needed any medication. I hadn't taken any antidepressants for several months. I was still seeing my psychotherapist and was still pretty sensitive and moody. I would sometimes drop into some very low times for several hours, but it wasn't every day now. Now I only got depressed after I let my guard down or had a stressful concert. I was still practicing and had decided to enter the Naumberg competition again. I even went down and played for Miss DeLay. She gave me a few lessons and was nice to me, but I knew that I was finished with any more schooling.

My therapy sessions were going well, and God was showing up in the middle of them. I was going through an intense healing process that involved my being totally honest and telling my therapist what I was going through. Then, like a pressure valve, there would be a release of some area of pain or hurt. Over the months, I had gotten much better, and I could function much better. The most difficult thing for me was letting go of my identity as a "depressed person." It had been a security blanket for so long. I had to see myself as a whole person again, pick up my life, and go on.

I made tremendous strides during the first couple of months of 1988. The cloud that had hung over me was beginning to lift, and joy was beginning to rise up in me. All that Word was beginning to take root and sprout inside my spirit at a tremendous pace, and I was daily growing more and more into a whole person.

Meeting Deborah...and getting married

That spring, a wonderful thing happened—I met my wife to be. I had prayed over my wife ever since I had started going through Larry Lea's prayer outline every day. In fact, even during the time I had lived in Houston in the early- to mid-'80s, the Holy Spirit had come on me several times and I interceded for her, even though I didn't know who or where she was.

I said to the Lord, "I want You to choose her for me because I would probably blow it. Please pick the right one for me and let me know as soon as I meet her."

I had forgotten those prayers I had prayed so intensely years before, but God hadn't. And He had a surprise up His sleeve for me that I never expected! Actually, I had already met her, but I just didn't realize it.

On Sunday, April 10, 1988, I was playing in the music group for praise and worship. As the pastor got up and began his message, I noticed this girl—right in my line of vision—who was staring at me. She wouldn't look away. I tried to ignore her at first, but I kept glancing over at her. Finally I recognized her as the girl who volunteered in the church library. It was Deborah Salatti. I couldn't take my eyes off her. We just sat there and looked at each other for the entire service. The more I looked at her, the more interested I was. I just had to meet her and talk to her!

I had never noticed how beautiful she was! She was the prettiest girl I had ever seen. I don't remember a word of the sermon that morning because I was concentrating on that dark, olive-skinned girl on the other side of the room with the pretty brown eyes. I kept waiting for the service to end, so I could go over and talk to her! She smiled at me, and I just about fell off my chair!

As soon as the service was over, I went over to her, introduced myself, and asked if she would like to have lunch with me. We ended up spending the whole afternoon together. She told me she was from Long Island, but she now lived in the city where she was a nanny for a wealthy Jewish family. I didn't care much what she said; I just kept staring into those beautiful brown eyes of hers. She was spectacular! I wondered why I had never noticed her before. Every move, every gesture she made just captivated me. I also noticed that she seemed to really enjoy being with me, too. She returned my interest at least as much, if not more. We both felt the sparks flying, as it were. It was awesome!

I was concerned when I got back to my apartment. Why was I so interested in this girl? I mean, it didn't make any sense. She was so different from me. She was really pretty, but not in a way that made me notice her before. It was something about her on the inside that made my insides do cartwheels. I could tell she was interested in me, too. In fact, she told me she had been trying to meet me for about two months, but I hadn't noticed her before. All of her blinkers were on, so to speak. She made no effort to hide her feelings. It was scary. Debbie Salatti was after me, but I didn't mind. And that bothered me. Still, I felt so wonderful inside after being with her that day, and I never wanted it to end.

Right from the first week we met, Debbie and I were very close. The Lord was in the middle of our relationship from the start, and I needed her companionship in a great way. I had a deep sense of peace whenever I was with her, which was nearly every moment she wasn't working. Exactly ten days after I had met her, I asked her to marry me! Even more amazing was that she said yes. We both knew that we were supposed to be together.

We got married November 26, 1988. We got a small, three-room apartment on the fourth floor of an old brownstone around the corner from where Debbie worked in Spanish Harlem. It was a big adjustment for us to live in such an environment, especially for me. I vowed that I would not be a poor man and began to confess the Word like I never had done before. The Lord supplied our finances, and we always had enough, although it was really tight that year. I had a good amount of freelance work, playing in the city, and with Debbie's salary we had enough to make ends meet. As humble a beginning as it was, at least I was beginning to live my own life. For the first time, I was no longer bound and controlled by my father's obsession for a solo career.

I had developed a strong pattern of prayer and confession of the Word every morning. I was still listening to my teaching tapes and doing all I had been doing before, and gradually I saw some changes taking place in my life as my own faith took over. I often had a little money left over, and Debbie and I would go out to eat or to see a movie every once in a while. When we would take the bus downtown, I would dream of a time when I would have enough money to have a nice apartment or condominium somewhere in a nice part of town. I wished for enough money so we wouldn't have to just scrape by, but having Debbie was a great source of comfort for me. If I was feeling low, she would help me in her quiet way. I no longer felt alone in this world.

During that time, the Lord spoke to me and said, "I am going to bring you deeply into My presence, and you shall live and abide there, just as the Levites dwelt in the Holy Place of the temple. Your music is to minister to Me. You belong to Me. You are Mine. I will take you out of the music world and bring you very far into My presence in the Holy of Holies. There you shall find your place. You shall minister to Me with your violin.

"Then I shall cause you to go out from there and minister to My church. That is the holy place. That is where I am calling you to live. From there you shall go out and minister to My people, the Jewish people in the outer court, and then, lastly, I shall send you out to minister and perform for the world on the classical concert stage. But you shall no longer live there in that world. I am separating you for myself, and from this day forward, you shall no longer be a slave to this world's music.

"I will bless your marriage and family and keep you myself and cause your lives to flow together into My goodness and grace. Rejoice and know that from this day forward, the curse is broken and you shall see My faithfulness extended toward you and your family from now on."

I bowed my head and wept before the Lord and thanked Him for His wonderful goodness toward me.

Chapter 21

A New Life In Tulsa

*T*hings did not improve for us economically, so Debbie and I left New York City after a year and moved to Louisiana. I planned to enter some international competitions and knew I wouldn't have time to do this with my free-lance schedule. So we decided to move to Baton Rouge. I also knew the Lord was leading us there to reach out to my dad. His marriage was not doing well, and he seemed to want me to be close to him. I had been praying through the part of the Lord's Prayer nearly every day that says, *"And forgive us our debts, as we forgive our debtors"* (Matthew 6:12). I wanted to honor my father and my family, no matter how scattered they were.

During my breakdown, I had spoken very little to him, but he seemed to be at least somewhat open to reestablishing a relationship. Our conversation flourished once more as we dusted off the old, well-worn paths of my establishing a classical music career. Of course, both he and I knew that things were different now, and we kept a close watch on straying into any "religious" areas that would break down our connection. I had heard from the Lord about moving there, and I knew it was more to minister to

my father and my family than it was to enter those competitions.

I never allowed my dad to control me in the same way he
had before, and I refused to submit to any manipulation
that might allow it to happen. Because of prayer, my knowledge of spiritual warfare, and the Word, Dad no longer
could take me over as he once had. He couldn't control me
with money. He couldn't control me by shutting off all
options other than the solo career. So we got back together with an unwritten and unspoken truce that the violin
career was in my court now. I had finally worked through
enough that I could now offer my dad an adult relationship
on my terms—with an understanding that I still loved him,
separate and apart from the violin issue. Of course, old
habits die hard, and there were still times when he attempt-
ed to control me again, but I think it was unconscious on his
part. And it gave me even more exercise in daily forgiveness toward him.

Debbie got a teaching job, and I began practicing a lot.
We also got involved in a wonderful church.

The first competition I entered was in Japan. It was a
grueling experience, but I believed the Lord would give it to
me. I played and thought I did quite well, but I was dropped
from the first round. I was shocked. I didn't know what to
do. I had never felt more like a failure than I did returning
from Japan. It was devastating for me. I had now lost every
competition I had been in for the last three years. My confidence had been shattered, and I had serious doubts about
my playing.

Even deeper than that, my faith in God had been really
shaken. I had been convinced that the Lord was going to
give me that competition and that He had led me to do it.
Why was I eliminated in the first round? It took me several
months to get over it. Because of it, I had no desire to enter
any of the other competitions. It was the last violin competition I ever entered. I never continued on with my plans
to enter the big ones. I had no grace or strength of heart to
follow through. After the Japanese competition, my competing days were over forever.

I was really broken up about losing that competition and
not even making the second round. It really hit me hard.
Something changed on that flight back home. I suddenly
knew I wasn't ever going to try to make a solo violin career

happen again. It was over. I told God, "If I ever have a solo
career, it will only be because You give it to me. I am finished from this day forward. I will never enter another
competition again. It is too much for me."

Then the Lord spoke to me and said, "In My sight, you
won that competition. You are not a loser, and you are not
finished. You haven't even started yet. I have far more for
you than just a music career. I will reveal more of it to you
in the next few months. I will give you more than you ever
could have had in this realm, and you could have had much
that this world offers. But since you have chosen Me, I will
give you the souls of men as your eternal reward. You will
see that I am your Father now. I will provide for you myself
out of My goodness. And your music career will never pass
away, but it shall go on forever and ever."

Reaching out to Dad

On Christmas day that year, Dad and his wife, Susan,
invited us over. We had a nice dinner together with them
and their children, Rachel and Ben. Dad and Susan were
not getting along well at all. They were constantly at each
other's throats. After about an hour, the strife in that house
got so thick that I just wanted to leave.

After dinner, my father asked me to go upstairs with him.
He wanted to talk with me. When we were alone, he said,
"It just isn't working with Susan and me. I have tried and
tried to resolve our problems, but Susan just won't listen or
cooperate with me at all. I think I am going to separate from
her."

When he said that, I felt an anointing from the Holy Spirit
come all over me. I said to him, "Dad, are you sure that's
the best thing? You have been through so much devastation with this in the past. Think of Rachel and Ben."

He said, "I know, Maury. I have thought about it for
months. I'm glad you're here, at least. But I don't think I
have any other choice. I can't stand the pain any more. It
has gotten unbearable in this house."

I said, "I know. I could feel it when I walked in here."

He said, "I have decided to leave Susan and to get an
apartment."

I said, "Dad, there is one way your marriage can be
saved. God doesn't want you to do this—I know He does-
n't. You can't make this marriage work, but He can. If you

will give your life to Jesus and surrender and repent of your sins, God can change everything and turn it around, even as far gone as it is. The Lord sent me here to live in Baton Rouge so that I could be here to help you. If only you will give your life to Him, He can turn it all around. God is telling me this right now as I sit here. It is your only hope at this point. God has changed me and so much in my life. Dad, you don't have to try to work it out all on your own. God loves you so much, and He wants to heal and restore you. Please let Him in. Let Him help you. That is the real reason why I came back here—so that Debbie and I could be here to help you at this time. It isn't hopeless—Jesus can heal your marriage, even now. Will you turn to Him? Will you give your life to Him now?"

Those words just poured out of me before I could even think about what I was saying. The presence of the Holy Spirit in the room was so thick that it seemed to be a mist all around us. Dad was staring down at the floor. He didn't look up for a long time. Finally he looked up at me, and I could see the tears in his eyes. He seemed like the most broken and hurt human being I had ever seen.

Then his countenance changed, and he got that steely look in his eyes. He glared at me and said, "That's fine if you want to be religious. If it works for you, that's great. But I've had enough of your preaching at me. I don't want to become a Christian. I don't ever plan on becoming like you. I'm through with listening to this out of your mouth. I don't believe in Jesus. I will never become a Christian. And I am finished with ever hearing about it from you again. DO YOU UNDERSTAND?"

I sat staring at him for some time. The Holy Spirit had been so grieved that He had left the room. I didn't know what to say, so I said, "Okay. I am finished with telling you about Jesus. Have it your way. The only reason I said what I did was that you seemed to be asking my advice about what to do. That is the only advice I have. I don't have any other advice or answers other than what I have found in Jesus. I was only trying to help you."

When I said that, suddenly the Lord spoke up inside of me and said, "You are now released from your father. I sent you here to minister to him. He has rejected Me and you. You are no longer responsible for him. You have done all you could to honor him as I have asked of you. I release you NOW."

Then I felt something just leave me. I had carried such a burden for him ever since I had come to Baton Rouge. I knew I would continue to pray for him, but all sense of duty and ministry toward him just left me—like a bird flying away and disappearing. It was like he had crossed a line in the Spirit. He had made his choice, and it was over.

I let him know exactly what I had just heard from the Lord. I said, "The Lord has just released me from you. I have done what He has asked me to do. I came here because the Lord wanted me to reach out to you. He wanted to save your family. He wanted to rescue you, but since you have once again rejected Him, you have no choice but to reap what you have sown."

Dad was red in the face as he glared at me, but I was full of peace. I said to him. "You will lose your marriage and family again. This house is left to you desolate. I pray that you do not lose your soul also." And with a sad heart, I got up and walked down the stairs and out of the house with Debbie.

Although we've only had limited contact since that time, I believe the Lord has never stopped reaching out to my dad. But on that Christmas Day in 1989, I was released from the assignment the Lord had given me toward Charles Sklar. It was over. I was free. Those chains of bondage fell off, and he would never again be able to rule over me. He knew it and I knew it. His hold on me was broken once and for all. I will always honor him as my father, but never again will I submit to the spirit of control that kept me bound for many years.

Unfortunately, he did lose his marriage to Susan, and he did indeed reap what he had sown. All of his children have been hurt by him, and our relationships with him are somewhat strained. What a terrible tragedy.

Even so, the Lord had mercy on him and gave him yet another wife a year or so later. He asked me to play for the wedding, and I did—but it was one of the most difficult things I've ever done. His wife has treated him very well, but they have become a deceived hybrid of what could best be described as "New Age Jews." Their present relationship reminds me of Ahab and Jezebel. Dear reader, please pray that they will not perish, but that somehow they will be rescued out of their deception and come to repentance. I still believe that God can do what seems impossible to us.

Lunch with the Lord

One afternoon some time later, the Lord came to our apartment in Baton Rouge. I can't tell you that I saw Him like I saw the furniture, but I knew He was there! He said to Me, "Maury, will you come and have lunch with Me?"

I began to tremble all over and fell on my face on the floor. I said, "Lord, I am so unworthy! Please forgive Me for all I have done wrong!"

I was crying so hard, and somehow I felt so dirty. He just kept standing in front of me and looking at me with such love that I felt even more lowly before His majesty. He picked me up off the carpet, looked me in the eyes, and said, "I have already forgiven you. You are clean in My sight. I have washed you in My blood."

His eyes were so indescribably beautiful, like the sunrise and the sunset at the same time! Like pools of liquid love that just melted me. Like every wonderful experience of peace, love, and joy that I had ever experienced. I knew that it had all come from Him, that He had been the source of every good thing I had ever known. I couldn't stop crying. Then He reached His hand toward my face and touched me, and suddenly I stopped.

He said to me, "You don't have to cry anymore. I am with you now. I have felt every hurt that you've ever had and seen every tear that you've shed. It will be better from now on."

Then I noticed that He had been crying, too.

As I began to regain my composure a little, I sat down on the couch. He sat in the chair next to me. I was speechless! What was the Lord doing here? He had on a beautiful white robe that had blue in it, and it shimmered when He moved. And yet, was He really there? I realized that I was seeing in the Spirit realm and the natural at the same time. He was there, but I still had to stay in the Spirit to see Him. I couldn't take my eyes off of Him. He was so wonderful to look upon.

Then the Lord Jesus said, "Let's go have lunch together!"

I said, "Okay."

He motioned toward the door and said, "You like the Drusilla Seafood Restaurant, don't you?"

I mumbled back, "Yes, that's fine."

Then we both walked out the door and went to that restaurant, which was about a ten-minute walk from our apartment. All along the way, I just kept worshiping Him and telling Him how much I loved Him. He received my worship and put His arms around me. He told me, "You are very precious to me. I love you so much. I have come to visit with you and to tell you what is coming in your life. But let's go into the restaurant first, and you can eat."

We finally arrived and I got a table. It was around two o'clock in the afternoon, so there was hardly anyone in there. I realized that no one could see the Lord except me. It kind of felt like that movie "Harvey." No one but me could see Him. And when I would move back into the natural very far, I couldn't see Him either. As soon as I reached out to Him in faith, however, there He was again. He just sat with me while I ordered some food, and then He started to speak to me.

He said, "I am sending you to Tulsa, Oklahoma. And I am giving you a ministry that will touch the world in the years to come before I return to the earth. You will base out of Tulsa and travel from there."

Then He showed me what looked like a picture of an airline map with red lines going out in every direction from Tulsa to other cities in the U.S. and even other nations. There were so many lines that it was just all red in the vicinity right around Tulsa. Then He spoke to me about other things that I cannot write about here—things concerning the kingdom of God and what He has planned for the earth before His return.

Then He started pouring out His love on me again, telling me that I would not fail Him and that My reward would be great because I was willing to obey Him fully. I burst into tears again, and I was embarrassed because I thought the waitress would see me. I tried to talk to the Lord as subtly as possible, since I knew that if anyone saw me, they would think I was crazy or something. Fortunately, I was behind some plants at a quiet table, and no one was around. But it really didn't matter because I was so overwhelmed. The whole restaurant was lit up by His presence.

The waitress got nervous whenever she approached our table and started shaking. She could hardly put my plate and drink on the table. She turned red in the face and said,

"I don't know why I am shaking like this. Something is around this table!" Then she nearly ran away from me (us), and she didn't come back except to bring the check. So I was left alone with the Lord.

After I ate, I paid the check, then I noticed that the waitress was gone! I don't know where she went. Then I looked back where Jesus had been sitting with me, and He was gone, too! He had disappeared!

Following God's plan

For several days, I felt like I was enveloped in a cloud. It was hard to think. I felt like I was drunk in the Holy Spirit. Gradually it lifted, and I went on with my life. All I could talk about to Debbie was how the Lord had spoken to me that we were going to Tulsa, Oklahoma. She wasn't too crazy about moving again, so after a few weeks, I just stopped pressuring her.

I decided to audition for an orchestra somewhere. I sent out résumés for several auditions and auditioned for the Associate Concertmaster position in the Philharmonic Orchestra in Tulsa, Oklahoma. We had found out just before Christmas that Debbie was pregnant, and I was determined to support her and my family now so she wouldn't have to work.

I traveled to Tulsa at the end of April 1990 to audition for the position of Associate Concertmaster, and I was hired. I signed a one-year contract for enough money so that Debbie wouldn't have to work. I was so thrilled! I knew the Lord had given me the position! What a great day that was for me. I knew we were going to love Tulsa. I had a job, and I could provide for Debbie and our new baby that was on the way.

Before I returned to Louisiana, I wanted to see the Oral Roberts University that I had heard so much about. When I saw it, it nearly took my breath away! It looked like something from a science fiction movie. All the buildings are so modern! I was blown away as I walked around that campus on that perfect day with the sun shining and reflecting off the glass buildings. The presence of the Holy Spirit nearly knocked me down as I approached the Prayer Tower in the middle of the campus.

As I was about to leave, the Lord spoke to me and said, "Go over to the music building."

I said, "The music building? Do they have a music building here?"

I asked someone where the music building was and headed toward it. I marveled at the thought of those ORU students being able to study music in such an atmosphere of faith and the Holy Spirit. What an amazing place this was.

I went to the music office and met the dean of the Music School. He showed me around and said, "This is a unique school because it focuses on educating the whole person from a biblical perspective, not just the mind but the spirit also."

My heart leaped in me as I saw the classrooms and the performance hall. I blurted out, "Do you need a violin teacher here? I am a Spirit-filled Christian, and I would be interested in teaching here!"

He looked at me intently and said, "Well, actually, our violin instructor has just informed us that he will not be returning in the fall, so it is interesting that you should mention it. Let me take down your name and address so I can contact you when school is out."

Then he shook my hand and said, "Would you mind if we pray and ask the Lord's blessing on your relocation here? I have a witness from the Holy Spirit that you may be the one God is sending to teach violin here."

We joined hands and prayed that God would help me and my family as we moved to Tulsa and undertook a new job and direction for our lives.

That day was one of the best days of my life! I flew back to Baton Rouge with a new job, an apartment, and the possibility of a teaching job at ORU. The Lord had come through again! It was like all those years of praying in tongues had finally given birth to a wonderful new life that I had only dreamed of.

That summer our daughter, Rebekah Abigail Sklar, was born. I was given a teaching job at ORU and started my job with the Philharmonic. Day by day, I was able to rebuild my life—or more accurately, God restored me to a normal life as a professional musician.

Then, after a year of working for the Tulsa Philharmonic, I felt the Lord leading me another direction, into ministry for Him. It started one day the following spring when Richard Robert's office contacted me and asked if I would play a song with soundtrack for his TV program. He wanted to advertise the music department and thought it would be good for me to do that. I managed to find a soundtrack of "Great Is Thy Faithfulness" and went to the studio and recorded it one afternoon when no one but the camera and audio guys were there.

I was grateful to get it over with and left as soon as I could. After all, I was used to playing "real music," like Bach, Mozart, Brahms, Beethoven, and other classical composers. This seemed like such a joke, but it was a good deed to do, and I did it out of respect for Richard. I forgot about it and went on.

A few days later, Richard called me and said, "Maurice, your playing was so anointed when we aired it on our show yesterday. We were all crying! Can you come and play it again for us at our annual alumni meeting next week?"

I said, "Well, sure, I guess so. Was it really that good? It was just a short hymn."

Richard said, "I have never heard a violin sound like that before. God has His hand on you!"

The very next day, the personnel manager of the Philharmonic handed me a white envelope. He said, "We are very pleased with your being a part of the Tulsa Philharmonic. You add so much to the first violins. This is your contract for next year. I think you will be pleased."

When I got back to my car, I got the contract out and read it. They had given me a raise of more than $5,000 for the next season! I was so excited. The raise would help us get out of some debt that we had. As I headed home, I couldn't wait to tell Debbie.

Suddenly a cloud filled the car, and I could hardly see. It seemed like a fog was all around me. I broke down and started weeping. Then I heard the Lord say to me, "Son, don't sign that contract. It is not My will for you to play in this orchestra past this season."

I sat there stunned. I said, "But, God, You don't understand. This is a good contract. I can finally make a little money from playing the violin. What will I do if I don't play in the orchestra?"

The Lord said, "Son, you can entertain people for a night, and that's okay. There's nothing wrong with that. But if you will go and minister and perform for Me, I will do more than just entertain people for a night—I will change lives forever! WHICH DO YOU WANT?"

I started weeping again and said, "Lord, I'll do whatever You want. I won't sign the contract if You don't want me to."

Then He spoke again. "Are you willing to play simple things? For I use what the world calls simple and foolish to do My greatest works on the earth."

I replied shakily, "Yes, I am willing to do whatever You want."

Then, just as suddenly as it had come, the awesome presence of the Lord lifted off of me, and I could see clearly out of the windshield again. When I arrived home, I couldn't move for about ten minutes. Then I went inside, fell into bed, and went to sleep.

The next few days flew by. I played in that ORU alumni meeting one night shortly after my "debut" on the Richard Roberts Show. I played the song "We Shall Behold Him" with soundtrack. I felt really awkward and stupid the whole time I was playing the song. I think it was like what a Shakespearian actor would feel if he had to perform in a TV soap opera. That is what I felt like artistically. I kept thinking, *This is ridiculous! What are you doing! This is a disgrace to your profession! Just think what your father would say if he saw you doing this! You're throwing it all away—everything you ever worked for...all that you hold dear! Is THIS what you spent your whole life practicing for! You are a disgrace!*

I couldn't stop the thoughts no matter how hard I tried. Then, about halfway through my song, all the negative thoughts suddenly ceased.

God moves through my music

After I finished playing the song, I stood there looking out over that big crowd with my mouth hanging open. To my utter amazement, after I finished playing, everyone was on their feet with their hands in the air, praising God. Many of them were weeping, and they didn't stop for about five minutes. No one was paying any attention to me at all. They were all worshiping God. I didn't know what to do! This had never happened to me before in a concert, at least not to this magnitude! They hardly even clapped! I was almost offended! It was like I wasn't even there!

Then the Lord spoke so sweetly to me and said, "You see what I can do when you yield yourself totally to Me?"

I silently replied, "I never knew this kind of music even existed! Thank You for being willing to use someone like me!" Then I also lifted my hands and began to worship with the others.

It was an awesome experience for me. I went home that night really shook up! Something big was happening, that was for sure! Spiritually speaking, a baby had been born. Maybe this was what the Lord had been speaking to me about all of those years.

Things began to happen. I spoke to Steve Strumbeck about finding some soundtracks that might work well for playing the violin in churches. He sent me ten songs on tape, with copies of the vocal lines and a letter. He explained that it was important to find hymns and songs people were familiar with and knew the words to. Out of those original tracks came four of my most powerfully anointed hymns and songs: "Amazing Grace"; "Holy, Holy, Holy"; "Turn Your Eyes Upon Jesus Medley"; and "How Great Thou Art." In addition, the other vocal track—which is still the most anointed song I play—was "We Shall Behold Him."

These five songs were birthed out of my first six months of stepping out to play for the Lord in meetings and churches. The arrangements are not written down in any way. They came directly from the Holy Spirit as I practiced and played through them over and over in my bedroom with our tape machine "boom box" playing on our night table. The arrangements kept growing through the anointing of the Holy Spirit until they became almost profound. These songs aren't Brahms or Tchaikovsky by any means, but they have something in them that came fresh from heaven. They still have the same impact today as the first time I played them.

I'll never forget the glory of God that descended in that room as I learned these songs! It got so hot that it was like a furnace of fire in there! My body heated up so much as I was playing that I had to put my violin down several times so I wouldn't drop it! I fell on the floor twice and couldn't get up one afternoon for an hour. I was just pinned there on the floor by the bed! Like a sword that has gone through the fire, the anvil, and the smelting furnace, these songs came forth to bless the body of Christ in glory and power like no others I have done since! These five songs are "the big guns" that the Holy Spirit still uses in meetings around the world.

Later that spring, Evangelist Benny Hinn visited ORU and held an all-day healing meeting in the chapel for students and faculty. I hadn't planned to attend, but the Lord woke me up and practically shook me out of bed. He said, "Son, you are to go to Benny's meeting this morning. Get up! And take your violin and sit on the platform with the faculty."

I did, but I felt pretty embarrassed. I went up and sat in the last available seat on the platform. It was right in front of Benny Hinn!

When Richard saw me there, he motioned for me to get out my violin and to go stand with his worship team, so I did. I played a little with his group and then sat down as Benny Hinn began to preach. Later, as he was praying for people, he spun around and pointed at me. He said, "Come here, young man!" Then he shouted to the people, "Stretch your hands toward him and pray!" To me, he said, "I see that God has a special anointing for your hands!" He motioned for me to put my hands out face up in front of me. To my astonishment, he slapped both of them with his two hands so hard that they stung for a long time! When he slapped them, I fell over like I was hit with a wrecking ball.

Then he said, "Pick him up, Charlie!" And a heavy-set, gray-headed man picked me up as he had done with about twenty people before me. Benny threw his coat toward me, and when it fell on top of my head, I hit the floor again. I was on the floor for some time with that coat over me. I felt as if God had put my whole body into a huge electric generator! I couldn't stop shaking from all of the power that seemed to flow out of Benny's fancy white coat that was on top of my head.

Finally, Charlie pulled the coat off of me and pulled me up into a chair. Then, at the end of the service, I once again got out my violin and played when Oral Roberts stood up and gave Benny a prophecy. What a service! I'll never forget that day!

It just so happened that Debbie and I had planned a vacation to Disney World right after school ended that year, which was only about a week and a half after that meeting took place. The first week of May, we were scheduled to be in Orlando, which is where Benny's church is, and he invited me to play for his services that Sunday morning. The church was packed, and I played, "We Shall Behold Him." When I finished, the people were all on their feet with their hands in the air, praising God.

Pastor Benny got up and hit his podium with his fist and said, "My God, what an anointing! Why didn't God give me that gift?"

Then he turned to me and said, "Maurice, why don't you come to the Tulsa Healing Crusade next week! I would like you to play there!"

I nodded that I would be happy to come. (After all, I didn't have far to go—I lived in the apartments right across the street from the Mabee Center where it was being held!) And so began my wonderful and intense relationship with Pastor Benny Hinn. I've played in many of his meetings over the past several years. I thank God for his ministry and the impact it has had on my life.

Many other ministers have also invited me to play the violin in their meetings, both here in the United States and abroad. I could go on and on with one story after another of the great adventure my ministry has been for me. (Perhaps that is for another book in the future.) The Lord has truly opened up to me "a door that cannot be shut" and given to me supernatural favor. Because of God's grace, I have been in hundreds of churches, from the smallest to the largest. I have preached, played my violin, taught the Bible, and seen a constant stream of healings and other gifts of the Holy Spirit flow during my concerts and meetings throughout many nations.

The first few years it was hard to pioneer the violin into the church, but God has done it by His grace. I have seen thousands upon thousands of lives touched and changed as I have ministered and performed for the Lord, just as He told me. I have found my purpose for being on this earth.

God blessed Debbie and me with a son—Josiah Israel Sklar—on September 23, 1993, and has shown his goodness to our family in a multitude of marvelous ways. What a miracle and honor it is for me to be part of a family who loves God and lives their lives according to His great plan! I have been so blessed to see how the Lord has miraculously provided for my family and my ministry during the last few years. I thank God for His constant faithfulness to us!

I have seen a continual unfolding of the restoration of God in my life as He has begun to "restore the years that the locust have eaten," and I have seen Him satisfy me time and again with the goodness from His hands and heart. With a grateful heart, I thank Him for restoring my soul, and I look forward to all that He has planned for me in the short time we have left before the Messiah's return to this earth.

Epilogue

Are you ready for your life to change? Do you want success and victory in every area of your life? Do you want it enough to do something about it? I have found the way out of defeat and into victory, both in my personal life, my family, and my ministry and music career. I have proved that it works, and I continue to prove it every day of my life. This isn't just a formula I have heard about somewhere. This is a Bible truth that has totally transformed my life—and it will transform your life, too.

I have gone from poverty to wealth. I live in divine health and so does my family. Such enormous favor from the Lord has come upon my life and ministry that doors have literally flown open to me from nearly ever leader in the body of Christ in the few short years that I've minis-tered. I have gone from suicidal depression a few years ago to a life that is filled with joy, peace of mind, and tremen-dous prosperity in many areas. Without a doubt, God has given me *beauty for ashes, the oil of joy for mourning, the gar-ment of praise for the spirit of heaviness* (Isaiah 61:3). I can indeed say, *"The Lord is my shepherd; I shall not want...He restoreth my soul..."* (Psalm 23:1,3). I have gone from total bondage into the abundant life Jesus promised to us in His Word. Praise Him forever!

As God is my witness, the things I have written here are true.   Does this mean I'm in such victory that I never have any problems or opportunities for defeat? No. Did this happen to me because I was born under the lucky star or something? No—absolutely not! God is no respecter of persons. He wants to do the same for you and for all of His precious children. Every day I have to stand in faith and apply what I am about to share with you. If I don't do it, the enemy would have much more access to my life and would probably steal, kill, and destroy most of the victory that I enjoy today.

I am about to share with you what to do to enforce your covenant rights in Christ on this earth. As Christians, there is a way to win over the enemy in every conflict and to maintain your position of victory, no matter what the circumstances may be. There is a way out of the defeat you may now be experiencing. You can experience the manifestation of all of God's promises in your life!

I don't know if you are like me, but when my back was up against the wall—when the devil was beating my brains out and I was seemingly helpless under his cruel and merciless blows—**I cried out to God and asked Him to show me what to do**. As I have shared with you in this book, I wanted to know how to overcome in the daily fight of faith in my life, but for much of my life, I felt there was no way out. But there is, praise God! Do you want to know what I have discovered? Here it is:

So Jesus answered and said to them, "Have faith in God. For assuredly, I say to you, whoever SAYS to this mountain, 'Be removed and be cast into the sea,' and does not doubt in his heart, but believes that those things he SAYS will come to pass, HE WILL HAVE WHATEVER HE SAYS. Therefore I say to you, whatever things you ask WHEN YOU PRAY, believe that you receive them, and you will HAVE THEM (Mark 11:22-24, NKJV).

DEATH AND LIFE are in the power of the TONGUE, and those who love it will eat its fruit (Proverbs 18:21, NKJV).

...your faith may become effective by the ACKNOWLEDG-MENT of every good thing which is in you in Christ Jesus (Philemon 6, NKJV).

And they overcame him [the devil] *by the blood of the Lamb, and by THE WORD OF THEIR TESTIMONY...* (Revelation 12:11).

Right now you might be saying, "Oh, great! Another message on THAT! I have heard about that for the last twenty-five years."

Well, you need to hear far more about it. Remember, *...the just shall LIVE by his faith* (Habakkuk 2:4). If you want to live, you must do it by faith and upon your confession of agreement with God's promises...or you will DIE because of your unbelief and your confession of Satan's lies.

You decide by what you believe in your heart and confess with your mouth. Jesus said, *"...out of the abundance of the heart the mouth speaks"* (Matthew 12:34, NKJV). I can be with a total stranger and listen to them talk, and within five minutes, I will know where they are in life. Why? Because their mouths will express exactly what is in their hearts. The Bible says of man, *"...as he thinks in his heart, so is he"* (Proverbs 23:7, NKJV).

What if your heart is full of doubts, fears, and negative thinking from years of listening and speaking the devil's lies out of your mouth? What if your mouth habitually speaks death instead of life? What can you do? You have to change what is in your heart by God's Word. There is only one way to do that: You must plant the promises of God in your heart by MEDITATING ON THEM and SPEAKING THEM out of your mouth and into your soul and spirit (your heart).

Maybe you know this already. So what can you do on a daily basis that will cause this wonderful spiritual law to work in your favor instead of working against you? I am about to share with you what I discovered and applied in my life in spite of all hell breaking loose against me. It has brought tremendous results in my life.

I found several scriptures concerning who I am in Christ and began to confess them every day over my life. I also took a number of prayers from the book *Prayers That Avail Much* (Vol. 1 and 2, published by Harrison House, Tulsa, OK), and began to pray those out loud daily. Then I wrote out all of the prophetic words the Lord had promised me at different times in my life, concerning my calling in music and in ministry. Then I put these prophetic words into a form that I could confess over my life in faith—in the first person. Then I added confessions from these passages of Scriptures found in *The Amplified Bible*: Deuteronomy 28:1-14; Psalms 23, 27, 34, 37, 91, and 103:1-6; Isaiah 54:11-17, The Lord's Prayer from Matthew 6:9-13; 1 Corinthians 13:4-8; Paul's prayers from Ephesians 1:17-23 and 3:14-21; Paul's prayer from Colossians 1:9-14; and Ephesians 6:10-18, which admonishes us to put on the whole armor of God.

I put all of these scriptures into confession form and pray them over myself and my family. Instead of saying "I," I say "we," so I can include my family and anyone else the Lord wants to be in these prayers from God's Word. I pray to the Father in the name of Jesus, just as the Lord tells us to do in the new covenant.

To some this may seem like a religious form that puts them under the law, but for me, this has saved my life. After many years of doing this, I can say that this one area of prayer has changed my life from defeat into victory! My prayer life also includes one thing that I have habitually put into practice: Every waking moment (when I'm not speaking to someone or involved in some activity that prevents me from doing so), I pray in the Spirit, speaking in my prayer language of tongues.

Thank God, this baptism of the Holy Spirit with the evidence of speaking in tongues is for every one of God's children who desires to have it in their lives. You see, every victory in our lives is a prayer victory. Every defeat that comes into our lives happens because somewhere there was a prayer breakdown or failure. When I pray in the Spirit, I know that the Lord is praying through me in a perfect way. Wouldn't it be good to have God Almighty praying through you for about three to six hours or more every day? Wouldn't that make a difference in your life? I can tell you that it certainly has made a wonderful difference in mine!

I pray and confess the Word for about a half hour to an hour nearly every morning. I also read the entire Bible out loud once a year. I go through one of the books of the Bible every week or so. I have a collection of confessions that I go through on a weekly basis, which takes a total of about three hours. Just as one works out in a gym and repeatedly does the same exercises to strengthen his muscles, I repeatedly pray these prayers and speak these confessions, and they strengthen me spiritually and protect me from the devil every time! Praise God forever!

I encourage you to try it. I promise you that it will be well worth your while to do what I have suggested here. I have done it long enough to know that it is one of the most neglected keys to victorious Christian living that there is. I urge you to put this into your life! Just knowing about it won't help you—you must DO it! When you believe God's promises in your heart and confess them over your life on a consistent, daily basis, they will produce the very divine nature of God in you and manifest His power that helps you to be victorious over the world, the flesh, and the devil. *Now thanks be to God who ALWAYS leads us in triumph in Christ!* (2 Corinthians 2:14, NKJV).

Talking with the Father

If you haven't yet accepted Jesus as your personal Savior, I invite you to pray the following prayer sincerely from your heart:

Father, I come to You, thanking You for the opportunity to receive salvation through the blood of Your Son Jesus Christ. I confess my sins and repent, asking You to forgive me. I now accept Jesus as Lord of my life, and I pray for divine help as I turn from my past life of sin into new paths of righteousness.

Jesus, I thank You for cleansing me and for writing my name in the Book of Life. I ask You now to fill me with the Holy Spirit and with power. In Jesus' name, I pray. Amen

Now I invite every reader to pray this prayer:

Father, I come to You now, in the name of Jesus, thanking You for Your love and faithfulness to me. I'm so grateful for all that You've done for me...and for all that You still have in store for my life. I want to reach out and access the victorious power that you have provided for me. I ask You now to help me and give me Your power as I begin to confess Your Word over my life and over the lives of those I love and care about. I thank You for Your transforming power, and I believe that as I continually confess the truth of Your Word and spend more time in prayer, You will release Your grace and power into my life. I thank You for it in advance, and I'm excited about the changes that are about to occur in my life. Amen.